Flying
America's Weather

*A Pilot's Tour
of Our Nation's
Weather Regions*

Flying
America's Weather

*A Pilot's Tour
of Our Nation's
Weather Regions*

Thomas A. Horne

A FOCUS SERIES BOOK

Aviation Supplies & Academics, Inc.
Newcastle, Washington

Flying America's Weather: A Pilot's Tour of Our Nation's Weather Regions
by Thomas A. Horne

Aviation Supplies & Academics, Inc.
7005 132nd Place SE
Newcastle, Washington 98059-3153

Published by Aviation Supplies & Academics, Inc.

Parts of this book were first published in periodical format in *AOPA Pilot* from
1990–1991. Maps, charts and other illustrations in this book are for explana-
tory purposes only and are not to be used for navigation or flight planning.

Printed in Canada

09 08 07 06 05   9 8 7 6 5 4 3 2

ISBN 1-56027-369-0
ASA-FAW

Library of Congress Cataloging-in-Publication Data:

Horne, Thomas A.
    Flying America's weather : a pilot's tour of our nation's weather regions /
    by Thomas A. Horne.
           p.   cm.
    "A Focus series book."
    Includes bibliographical references and index.
    ISBN 1-56027-369-0
    1. Meteorology in aeronautics—United States. 2. Airplanes—Piloting—United
States. 3. United States—Climate. I. Title.
    TL558.U5H67 1999
    629.132'4'0973—dc21   98-52372

01

Photo and Illustration credits (for full citations of the abbreviated source material in this list, see the Bibliography
starting on Page 319, also the Acknowledgments on Page vi): pp.xvii-xx, U.S.A.F. 4th Weather Wing; p.6, AMS; p.9,
NOAA; p.22, photo by Brooks Martner; p.27, Alaska Aviation Weather Unit, NWS; p.29, photo by Burke Mees; p.39,
NOAA; pp.74, T.T. Fujita; p.79, photo by Paul Neiman; pp. 82-83, T.T. Fujita; pp.85, 93, Carney, Bedard et al; p.94, photo by
Brooks Martner; pp.95, 102, AMS; p.108, T.T. Fujita; p.111, NOAA; p.119, AMS; pp.130, 142, photos by Steve Albers;
pp.144-145, AMS; p.149, T.T. Fujita; pp.151-152, NOAA; pp.158, 193, 197, 208, T.T. Fujita; p.211, NOAA/NWS; p.235, AMS;
p.236, NOAA; pp.249-250, T.T. Fujita; pp.252-253, 269, AMS; pp.272-273, T.T. Fujita; p.280, AMS; pp. 288-291, U.S.A.F. 4th
Weather Wing; p.293, CIMSS (Univ. of Wisconsin); p.294, photo by Paul Neiman, illustration courtesy Carney, Bedard et
al; p.295, photo by S. Horne; p.296, courtesy of Storm Prediction Center; p.297(top), photo by S. Horne; p.298(top),
courtesy of Storm Prediction Center; p.299-300, CIMSS; pp.304-305, NOAA; p.306, NWS. Maps were created in
Macromedia FreeHand with the aid of *Cartesia* mapping software by ASA's Graphic Design Department.

Contents

Acknowledgments

—National Oceanic and Atmospheric Administration (NOAA) and the National Weather Service (NWS), for meteorological data, charts, and illustrations which are available in NOAA publications and world-wide websites, in the public domain (website: http://www.noaa.gov).

—Dr. T.T. Fujita of the University of Chicago, and James W. Partacz of the Wind Research Lab at the University of Chicago, for permission to use Fujita material.

—American Meteorological Society (AMS), for permission to reprint journal and monograph illustrations; and Melissa Weston of AMS for assistance.

—for assistance in gathering illustrations and art: Dr. Alfred J. Bedard, Environmental Technology Laboratory (NOAA/ETL); Dr. Jason E. Nachamkin, Colorado State University; Dr. Conrad Ziegler, National Severe Storms Laboratory (NOAA/NSSL); James Wilson, National Center for Atmospheric Research (NCAR); Dr. David Levinson, Northwest Watershed Research Center (USDA-Agricultural Research Service); Dr. Robert Banta, NOAA/ETL.

—Stanley G. Benjamin of the NOAA's Forecast Systems Laboratory (FSL) for expertise on numerical prediction; Marcia Politovich of NCAR's Research Applications Program (RAP) for expertise on numerical prediction of icing conditions.

—Grant Goodge, NCDC, for help in researching historical weather data.

—Dr. Louis Uccellini, NCEP.

—Elliott Barske, NOAA, Alaskan Aviation Weather Unit.

—Lee Grenci, Pennsylvania State University.

—Dr. Edward Hopkins, University of Wisconsin.

—Thanks to photographers of weather phenomena: Steve Albers (NOAA/FSL); S. Horne; Brooks Martner (NOAA/ETL); Burke Mees of Dutch Harbor, AK; Paul Neiman (NOAA/ETL).

—the "GOES Gallery" by CIMSS (Cooperative Institute for Meteorological Satellite Studies) at the University of Wisconsin–Madison website (http://cimss.ssec.wisc.edu/goes); also, "Latest Cool Image" website by Roger Edwards of the NWS Storm Prediction Center. (http://whirlwind100.nssl.noaa.gov/~spc/coolimg/index.html)

—ASA's Book Production and Editing team: Jennie Trerise, editing; Dora Muir, design; Mayumi Thompson, illustration; Cynthia Wyckoff, layout.

Preface
WXpectations

We pilots sometimes expect too much from today's weather forecasts. Yes, they're good, and getting better each year. But in our heart of hearts, we're looking for highly specific, small-scale information, and our current weather system isn't quite yet up to the task. We want to know what the weather will be right along our proposed route of flight, at the altitude we've chosen to fly, from takeoff to touchdown. This narrows down to a few tiny corridors (allowing for alternate routes in the event a diversion is necessary), just a few miles wide and a few thousand feet deep. In short, we don't want any surprises. Pilots want a 1-800-Can-I-Make-It telephone number they can call for an unequivocal answer as to the weather's influence on the flight at hand.

But unless there's always another airplane, the same type we happen to be flying, a few miles ahead of us at all times, and at the same altitude, we'll never really know what weather awaits us. There's only one airplane in the world that has this luxury, and it's the specially modified Boeing 747 used to ferry the Space Shuttle from Edwards Air Force Base in California to the Kennedy Space Center in Florida. A lead airplane always flies ahead of the Boeing and its piggy-back payload. If any convective activity, rain showers, or even cumulus clouds pop up along the route, the lead ship tells the ferry crew and it's a 180-degree turn and another try on another day. (Why, you ask? The Shuttle's tiles are very durable when it comes to handling intense heat, but very brittle when flown into rain or even large water droplets.)

Fat chance any of us general aviation pilots will have this kind of service. Unlike shuttle ferry pilots, every pilot venturing out of the local traffic pattern, or flying in an unfamiliar part of the world, can never *really* know what's up ahead. It can be a guessing game if forecasts are in the least ambivalent, and there are no pilot reports to verify predicted conditions.

Yes, onboard equipment such as weather radars and lightning detection devices can be a big, big help—as long as pilots understand their limitations and know how to interpret their information. And yes, we can obtain a lot of good preflight information from the nation's system of WSR-88D Doppler weather radars, as well as the plethora of information available over the internet. The Terminal Doppler Weather Radar (TDWR) installations at many of the nation's busiest airports can provide invaluable information, too—such as detecting wind shear along runway approach and departure paths.

A new network of wind profilers—if approved and installed—will give us more and better information about winds and temperatures aloft, maybe even locate areas of icing, and do all this at six-minute intervals. That sure beats the twice-daily reports that today come from instruments launched by balloon.

What's more, computer modeling of the atmosphere is advancing by leaps and bounds. The latest models analyze 50 or more layers of the atmosphere, crunching such data as moisture, temperature, evaporation, wind, convergence, and divergence several times a day. This ability to process huge amounts of data should make for forecasts of ever-better accuracy, especially when it comes to forecasts involving storm systems and other mesoscale phenomena—that is, systems like low- and high-pressure zones, fronts, and thunderstorm complexes covering areas the size of many counties or states.

Meteorologists at the NOAA's National Center for Environmental Prediction (NCEP) in Camp Springs, Maryland have added a new computer model, the RUC (Rapid Update Cycle), to their existing arsenal of a dozen or so other models. The RUC makes new forecasts every three hours. To see what a RUC model looks like, check out the Unisys website at:

www.weather.unisys.com/aviation/index.html

More models are on their way to operational status. These include one very promising model, the "Stovepipe" model, which predicts the extent (horizontal and vertical) of icing conditions, and even identifies areas likely to experience the very dangerous large droplet icing conditions (such as those discussed in the chapter on the Great Lakes). This model is in the experimental stage, and was developed by the National Center for Atmospheric Research (NCAR). To view the Stovepipe model products, check out:

www.rap.ucar.edu/largedrop/national.html

To see other icing forecasts derived from the RUC models, go to the Aviation Weather Center's experimental neural net icing products at:

www.awc-kc.noaa.gov/awc/neural_net_icing.html

But even with all these developments, the weather reporting and forecasting system by itself can't make pilots weatherwise. In the end, it all boils down to someone sitting in a cramped cockpit somewhere, trying for all he's worth to figure out what meaning those clouds up ahead have for him. Or if he's in the soup, he's trying to arrange it so he comes out in one piece. The average general aviation pilot, for example, probably doesn't have weather radar, probably wouldn't know how to use it properly if he or she did, may not be instrument-rated, may not be instrument-current if instrument rated, and is shot through with doubt. Can you handle what's ahead? Should you turn around? Land a.s.a.p.?

As conventional teaching and testing methods have demonstrated, it's possible to know quite a lot about the weather, yet understand very little. Just force-feed the buzz words, memorize the prepublished test questions, and virtually anyone can pass the weather portions of a pilot knowledge examination. Pilots who learn about weather this way may actually reassure themselves this type of learning will make them safe in the air. But the most effective learning comes only from hard-won experience, and that takes time—and a willingness to accept risk.

Most of a pilot's formal weather education occurs at the macro level, where major concepts are discussed at some length. We first learn all about the importance of pressure systems, pressure gradients, fronts, lapse rates, dew points, atmospheric stability, fog, ice, and thunderstorms, to name just a few of the major recurring topics—all of which are very important elements of a pilot's weather knowledge. Then it's quick, on to the drudgery of memorizing weather abbreviations and symbols—all in preparation for that FAA Knowledge Exam.

Unfortunately, these discussions take place in a somewhat sterile environment, far removed from the microcosms pilots face in flight. Pilots learn about weather on a grand scale, then do their flying in small-scale, regional environments. Somewhere in the education process, a great opportunity is lost: The chance to relate larger meteorological forces to the weather taking place on a regional level. Understand what happens on this scale, and you've gone a long way toward reducing the risks of on-the-job training.

That's the aim of this book. Here, we'll rely on the certainties of weather, applying the climatological record of the past 30-odd years to areas of the United States that experience the same general weather patterns. Call it a regional climatology for pilots, if you will, or a book about expectations. Climate, goes a saying, is what we expect. Weather is what we actually experience. In the pages that follow, we'll talk about what you can expect from a region's weather—and do it in broad terms.

One key element in this presentation of aviation climatology is a series of charts that plot the frequency of instrument meteorological conditions (IMC—meaning ceilings less than 1,000 feet, and visibilities less than one statute mile). These charts came from a source which is, unfortunately, out of print: the United States Air Force's *Climatic Atlas of North America Flying Weather*, published in May 1969 by the 4th Weather Wing at Ent Air Force Base, Colorado. A four-season sampling (for the months of January, April, July, and October) of this information is presented after the introductory section (Pages xvii–xx). In the Appendix (Pages 288–291), another four-season series of Air Force charts shows where low IFR (ceilings below 500 feet, visibilities below one statute mile) conditions are likeliest to prevail.

Illustrations of a similar type of information, presented in a different manner, are featured in each of the chapters that follow the introduction. These charts identify areas of varying IMC probability within each chapter's region, collected from climatological data.

If these charts show one thing, it's that flying weather is mostly good. With a few exceptions, the nation's weather is VMC (ceilings better than 1,000 feet, visibilities greater than one statute mile) for a majority of the time. Even so, remember that VFR flying in bare-minimum VMC may be legal, but it certainly isn't safe.

We'll also look at some weather-related aviation accidents that took place under region-specific conditions to emphasize how some pilots experienced difficulties. In the interest of providing more recent examples of weather accidents, much of the accident data summarized in these pages is derived from accidents that occurred after 1990. In many cases, the National Transportation Safety Board has yet to determine official probable causes and contributing factors. Therefore, many of the report summaries you see here consist of preliminary information only. Nevertheless, the purpose of presenting these accidents is not to assign blame, but to make assessments about the weather at the time. Most times, the weather's influence on an accident scenario is obvious.

One of the great shortcomings of general aviation accident analysis and investigation is the absence of any information about the synoptic weather situations at the time of a weather-related crash. Sure, an analysis of a weather-related airline accident, or a high-profile general aviation accident of the type that killed seven-year-old Jessica Dubroff for example, may delve into the meteorology at work at the time of the crash. But for thousands of other weather-related general aviation crashes, weather analysis is conspicuously absent.

My methodology in analyzing the weather situations at the times of the accidents summarized here involved studying the *Daily Weather Maps'* 500-millibar, surface analysis, temperature, and precipitation charts for the days in question, then consulting *Storm Data* for any amplifications. *Daily Weather Maps* is a publication of NCEP; *Storm Data* is published by the National Climatic Data Center in Asheville, North Carolina. Of course, any mention of weather in the accident reports was also included.

For a more complete investigation of weather's influence on general aviation accidents, I would refer you to a publication entitled "Safety Review: General Aviation Weather Accidents— An Analysis and Preventive Strategies," published by the AOPA Air Safety Foundation in 1996 and authored by yours truly. This is a comprehensive review of accidents associated with all types of adverse weather, together with instructional materials. To place an order, contact Sporty's Pilot Shop at 1-800-LIFTOFF.

At this juncture, it's only fair to mention that I'm not a meteorologist. However, I've had formal study in meteorology at the Ohio State University, and taken meteorology courses from the University of Wisconsin. The rest of my weather knowledge has come about through years of research in the course of writing about aviation weather, the insight granted me by direct or indirect contact with scores of talented meteorologists well known in their field—and through personal experience flying in all sorts of weather conditions.

A few of the chapters that follow are adaptations of a series of articles I wrote for *AOPA Pilot* magazine, the monthly publication of the Aircraft Owners and Pilots Association. As originally published, the articles appeared in my "Wx Watch" column on aviation weather, and were spread out over a two-year period. Here, they are joined together in another incarnation, and in a new, expanded and improved format. I hope you find them useful and entertaining.

Thomas A. Horne

New Market, Maryland
February 1999

Introduction

With the Jet

For several reasons, fronts and other weather phenomena in the northern hemisphere move from west to east.

The principal reason for this is the movement of the jet stream—often called simply "the jet"—which is a high-altitude flow of high-speed winds that blow from west to east. Jet streams most often can be found in the 30,000- to 39,000-foot altitude range, with wind speeds ranging from lows of 50 knots to upper limits as high as 200 knots.

When jet-stream flows dip southward they create troughs in the upper atmosphere. This causes jet flows to shift direction to the southeast, then switch around to the northeast after rounding the southernmost terminus of the jet's journey to the south (*see* the illustration on the next page). In other words, winds of jet-stream strength blow around the periphery of the southward bulge of troughs aloft.

Jet-stream flows are not confined to the upper troposphere. Low-level jet streams can rip along at 3,000 to 5,000 feet MSL, and sometimes lower. This happens most often in the central portions of the United States, in advance of a cold front's easterly progress over the Great Plains or Central Lowlands west of the Mississippi River watershed. In these cases, the jet takes the form of a high-speed southerly flow—a surefire precursor of the fireworks to come when the cold front passes through, and a surefire surprise to pilots encountering such strong winds at such low altitudes.

Why the focus on the jet stream at this juncture? Because the following chapters make a west-to-east progression, following the jet stream, with each succeeding region carrying a unique weather imprint. As both upper- and lower-level airflows march eastward, their nature and interactions change, modified by terrain and latitude, and so produce the climates

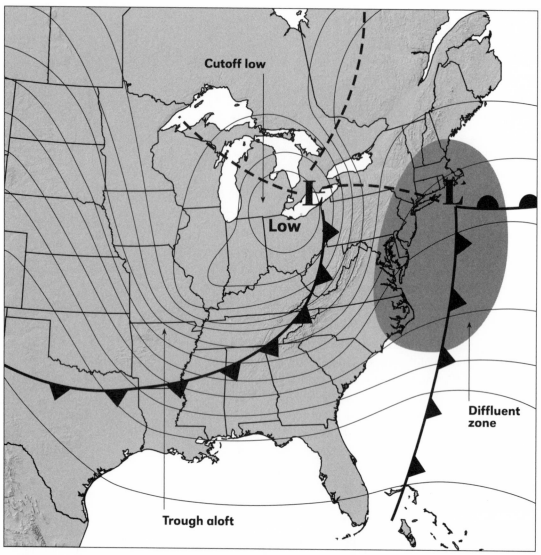

January 10, 1997: Here we have great examples of both a cut-off low aloft and diffluent flow. The cut-off low is over western Lake Erie at 500 millibars, or about 18,000 feet MSL. To its northeast is a surface low trailing a cold front and three troughs. Meanwhile, the diffluent, or fanning-out, pattern of the 500-millibar height contours over the eastern seaboard has set up the right conditions to feed a surface low off the southern New England coast. Surface lows often crop up in these regions "downwind" of a trough aloft. This trough remained in basically the same spot for three days, creating widespread precipitation and poor flying weather around the Great Lakes and most of the rest of the eastern United States. Three days earlier, the low off New England was in the Gulf of Mexico. It tracked to the northeast, following the trough aloft's southeasterly margin.

we fly in. Upper-air patterns create low-level weather, and low-level weather influences upper-air flows in an arcane dance that is still not fully understood.

What is understood is that the jet stream is more than just a whole lot of wind. Here are some known facts:

➤ It marks the boundary between colder air to the north of it, and warmer air to the south.

Therefore, it's a kind of high-level front—it's even called the circumpolar front by some meteorologists—complete with rising and descending parcels of air that exert immense influence over the weather below. When a strong jet teams up with a mean surface front, expect severe weather. That's because the jet and/or its associated trough provides the lifting force aloft that produces the strongest convection. It does this via temperature differentials. A trough is nothing more than a batch of cold air aloft, shuttled south by a willing jet. If it slides over warmer, moist, unstable air, the stage is set for explosive convection as the warm air below accelerates through the trough's cold cover. Sometimes, the upper-air circulation in a trough aloft becomes cut off from the trough's general flow. This is what meteorologists call a cut-off low, or closed low aloft; an example of a cut-off low is shown in the illustration at left. A cutoff-low aloft is a strong indicator that the low pressure aloft has deepened and has reached a mature stage that precedes its breakup. It's also a sign that the surface weather's movement across the ground is slowing down. (This is what television weathercasters are talking about when they refer to "upper-air disturbances," or "cold pools of air aloft" as causes of rotten surface weather.)

Other dynamics within the jet's core of strongest winds help set up squall lines and huge mesoscale thunderstorms in summer, and snow and ice storms in winter. The chapter on "Tornado Alley" delves into the details of the mechanics at work within jet cores.

➤ Jet streams steer surface weather.

In addition to creating the weather below it, jets shove it along. If you know where the jet is going, you have a fairly good idea of where the weather is going.

See "Height Contours: What are They?" on Appendix Pages 306–307 for an explanation of what height contours are, and how they are labelled.

➤ Jets identify locations likely to experience fronts and other significant weather.

On a 500-millibar chart (in which "height contour" lines represent the relative heights of the 500-millibar pressure surface at approximately 18,000 feet MSL), you can glean predictive information from a jet stream's early effects. At the southeast corner of a trough, for example, you can frequently observe a divergence of height contours. This frequently marks a jet stream's impingement point—the zone of highest temperature contrast between the trough's cold and the surface-influenced southern air masses, and the zone where lifting forces are greatest.

Find this "fanning-out" of contours (or, "diffluence"), and you'll know where to find the significant surface weather, goes a sixty-year-old forecasting rule of thumb. About fifty percent of the time, according to one meteorologist's recent case study work[1], diffluent upper-air flows are associated with deepening of surface low pressure. A representative example of a diffluent upper-air flow is also shown in the illustration.

With this as background, let's start our trip across America's flying weather beginning with Hawaii and flying east, riding on tailwinds strong and weak, high and low. As we go, we'll show some of each region's typical bad weather scenarios, as revealed through both surface and upper-level, constant pressure charts.

[1] Sanders, Frederick, "Upper Level Geostrophic Diffluence and Deepening of Surface Lows." (See Bibliography, Page 322.)

Percent frequency of instrument meteorological conditions (IMC)—ceilings less than 1,000 feet, and/or visibilities below three statute miles

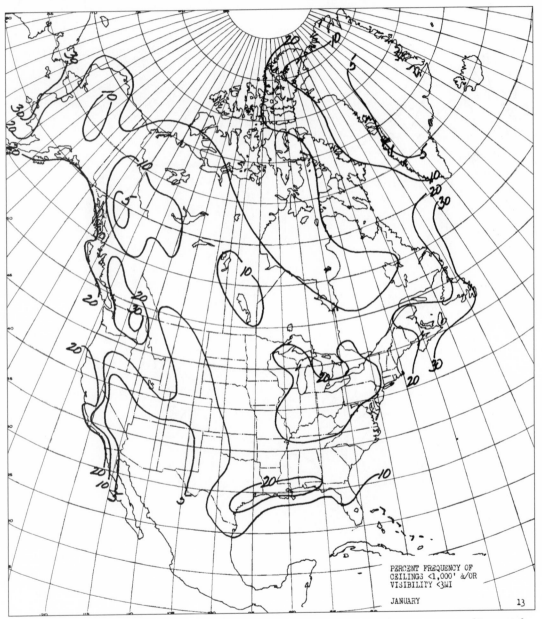

PERCENT FREQUENCY OF
CEILINGS <1,000' &/OR
VISIBILITY <3MI

JANUARY

13

Percent frequency of IMC for January. The highest frequency of instrument weather is concentrated in coastal areas and the Ohio Valley.

Percent frequency of instrument meteorological conditions (IMC)—ceilings less than 1,000 feet, and/or visibilities below three statute miles

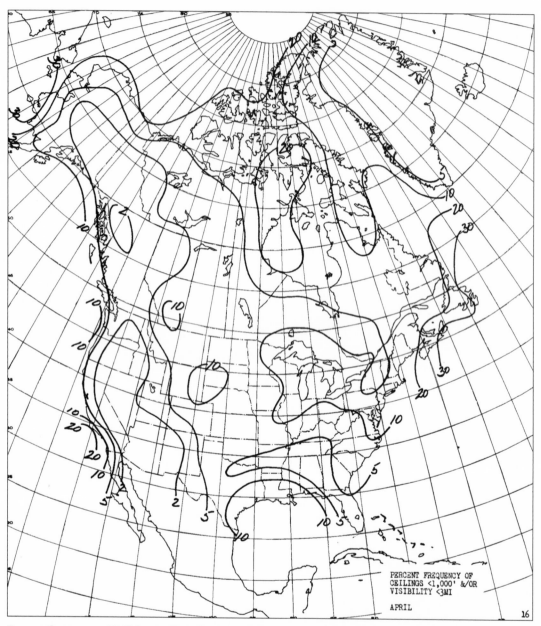

Percent frequency of IMC for April. *With spring's slightly warmer temperatures, instrument weather slackens off a bit, though coastal regions and the Ohio Valley experience less than in the winter months.*

Percent frequency of instrument meteorological conditions (IMC)—ceilings less than 1,000 feet, and/or visibilities below three statute miles

PERCENT FREQUENCY OF CEILINGS <1,000' &/OR VISIBILITY <3MI

JULY

Percent frequency of IMC for July. Now southern California and the western Alaska coast are the problem areas, while in climatological terms the rest of the nation is almost IMC-free. California's and Alaska's IMC is the product of onshore flows of relatively cool, moist air from the Pacific.

Percent frequency of instrument meteorological conditions (IMC)—ceilings less than 1,000 feet, and/or visibilities below three statute miles

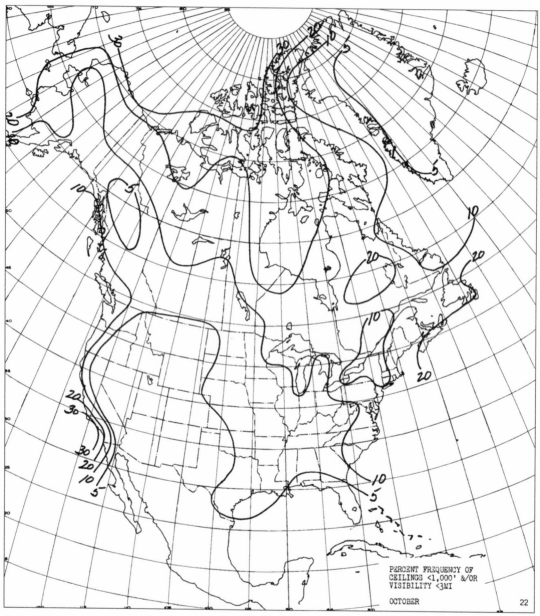

Percent frequency of IMC for October. *Cooler fall temperatures bring a greater chance of IMC to western New England and New York. Marine inversions and other coastal effects persist as IMC causes fog in coastal California.*

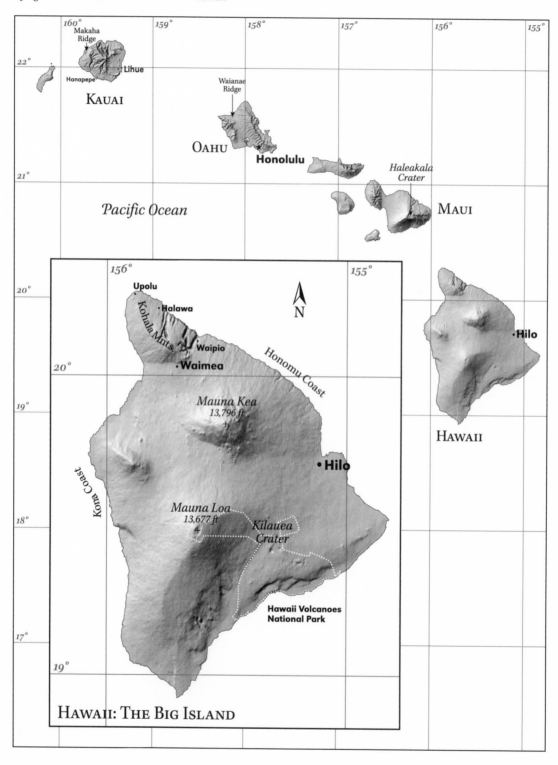

KAUAI

Makaha
Ridge

Hanapepe

•Lihue

OAHU

Waianae
Ridge

Honolulu

Haleakala
Crater

MAUI

Pacific Ocean

Upolu

Halawa

Kohala Mnts.

Waipio

•**Waimea**

Honomu Coast

Mauna Kea
13,796 ft

•**Hilo**

Kona Coast

Mauna Loa
13,677 ft

Kilauea
Crater

Hawaii Volcanoes
National Park

HAWAII: THE BIG ISLAND

HAWAII

•Hilo

Hawaii
And Hawaiian Breezes

Predictability is hard to come by when it comes to day-in, day-out weather, but the Hawaiian Islands have some of the world's most regularized meteorological events. Luckily for pilots, this predictability works in favor of VFR operations—with certain exceptions, as we'll soon find out. My familiarity with Hawaiian weather precedes my flying experience by several years, thanks to a job that necessitated a three-month training period there, back in the late 1960s.

My first memory of Hawaii involves arriving there on an airliner, and being bombarded by rainfall of Biblical proportions during the instrument approach to Hilo International Airport. The rainfall was so heavy that a missed approach was performed. Missed approaches can be scary for experienced pilots, let alone unwitting passengers, so the image of Hawaii-as-raging-storm was burned into my brain. Just minutes after landing, however, the heavy rain slowly subsided, the skies turned blue, and in the distance a rainbow graced the Big Island from horizon to horizon.

The Hawaiian Islands, where forecasts rarely have a discouraging word…courtesy of trade winds, Kona storms, and steep terrain.

More recent trips to Hawaii have given me great opportunities to check out this state's weather from a pilot's seat. Where before I spent a rain-drenched winter and spring studying on the Big Island's eastern, Honomu coast (with a few side trips to the sunny and dry western Kona coast), now I could quickly roam around at will. But some things never change. From my earliest visit, I seemed to recall it always being rainy on the east coast, and dry on the west. Those observations were as true then as now.

3

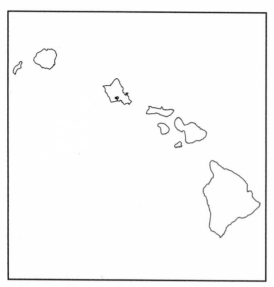

*Percentage of hours in **Spring** when ceiling is below 1,000 feet and visibility is less than 3 miles*

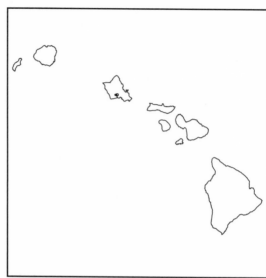

*Percentage of hours in **Summer** when ceiling is below 1,000 feet and visibility is less than 3 miles*

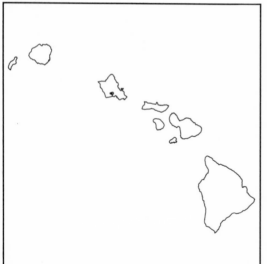

*Percentage of hours in **Autumn** when ceiling is below 1,000 feet and visibility is less than 3 miles*

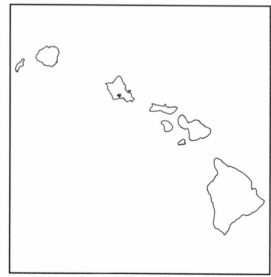

*Percentage of hours in **Winter** when ceiling is below 1,000 feet and visibility is less than 3 miles*

50% or more   **40-49%**   **30-39%**   **20-29%**   **10-19%**   **Less than 9%**

Note: Approximations based on derivations from the Climatic Atlas of the United States.

Trade Winds

This predictability is a direct result of the trade winds. These winds blow almost unceasingly, thanks to a semipermanent dome of high pressure that controls the North Pacific for all but a few weeks a year. Because the center of highest pressure is usually to the north and west of the Hawaiian chain, the clockwise flow of air around it brings surface winds (and winds up to about the 6,000- to 7,000-foot level) out of the easterly quadrants of the compass. Most often, the winds are out of the northeast. They're strong, too. Average speed is about 8 MPH, but fastest winds over one minute are regularly clocked at 30 MPH, and peak gusts have reached 47 MPH.

Imagine this flow of warm, moist ocean air coming up against mountains thousands of feet high, and you get a pretty good idea of what happens almost every day in Hawaii. The air rises as it strikes the easterly, windward slopes of the mountains, cooling as it goes. At about 1,000 feet this air cools to its dew point, creating layers of clouds that usually end up giving a more or less constant rainfall. To a certain extent, **diurnal heating** of the islands' surfaces aids the formation of clouds and precipitation, with this heating reaching its maximum in the late afternoon. This is especially true of the Big Island, with a land mass larger than the state of Connecticut.

diurnal heating. A daily cycle of surface temperature patterns, with maximum temperatures in mid-afternoon, and minimum temperatures in the early morning. (*See also* "diurnal," Glossary, Page 312.)

On the leeward, western slopes of these volcanic mountains this same flow of air descends, causing a **Chinook effect.** Just as air cools and condenses into clouds as it rises, it warms and loses its moisture as it descends. So, most of the western half of Hawaii—as well as the western slopes of most every other mountain in the Hawaiian chain—is sunny and arid.

Chinook effect. The temperature response to downslope winds (*see* Glossary, Page 310).

On all islands, land and sea breeze effects are frequently also at work. With the heat of the day, cooler, damper ocean air is drawn inland, to fill the "vacuum" created by warm air masses rising from the islands. The result: onshore winds and upslope clouds. At night, the process is reversed. The islands' surfaces cool, and breezes flow from land to sea, where temperatures are relatively warmer. Now, winds blow any upslope clouds out to sea. There, these clouds tend to organize in miles-wide bands of rain, lying offshore and stationary. There, they seem to lie waiting for the wind patterns to reverse, which usually occurs shortly after sunrise. This is especially true in the winter and spring months.

When they exist, cloud bases and visibilities rarely reach low (or IFR) levels. Because of lapse rate effects, the Hawaiian Islands seldom experience clouds below 1,000 feet MSL over the ocean or coastal regions. (The same is also true in the Caribbean.) Because most Hawaiian airports are near the shore, this means that IFR conditions are not usually a problem during the final approach course segment.

Ahem—except for windward-shore airports like Hilo International, on Hawaii, or Lihue Airport on Kauai. These airports face due east, and experience a good deal of rainfall, low clouds, and visibility restrictions in the heavier rains. These can come on suddenly, so an unwary—or unprepared—pilot on a VFR flight from a leeward-coast to a windward-coast airport can find him/herself confronted with instrument meteorological conditions, turbulence, and mountainous terrain all at once. Therefore well-honed instrument flying skills can come in handy, even in Hawaii.

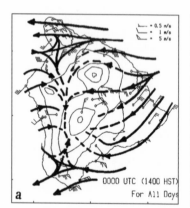 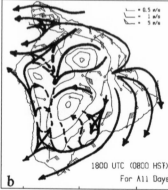 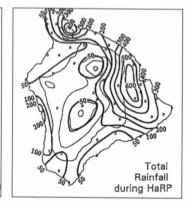

Figure 1-1. *A look at the wind flows and precipitation totals for the Big Island of Hawaii sums up what pilots can expect on all the Hawaiian islands. In (a), consistent sea breezes of around 10 MPH come on shore during the heat of the day, but at 8:00 A.M. (b), it's a different story, with land breezes flowing down the island's slopes and valleys to the sea. At right: During the University of Hawaii Department of Meteorology's Hawaiian Rainband Project (HaRP) of July and August of 1990, rainfall accumulations as high as 600 millimeters were recorded in the slopes to the west of Hilo—the area with the island's heaviest rainfalls.* (Diurnal Variation of Surface Airflow and Rainfall Frequencies on the Island of Hawaii, *Chen and Nash;* Monthly Weather Review, *January 1994, AMS.*)

A Volcano Special

Even native pilots can be caught off guard by instrument weather. A good case in point involves the April 1992 crash of a Scenic Air Tours Beech E18. The pilot was flying eight passengers on a "Volcano Special"—an aerial tour of Hawaii's picturesque volcanic landscapes. The flight passed over the Big Island's Kilauea volcano, then landed at the Hilo International Airport so that the passengers could have a land tour of the nearby Hawaii Volcanoes National Park. Six hours later, the Beech departed Hilo. The tour itinerary called for overflights of Akaka Falls on the Big Island's steamy Honomu coast, then a passage over the spectacular Waipio Valley at the island's northeast coast. From there, the pilot was supposed to track the 294-degree radial of the Upolu VOR and fly back to Honolulu. For whatever reason (probably to give the passengers a better look at Maui's Haleakala crater) the airplane took up a track of 310 degrees.

What did the pilot expect the passengers to see? Haleakala was surrounded by clouds and rain showers, and the pilot must have known it. The pilot of a subsequent Volcano Special that left Hilo 30 minutes after the Beech reported multiple layers of clouds, with estimated tops at 8,000 feet. This pilot said that Haleakala was totally obscured by haze.

Flight Service advised the Beech pilot that VFR flight was not recommended over the interior sections of all islands, and forecasted areas with visibilities as low as three miles in haze and rain showers.

Even so, the pilot flew into Haleakala, crashing just above the 9,600-foot level. A later compilation of weather reports concluded that the cloud bases around the crater were at approximately 1,000 feet AGL, and the tops were at about 10,000 feet—which would make them level with the crater's peaks.

The moral is to keep your distance from Hawaii's steep slopes when upslope winds are blowing, and when Flight Service issues one of its few warnings against VFR flight.

Some windward coast rainfall can be positively torrential. In February 1979, for example, Hilo recorded 45.5 inches of rain. I've seen this kind of rain, and it comes down in the kind of cascades that reduce visibility to IFR levels in a matter of seconds.

Hilo's mean annual rainfall is 128 inches (*n.b.*: Hilo's 1990 total rainfall was 210 inches), and Lihue comes in a distant second with 44 inches of precipitation. Honolulu International, protected by steep terrain to its east and west, only receives an average of some 23 inches of rainfall per year.

upslope effects. These weather-makers are also hard at work in other mountainous areas of the nation, as evidenced on Page 39.

Because of the **upslope effects** we discussed earlier, Hawaii's precipitation is greatest in the zone between 2,000 and 4,000 feet. Stations at those altitudes on the volcanic mountains of Mauna Loa, Mauna Kea, and Haleakala can rack up averages of as much as 300 inches per year—that's about 25 feet, to put things in perspective. It's the Big Island's unique combination of elevation, temperature, and wind flows that make the Big Island's Honomu coast annual rainfall totals the second highest in the United States. The award for highest normal annual rainfall goes to Kauai's east coast, with 400 inches of rain.

Even though Hawaii's average high temperature hardly ever deviates from the 72°F to 78°F range, there is a winter of sorts. Actually, it's more of a wet season than a bona fide winter. The months from November to April bring a northward migration of the Pacific high. This allows low pressure and cold fronts to affect the islands. In an average year, six to eight cold fronts can pass over the islands, dumping heavy rains.

Kona Storms and Hurricanes

Another phenomenon is the Kona (Hawaiian for leeward) storm. Kona storms are well-developed lows that usually station themselves west of the Hawaiian Islands, sending winds and rain from a westerly direction. It's a reversal of the usual tradewind pattern, and these storms often remain stationary for days, sending successive bands of rain showers and thunderstorms shoreward. Usually, one or two Kona storms occur each year. Hurricanes, which by definition carry winds of 64 knots (73 MPH) or greater, are extremely isolated events in the Hawaiian chain. In 63 years, only four have struck. The Hawaiian hurricane season corresponds in time to that of the Atlantic hurricane season, between the months of June and November. Peak hurricane activity often occurs in September, when sea surface temperatures are highest.

Microbursts. Details about "microbursts" (shown in Figure 1-2b) will be covered in later chapters (Pages 82*f*, 157*f*, and 192*f*).

The most devastating hurricane to hit the Hawaiian Islands in recent years was Hurricane Iniki. On September 11, 1992 it hit Kauai dead-on, its eye pausing north of the town of

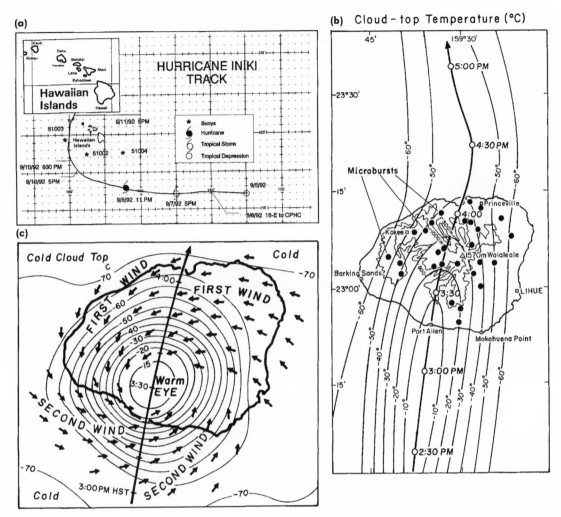

Figure 1-2

(a) *Track of Hurricane Iniki. Most hurricanes recurve, or take a turn to the east, once they reach high latitudes. Iniki followed this rule, but for Hawaiians the turn was ill-timed. By September 8, 1992, Iniki was starting its turn. By the evening of September 10, its course toward Kauai was set.*

(b) *Cloud top temperature. Iniki's track, eye-, and eyewall passage over Kauai shows that the hurricane spent less than an hour over the island. In that time frame, at least 24 microbursts—localized, extremely intense downdrafts—hit locations all around the strike zone.*

(c) *Cold cloud tops, warm hurricane eye. Super-cold cloud tops rotate around the warmer temperatures in Hurricane Iniki's eye. The first of the hurricane's counterclockwise-rotating winds struck the island of Kauai from a northerly and easterly direction as Iniki approached and then first hit land. The second winds, from the south- and westerly quadrants of the compass, came later, when Iniki crossed Kauai and moved back out to sea.*

*(*Damage Survey of Hurricane Iniki in Hawaii, *by T. Theodore Fujita.* Storm Data, *September 1992; NOAA)*

Hanapepe at 3:00 P.M. The first blast of winds came from the northeast. Then, as the hurricane passed to the north-north-east, subsequent winds blew from the northwest and south-west, reflecting the intense counterclockwise flow of air around Iniki. At the Makaha Ridge Naval Radar Site on the northwest coast of Kauai, an unofficial wind gust maximum of 215 MPH was recorded. Iniki was distinguished by some 26 intense microbursts, most of which were located in the interior regions of Kauai. These were studied and mapped by the National Oceanic and Atmospheric Administration (NOAA), as well as by noted microburst theorist and researcher, T. Theodore Fujita of the University of Chicago.

By a quirk of fate, the Lihue Airport went unscathed by truly destructive gusts. Pilots, apparently taking good heed of the National Weather Service's accurate warnings, stayed down the day Iniki blew through Hawaii, and no in-flight accidents were recorded on the fateful day.

Roaming the Big Island

A sightseeing flight around the Big Island of Hawaii is a great way of learning about Hawaii's usually benign, but blustery, weather. Take off from Hilo International Airport, for example, and you'll immediately run into those trade winds. Healthy crab angles will be needed to maintain ground tracks, and there'll be a fair amount of turbulence—some of it from sur-face heating, some of it mechanical, caused by flows of air over and around the nearby mountains and ridges.

By midday, clouds will form. They'll be scattered, at the 1,000-or-so foot level. Later in the day, the clouds may thicken and move onshore, bringing rainshowers—heavy at times—as they move up the island's volcanic slopes.

En route to look at some of the volcanic calderas in the Volcanoes National Park, you'll slowly climb as the cone-like terrain of the volcanic shield rises in elevation. If there are cloud bases, you'll see them rise with the terrain. A popular objective is to circle Puu Oo Crater in the Park. It's filled with a churning pool of molten lava (very impressive at night), and it's at the 3,600-foot level. The Kilauea crater, some 1,500 feet higher in elevation, is also a wonder to behold. But at that level, it can often be obscured by clouds.

There are a wide variety of climates on the Big Island, all in close proximity to each other. The northeast coast is lush, humid, jungly, and covered with sugar cane and ginger root fields. Waipio Valley, at the northeast tip of the island, has all the attributes of a rain forest. Fly five miles to its southwest, however, and you see upland prairie, vast grasslands, and large cattle ranches. You also see 45-knot tailwinds as you fly through the Waimea saddle, a pass between the Kohala Mountains and Mauna Kea. These winds are produced by the venturi-like funneling of the trade winds through the area near Waimea.

The Kona coast is full of beaches. And there's a desert south of Mauna Loa. Fly for the better part of a day, however, and you'll see some rain shafts offshore, and know that it won't be long before Hilo will have yet another dousing.

A trip to the Mauna Loa Observatory, near the summit of Mauna Loa can provide you with some additional insights to Hawaiian weather. From the observatory (elevation 11,150 feet) you'll see very uniform cloud tops hovering at 6,000 feet. This confirms another Hawaiian truism: except when Kona

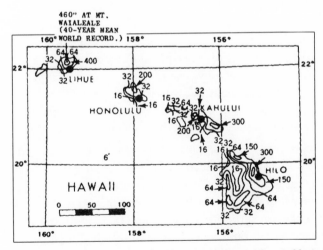

Figure 1-3. The Hawaiian Islands are located at trade-wind latitudes, where precipitation is normally scarce. But the abundant low-level moisture around the islands, the orographic lifting forces generated by the trade winds, and the heating of the high-elevation terrain combine to make these islands some of the rainiest on earth. With an annual total of 460 inches of rain, Mt. Waialeale on Kauai set a 40-year world rainfall record. The eastern coasts of the other islands also rack up some serious rainfall amounts; if IFR conditions ever prevail, there is where it happens.

storms prevail, count on what clouds there are topping out at about 6,000 to 8,000 feet.

These cloud tops are visible proof of Hawaii's inversion layer. They mark the boundary between the low-level air rising up the mountain slopes, and the descending air mass coming from the high pressure system aloft. The inversion layer also marks the transition zone in the direction of winds aloft. Below it, easterly trade winds prevail. Above it, winds are out of the west.

This means that on inter-island flights with courses running east and west, you can have tailwinds on each leg. Simply fly above 6,000 feet MSL on easterly courses, and below 6,000 feet MSL when flying west.

It's this inversion layer that holds pollutants and other particulate matter well below 6,000 feet. Above the inversion layer, skies are usually crystal clear—especially at night. This clarity, along with low humidity and a summit of 13,796 feet, is what makes Mauna Kea such an ideal location for the world's most sophisticated telescopes. Mauna Kea has several of them, along with a small community of astronomers.

The Mauna Loa Observatory makes the usual meteorological observations, but its real purpose is to collect data for numerous experiments. Some of their findings are disturbing. No question about it, says physicist John Chin, atmospheric ozone *is* increasing annually by .02 to 10 parts per million. That's a growth rate of one to three percent per year. Carbon dioxide is also on the rise. Apparently, global warming is a fact.

Hawaii promises a lot for any visiting pilot. Just be prepared to dust off your crosswind takeoff and landing skills, pay attention to your ground track and nearby mountains, and keep a sharp eye out for rain showers. If you're planning on island-hopping, make use of the FSS's inter-island flight following and reporting services. It rarely happens, but if IFR weather is encountered over the ocean, or an engine failure or other emergency occurs, Hawaii's excellent inter-island services can make all the difference.

As on the mainland, always obtain a complete weather briefing before every flight. The more information, the better. Just don't be surprised—like I was—if your request for a forecast is prefaced by a casual, "Oh, the usual."

Accidents

December 12, 1991, at about 10:00 A.M. At the Big Island's Waimea-Kohala Airport, a Cessna 172 was blown over while taxiing from the active runway to the parking area. There were no injuries. Weather was VMC with a scattered cloud layer at 1,500 feet. However, surface winds were from 060 degrees and blowing at 20 knots, with gusts to 42 knots. Typical tradewind activity at the Waimea saddle.

November 1, 1996, at approximately 7:07 P.M. A PA-34-200 Seneca I with five aboard crashed into mountains west of Halawa on the Big Island's northeast coast during a flight to neighboring Maui. Night IMC prevailed, with ceilings estimated at 1,000 feet MSL and visibilities of just over one-tenth of a mile. The pilot was non-instrument-rated and no flight plan was filed. All aboard were killed. The weather is consistent with the windward clouds and rain so frequent in this location at this time of year.

August 8, 1992, at 2:12 A.M. A Cessna 310 crashed into the ocean roughly eleven miles off the Honolulu coast. A local, personal flight, the pilot and a passenger took off from Honolulu and apparently ran into thunderstorm and rain shower activity, which was reported in the area. Controllers saw the airplane make a 270-degree turn while descending from 1,500 to 700 feet MSL, then disappear from their scopes. Both occupants are presumed dead. This time of year is characterized by tropical convective activity, and nocturnal storms off shore are common. Meanwhile, at Honolulu conditions were 4,000 scattered, 20,000 broken, visibility 10 miles, and winds out of 060 at 7 knots.

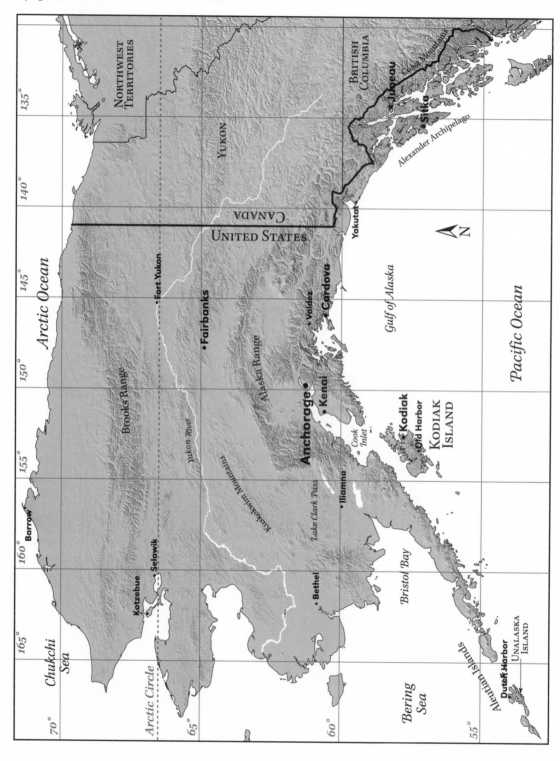

Alaska
Flying to the Frozen Zone

To a typical inhabitant of the coterminous United States, Alaska frequently conjures up the image of a solid block of snow and ice, interspersed with vast, forbidding mountain ranges. For portions of Alaska, that mental picture is correct. But there are many, many other aspects of the Alaskan climate that contrast strongly with this stereotype. Anyone planning on flying in Alaska needs to know the extreme variations that our 49th state has to offer.

A Land of Extremes: Visiting an arctic zone with an interesting mix of weather patterns

But first, let's deal with the stereotype. Yes, Alaska has cryogenic temperatures and rugged, bleak landscapes. But these conditions are characteristic of the terrain north of the Arctic Circle (the latitudes above 66½ degrees north), and the interior, mountainous portions of the state. Climatologists identify the northernmost Alaskan climatic division as the Arctic drainage; it's north of the Brooks Range, and bounded on the north by the Arctic Ocean. To the west is the Chukchi Sea. In this region, which most know as the North Slope of Alaska, Weather Service Offices are at Barter Island and Barrow on the northern coast, and Kotzebue on the western coast.

It should come as no surprise that winters in the Arctic Drainage zone are serious business. Take Barrow's Wiley Post-Will Rogers Airport. In January, the normal daily maximum temperature is −8°F; the normal daily minimum is −21°F. Record lows and highs were −53°F and 36°F, respectively. Mean wind speeds are 11 mph, which gives wind chill factors that fall off the chart. Kotzebue, being farther to the south, is just a bit warmer, with normal January lows and highs of 3°F and −11°F. Small wonder that Alaskan pilots have perfected the art of preheating their engines.

A big part of the reason for such low winter temperatures at these latitudes is that the sun is below the horizon continu-

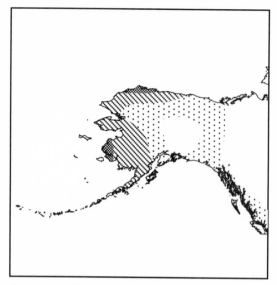

Percentage of hours in **Spring** *when ceiling is below 1,000 feet and visibility is less than 3 miles*

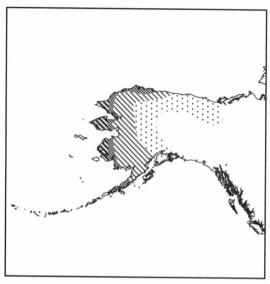

Percentage of hours in **Summer** *when ceiling is below 1,000 feet and visibility is less than 3 miles*

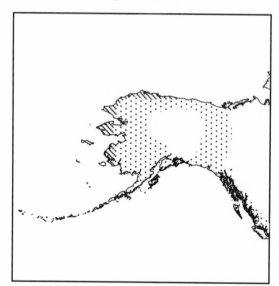

Percentage of hours in **Autumn** *when ceiling is below 1,000 feet and visibility is less than 3 miles*

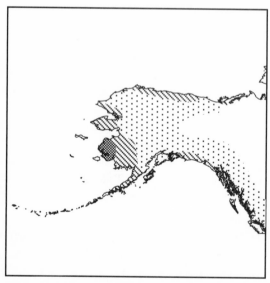

Percentage of hours in **Winter** *when ceiling is below 1,000 feet and visibility is less than 3 miles*

50% or more   **40-49%**   **30-39%**   **20-29%**   **10-19%**   **Less than 9%**

Note: Approximation based on derivation from the Climatic Atlas of the United States. Data unreliable at higher elevations.

16

ously from November 19 to January 23. With zero solar insolation, sea ice along the coast, and winds that can range anywhere from 10 to 60 MPH, the winter darkness goes a long way toward making life on the northern coast a reasonable facsimile of a survival existence.

But natives and visitors alike have come to terms with these rugged extremes, and winter air operations are usually not hindered for lengthy periods of time. The biggest winter problems in the northern areas usually come not from low ceilings—it's usually too cold for moisture to condense into clouds—but from blowing snow and ice fog. Ice fog forms in very low (–30°F or colder) temperatures when winds are light and particulate matter creates condensation nuclei. Any moisture in the air coalesces around these nuclei, and before long visibilities can be reduced to MVFR or even IFR levels. And once it forms, ice fog tends to persist. What's worse is that airplane exhaust (automobile exhaust, too) is a great cause of ice fog nuclei; this means that airports in the far north can, unfortunately, be plagued by ice fog for hours or even days.

Snow accumulations north of the Brooks Range are relatively meager, compared to the rest of the state. The annual average runs from 28 to 47 inches, which is a far cry from the 60 to 200 inches of annual snowfall that affects Alaska's south

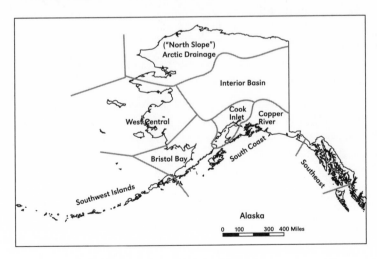

Figure 2-1. The National Weather Service divides Alaska up into an astonishingly meager nine climatological regions. While useful for quickly identifying the broadest sectors with the most homogenous weather, Alaskan weather is too complex to have so few regions. Each mountain range, mountain pass, bay, cove, inlet, or river can have its own distinct microclimate, and being familiar with this kind of small-scale local weather is essential for safe weather flying in Alaska. A more detailed analysis of the next-lower level of Alaskan microclimates can be found in Figure 2-4.

coast and southeastern climatic divisions. This is because a huge, very dry, semipermanent dome of high pressure is located north of the Arctic Circle in the winter months. The pressure can be so high that local altimeter settings can literally go off the top of the Kollsmann scale. At times like these, the regulations require the altimeters of aircraft flying below 18,000 feet MSL to be set to 31.00 in. Hg.

In Alaska's interior basin, a continental climate prevails. This region lies between the Alaska Range and the Brooks Range, receives an average annual snowfall of some 60 inches, and is also marked by wide temperature swings between winter lows and summer highs. Winter lows in Fairbanks, for example, may dip as low as −61 degrees (as it did in January, 1969). But in June, July, and August, surface temperatures ranging from the 70s to the 90s are not uncommon. In fact, Alaska's all-time record high temperature—100°F—was set in Fort Yukon on June 27, 1915. So yes, Alaska does have a summer, and a very tolerable one at that. Even on the North Slope, summer highs can reach as high as the mid-70s (although the mid-40s are the normal summer maximums).

The Aleutians, and the Soggy Southern Coast

POES. *See* Glossary, Page 315.

Now for the flip side of Alaskan weather. The Aleutian Islands, southern, and southeastern coastal regions are far more warm and moist than the North Slope and interior regions. In terms of frontal activity, precipitation, fog, high winds, and extremely deep low pressure centers, the southwest coastal areas of Alaska are where the action is.

This is because the area around the Aleutian Islands is home to a large number of intense storms. It's a zone that's squeezed between the high pressure regions of the Arctic and the Pacific Ocean. Flanked on both sides by these semipermanent highs and energized by a fairly continuous, vigorous jet stream, pressure gradients in the Aleutians become very steep. This is what makes Aleutian lows so windy, feisty, and persistent. Once an Aleutian low forms, the usual pattern of events is that the storms intensify as they approach southeastern Alaska, and mature as they hit the coast. Winds start to hit gale force, and ceilings can go right down to the ground.

Many times, Aleutian lows will form in sequence, one right after another. Then you have a daisy chain of powerful lows

GIL 092:22:10:26 7578   V3F4474 02APR78 N5 01S 13W

Figure 2-2. *A Polar Orbiting Operational Environmental Satellite (POES) captures an occluding Aleutian low pressure center at the west of the Bering Sea. The Kamchatka peninsula can be seen at the left side of the image, which was taken in April, 1978. Lows like these line up to assault Alaska on an almost daily basis in the colder months of the year. Though known for high winds, low ceilings, rain, snow, and very low central pressures, this particular Aleutian low is in the process of dying. The tight, spiraling cloud bands of this system usually indicate that the surface low pressure center has moved north of a jet stream's core of strongest winds. Deprived of this sustaining force, this surface low is slowly spinning down as it fills with clouds. Eventually, higher barometric pressure will prevail — but not until the low and its fronts inflicts at least some IFR conditions on the southern portions of Alaska.*

training along the Aleutian archipelago, each one dragging along IFR ceilings and visibilities and howling winds. This makes the Aleutians no place for pleasure flying, particularly in the fall and winter months, when semipermanent lows in the Aleutians lodge themselves overhead.

After pounding the Aleutians and southeast Alaska, these lows and storms usually head for the state of Washington and the rest of the northwestern United States. This direction of movement is largely a product of the jet stream's southeasterly track.

While the North Slope experiences most of its precipitation as snow, Alaskan coasts to the southwest and southeast get hit with double doses of precipitation—rain and snow, in various combinations. Often, a heavy snowfall is followed by a lengthy period of continuous rain. This spells bad news because the

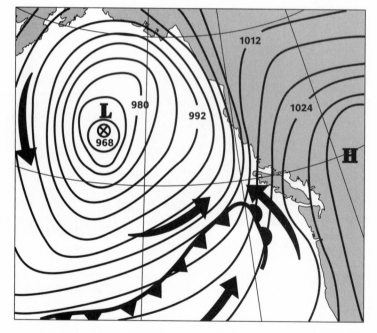

Figure 2-3. One type of low pressure system that affects the southern reaches of Alaska is the Gulf of Alaska low. These typically form somewhere to the south of the Aleutians, and then move toward the Alaskan Panhandle, intensifying as they go. The fronts they push ahead of them can lock the panhandle into IFR conditions and high winds for several days. Behind the fronts, the low's packed isobars signal surface winds that can reach 50 knots or more.

snow absorbs the rain. The resultant accumulations can become so heavy that roofs and hangars collapse. There have even been cases where boats have sunk under the weight of rain-soaked snow.

Advection fog is frequently present in Alaska's southerly climatic regions due to the movement of warm (relatively speaking), moist ocean air over colder land masses. These fogs can last for days, filling mountain passes and valleys, and reducing visibilities to low IFR levels. Compounding this trouble are the quirky microclimates that exist in the transitional zones between the warm coast and the frigid interior. One pass, fjord, bay, or inlet can be clear, while the next one can be completely socked in. Regularly flying in these conditions generates the kind of local knowledge that has made so many of Alaska's bush pilots and other charter operators such experts at always "getting through," no matter how horrible the weather.

advection fog. A type of fog caused by the movement of moist air over a cold surface, and the consequent cooling of that air to below its dew point.

The Bush Flying Syndrome

The ugly truth, however, is that this knowledge is many times abetted by dumb luck. Accident statistics prove that Alaskan pilots often come to grief because of the unique combinations of conditions they face. Sudden onsets of IFR weather, a dearth of weather reporting stations, practically no radar coverage, unimproved landing strips (gravel strips and makeshift runways on gravel bars are the scenes of many accidents), and nearby high terrain contribute to many of Alaska's high number of aviation accidents.

A 1980 special study conducted by the National Transportation Safety Board (NTSB), entitled *Air Taxi Safety in Alaska* (NTSB-AAS-80-3), delves into some of the unique safety aspects of Alaska's flying weather. In the study, the NTSB identifies what it calls a "**bush flying syndrome**" among many air charter operators and pilots—most of whom use single-engine airplanes. Air taxi and charter flying, it should be emphasized, is essential to Alaskan commerce. In a state twice as large as Texas, and larger than Washington, Oregon, California, Arizona, and Nevada combined, general aviation airplanes are vital to transporting people and cargo over long distances and

bush flying syndrome. A defect in judgment caused by overconfidence born of successful past encounters with adverse weather in Alaska.

geography that would in most instances be impassable by any other means. Since almost one-third of Alaska's population lives outside of the three major urban centers (Anchorage, Fairbanks, and Juneau), and since so many live in isolated villages and surroundings, small airplanes are *the* way to get around. This helps explain why there have been up to sixteen times as many active general aviation airplanes, and eight times as many pilots, per 1,000 inhabitants in Alaska than in the rest of the United States.

Take the pressure to reach a destination, throw in mountainous terrain, sudden onsets of fog and icing conditions, comparatively fewer weather reporting and forecast stations than in the contiguous United States, often unimproved landing strips, and long winter nights, and you've got a recipe for airplane crashes. The NTSB study, which took in the years from 1974 to 1978, found that there were more than twice as many non-fatal general aviation accidents in Alaska than in the rest of the United States (23.54 accidents per 100,000 flying hours, versus 10.74/100,000), and the fatal general aviation accident rate (3.65/100,000 hours in Alaska, versus 2.14/100,000 hours for the rest of the United States) was also higher. As for the air taxi industry alone, the Alaskan fatal accident rate was more than double the rate of fatal air taxi accidents in the rest of the United States (2.57 versus 1.11 accidents per 100,000 hours).

© B. Martner

Mt. McKinley and circular lenticular clouds

In the four-year period, there were 311 air taxi accidents in Alaska (45 of them fatal), and 1,251 nonrevenue general aviation accidents (168 of which involved fatalities).

Many of those accidents were attributed to collisions with trees or obstacles during takeoffs, or botched landings. Others relate to poor runway conditions, which inspire some wags to assert that Alaska's accident rates could be cut by a third if gravel strips were eliminated.

But two interesting facts emerge from this NTSB study. One is that pilot error was blamed for 85.1 percent of Alaskan air taxi accidents; the comparable figure for the rest of the United States was 70.4 percent. The other is that adverse weather was named as a cause or factor in 24.3 percent of Alaskan air taxi accidents; bad weather was named in just 10.1 percent of air taxi accidents in the rest of the United States. The NTSB explained these discrepancies by pointing to the bush syndrome.

This syndrome, the NTSB says, primarily seems to affect high-time pilots. The study indicated that 80 percent of pilots involved in accidents had more than 2,000 total hours of flight time; 80 percent also had more than 100 hours of time in type; 80 percent had instrument ratings; and 20 percent held Airline Transport Pilot certificates. Perhaps most important is what the study didn't say about these pilots: there is no mention of how much of their flying time was accomplished in Alaska.

Bush syndrome seems to cultivate a high tolerance for risk. In Alaska, the NTSB says, it's not uncommon for pilots to fly in extremely poor weather. Taking chances is simply considered a part of flying. Stories abound of pilots who always manage to get through to a destination, no matter the weather, and who have even crashed several times and survived. These pilots become near legends and are spoken of with reverence by some young pilots, especially those new to Alaska. And so the willingness to press on in adverse weather has become entrenched in Alaskan aviation. It doesn't just affect pilots, either. Many passengers, acclimated by prior luck flying in rotten weather, often demand that a flight be made when conditions plainly dictate otherwise. Pilots, not wanting to diminish their reputation (or their careers) can succumb to the bush syndrome all the easier when faced with this situation.

Does the bush syndrome affect airline and run-of-the-mill general aviation pilots, those not in the air taxi business? It's reasonable to assume so. A subsequent NTSB study, entitled *Aviation Safety in Alaska* published in November 1995, noted that of the 172 commercial and private aviation accidents that took place in Alaska during 1993, two types of accidents accounted for 131 crashes—or 76 percent. These accidents involved VFR-into-IMC situations (eleven accidents, six of them fatal), and takeoff and landing accidents (120 accidents, three of them involving fatalities). Then the 1995 study took a closer look at VFR-into-IMC crashes, and found that the 1989–1993 rate was vastly higher than the rate in the rest of the United States. Alaskan commuter airlines had .6 VFR-into-IMC accidents per 100,000 flying hours; the rest of the U.S. had less than .05/100,000 hours of these kinds of wrecks. For general aviation, the VFR-into-IMC rate was .62/100,000 hours; in the contiguous U.S. the rate was approximately .25/100,000 hours. Air taxi operations took the prize for the highest VFR-into-IMC rate: some .91 accidents per 100,000 hours, versus approximately .13 per 100,000 hours for the rest of the United States.

Alaskan Aviation Wx Services

The 1995 study singled out Alaskan weather reporting deficiencies as factors in Alaskan flying risks. Although Alaska has 122 weather reporting sites, the NTSB said that these provided inadequate coverage for VFR flight operations. For example, Lake Clark Pass has part-time weather observers at either end, but no observers for the 80 miles of its most mountainous portions. The corridor from Cordova to Juneau, the NTSB said, has but a single weather station—at Yakutat, halfway between the 400-mile-long route. Another VFR route—the nearly 400-mile-long stretch between Anchorage and Bethel—crosses two mountain ranges and also has a single reporting station. That's simply not enough information for decision making on any kind of flight, VFR or IFR.

Alaska's new network of Automated Surface Weather Observation Systems (ASOS) and Automated Weather Observation Systems (AWOS) are other subjects of concern. Ultimately, the plan is for 47 ASOS installations in Alaska, and 44 AWOS's. Pilots have sometimes complained about the inaccuracies and questionable technologies bound up in the technology behind automated weather observations, but in Alaska these concerns are particularly well warranted. Inaccuracies of ceiling and visibility measurements are the biggest complaints, along with these installations' inabilities to detect the clouds and precipitation surrounding (i.e., about to descend upon) an automated site. Where automated weather reports are augmented by trained human weather observers this is less of a concern. But as of 1995, there were only six sites with this kind of report augmentation. ASOS and AWOS

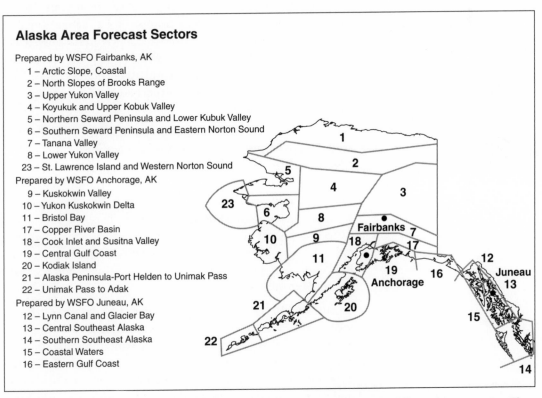

Alaska Area Forecast Sectors

Prepared by WSFO Fairbanks, AK
  1 – Arctic Slope, Coastal
  2 – North Slopes of Brooks Range
  3 – Upper Yukon Valley
  4 – Koyukuk and Upper Kobuk Valley
  5 – Northern Seward Peninsula and Lower Kubuk Valley
  6 – Southern Seward Peninsula and Eastern Norton Sound
  7 – Tanana Valley
  8 – Lower Yukon Valley
  23 – St. Lawrence Island and Western Norton Sound
Prepared by WSFO Anchorage, AK
  9 – Kuskokwin Valley
  10 – Yukon Kuskokwin Delta
  11 – Bristol Bay
  17 – Copper River Basin
  18 – Cook Inlet and Susitna Valley
  19 – Central Gulf Coast
  20 – Kodiak Island
  21 – Alaska Peninsula-Port Helden to Unimak Pass
  22 – Unimak Pass to Adak
Prepared by WSFO Juneau, AK
  12 – Lynn Canal and Glacier Bay
  13 – Central Southeast Alaska
  14 – Southern Southeast Alaska
  15 – Coastal Waters
  16 – Eastern Gulf Coast

Figure 2-4. Flight service station meteorologists dice Alaska up into a whopping 16 different forecast sectors. These sectors are used to identify synoptic weather features in Alaskan area forecasts (FAs). This can make a complete perusal of an Alaskan FA a long read, but it gives you a clear idea of the vastly different geographic features in that state—as well as an appreciation of the various microclimates indigenous to each one. Generally speaking, the worst flying weather occurs in the southern and western half of the state, and the coastal Arctic Slope (Sector 1) has generally VFR weather. Even so, ice fog and whiteouts sometimes plague the North and Arctic slopes.

deficiencies are legend, and while the National Weather Service is well aware of the problems of automated weather observation it has, to date, responded somewhat slowly and defensively to criticism.

As if this weren't enough, the FAA has seen fit to close many flight service stations in Alaska, as part of the FSS consolidation plan first enunciated in 1980. Where once there were 27 FSS's in Alaska, there are now 10. Some of these don't operate on a 24-hour schedule, so pilots flying near a temporarily shut down FSS often have difficulty calling up the next closest FSS once airborne. Four others are open on a seasonal basis. The three automated flight service stations—at Fairbanks, Kenai, and Juneau—are the state's centralized, flagship stations. If a nearby FSS in an AFSS's region is closed, then pilots can reach an AFSS for forecast information and other services. However, AFSS's are not required to issue airport advisories or make weather observations.

The 144 remote communications outlets (RCOs) in Alaska are set up to help relay VHF radio transmissions from pilots to AFSS's, and are designed to be usable down to 2,000 feet AGL along most of northern Alaska, and down to the surface in the south and southeast. Even so, pilots have reported problems establishing communications using RCOs. This is because an AFSS may be responsible for handling more than 75 different radio frequencies when seasonal or part-time FSS's are closed. It all adds up to potentially unsafe levels of timely and accurate weather information.

Suffice it to say that adverse weather and adverse terrain meet up in Alaska in such a way that avoiding the two must become the highest priority for anyone contemplating some stick time. This is especially true of the regions from Bethel to Kotzebue, and the area to the south and east of the Kuskokwim and Alaska mountain ranges. The NTSB identified southwest Alaska as the area with the highest (25 percent) number of accidents, followed by the zone north of the Arctic Circle (19 percent), the south central (16 percent), and southeast (14 percent) regions. The Aleutians and Kodiak Islands regions, with just eight percent of the accidents in the air taxi study, presumably reflect evidence of basic orders of sanity among the pilot population. No one with any sense would attempt to take on the weather in those parts.

Which brings us back to the Aleutian phenomena. Perhaps most troubling for pilots is that by the time an Aleutian low pressure system reaches the Alaskan mainland, it has matured to the point where an occlusion occurs. This melding of a cold front with a warm front (or more accurately, a cold front catching up with a warm front) is a sign that a frontal system is slowing down. This means that the occlusion's precipitation and icing can last for days before moving on, and affect the entire southern coastal areas of the state—right down to coastal British Columbia.

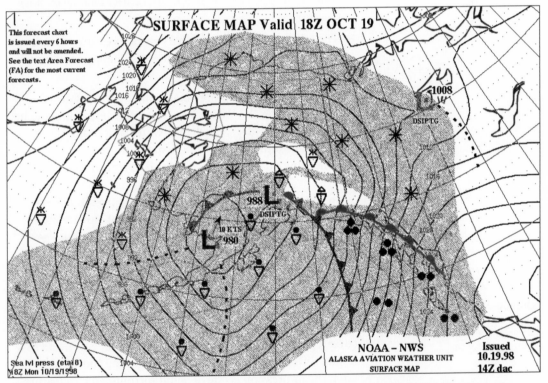

Figure 2-5. *Ah, autumn in Alaska, and double-barreled low pressure systems move from the Aleutians to the Bristol Bay and Cook Inlet regions. With them, they bring a warm front making landfall in the Panhandle, a cold front at sea, and a 400-mile-long occluded front stretching across the Kuskokwim Mountains. To the north of the fronts is snow, to the south and west, continuous and showery rain. This October 19, 1998 system covered much of the state with instrument weather conditions. (Surface map for October 19, 1998, courtesy Alaska Aviation Weather Unit, NOAA-NWS website.)*

To round out our picture, let's look at some typical southern Alaska weather events. First, a look at January 1990.

➤ On the ninth and tenth, a strong low with a central pressure of 28.35 inches of mercury (in. Hg) moved northeast from the Aleutians, then became stationary in the Bering Sea. Wind speeds at Shemya gusted to 53 knots. From the tenth to the thirteenth, a series of lows moved north of the Gulf of Alaska and into the Cook Inlet area, producing heavy snow. Valdez received 33 inches of snow on the tenth and another 11 inches on the twelfth and thirteenth. In Anchorage, visibilities dropped as low as one-sixteenth of a mile in blowing snow.

➤ The following day, a low with a central pressure of 28.30 in. Hg moved through the Aleutians. Winds gusted from 50 to 60 knots.

➤ From the fifteenth to the nineteenth, a series of deep lows once again hit the Valdez area, this time dumping 65 inches of snow in two days. In all, high winds and blizzards affected southern Alaska on 16 days that January. And this is nothing out of the ordinary for that time of year.

In the summer months, things slacken up a bit. For example, in August 1990, only five days brought violent lows. Still, these were enough to cause widespread flooding.

Whiteout!

whiteout. A loss of visual reference in conditions where all terrain and weather presents a white appearance.

Finally, no discussion of Alaskan weather would be complete without a mention of **whiteout**. A pilot can experience whiteout when flying beneath an overcast and over an area of solid snow cover. The sun's rays are scattered by the cloud cover, and this bright, diffuse light is in turn reflected off the snow. For the pilot, the impression is one of being surrounded by a featureless, radiant field of white—hence the name. It's rather like instrument flying in that no horizon is visible and no surface features are available for ground reference. Whiteouts are extremely dangerous. Not only can they lead to spatial disorientation, but there have been many cases where pilots have flown into terrain they simply could not discern in the enveloping brilliance.

A pilot in a whiteout will wish he was on the ground, and right away. If this isn't an emergency, I don't know what is. But without any ground reference, how could you time your flare, or know how high to fly your "pattern," if contemplating an off-airport precautionary landing? According to legend, pilots can deal with this if they drop dark-colored objects from the airplane, then use their relative sizes and positions to get an idea of the forced landing spot. There are stories of pilots who carried pine boughs in their airplanes expressly for this purpose. If a whiteout occurred, the pilot opened a door, threw out the boughs, and would then be able to see them clearly against a snow-covered surface. The pine boughs wouldn't exactly be up to Visual Approach Slope Indicator (VASI) standards of excellence, but hey, they'd be better than nothing in a whiteout.

None of these horror stories should discourage visiting pilots from flying in Alaska. The state is one of inspiring beauty, and one of the best ways to take in the sights is from the air. Because of its vast coastal area and plentiful harbors, the southern portions of the state are extremely popular with seaplane pilots.

Minimize your risk by constantly staying abreast of the latest weather. Another idea—always good when new to flying in a region as climatologically complex and fickle as Alaska—is to fly with a local instructor before heading out on your own in unfamiliar territory. The dual instruction will do you good, and a native pilot can help warn you against dangerous areas and microclimates, as well as direct you to locations with the best airports and the best flying conditions.

© Burke Mees

Dutch Harbor airport, in the Aleutian Islands

Accidents

On September 22, 1994 a float-equipped Cessna 185 crashed into mountainous terrain after a 9:30 A.M. takeoff from a private airstrip next to a river 34 miles east of Juneau. Marginal VMC to IMC weather prevailed at the time, but a VFR flight plan was filed. Witnesses said the weather was poor, with one-mile visibility in heavy rain. After takeoff, the airplane was seen making steep turns in a valley five miles from the airport. A witness lost sight of the airplane after it flew into a cloud. Both the pilot and his passenger were killed. A surface cold front, extending from a low in the Yukon, had just passed through southeastern Alaska.

On March 7, 1993 at 11:30 A.M. the pilot and two passengers aboard a PA-22 Piper Tri-Pacer were seriously injured after entering whiteout conditions and crashing into a lake 10 miles south of Iliamna in an inverted attitude. The pilot said he took off in IMC, but intended to navigate by reference to ground features along the shoreline of a lake. He said he climbed to what he thought was an altitude of 200 to 300 feet above ground level (AGL), but soon realized that there were no prominent features along the shoreline. He became engrossed in "trying to find the ground rather than flying the airplane," became spatially disoriented, then crashed. A surface low was some 300 miles to the southwest, leaving Iliamna in the moist southerly flow in advance of a weak occluded front.

The pilot of a Cessna 207 Stationair on an air taxi flight was seriously injured on March 25, 1995 when he crashed into terrain while trying to negotiate a mountain pass near Old Harbor at 7:40 P.M. He was trying to reach Kodiak. Ceilings were reported as being 1,000 feet. A pilot of another airplane told the Stationair pilot that the higher-elevation passes were closed, but he decided to fly into this pass to see if he could make it. He soon saw that the pass was closed by clouds, then turned right to reverse course, entering the clouds in the process. The left wing hit a mountain, and it and the engine broke off and remained at the summit. The rest of the airplane fell to a lower elevation. A weak cold front to the west of Old Harbor—which is on the east coast of Kodiak Island—was putting the accident site in a weak southerly flow of moist air with temperatures in the low 40s and dew points in the high 30s.

Another Cessna 207 on an air taxi cargo flight crashed into ice-covered terrain after taking off from the Kotzebue airport, bound for Selawik on April 17, 1996. IMC prevailed, a VFR flight plan was filed, and the pilot departed on a Special VFR clearance. Witnesses said that "flat lighting conditions" existed at the airport. The airplane was observed climbing to about 500 to 700 feet AGL. Then it entered a 90-degree bank to the right and crashed. A special weather observation taken at 12:51 P.M. (three minutes before the crash) reported: Sky and ceiling partially obscured; 2,800 feet scattered; measured 5,000 feet overcast; visibility 2½ miles, variable in light snow and fog; wind 310 degrees at seven knots; altimeter 29.41; remarks—snow covering one-tenth of the surface and visibility two to three miles. Surface analysis charts for the day in question do not permit a view of the Kotzebue region.

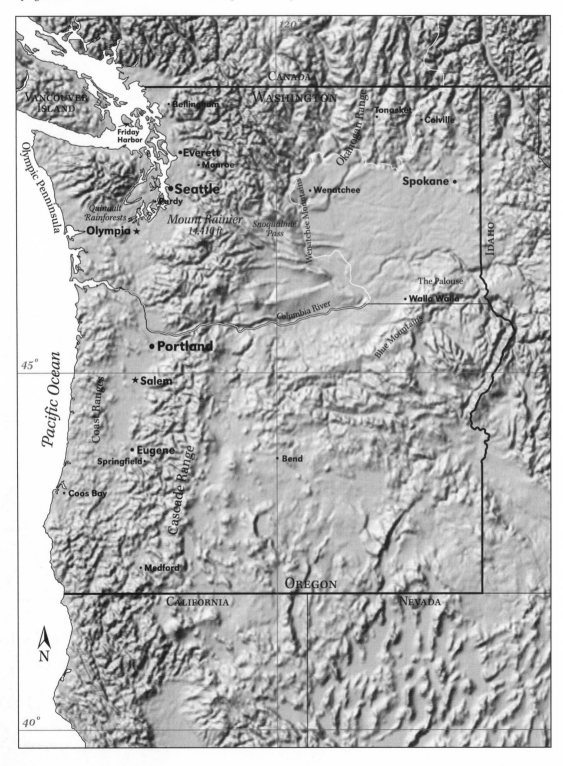

Washington and Oregon

Home of IFR

*VFR at its most glorious —
sandwiched between nine
months of IMC*

When high pressure ridges north over the Pacific Northwest, and the jet stream meanders up into British Columbia and Alberta, the states of Washington and Oregon can experience some of the most beautiful flying weather anywhere in the country. At lower altitudes, temperatures rarely become torrid in summer or bone-chilling cold in winter when ridging occurs, and sunny VFR days welcome a most appreciative pilot population.

Winters in the Pacific Northwest can sometimes provide surprisingly good flying conditions. One time I flew to Washington in a February, expecting pneumonia weather and nothing but IFR. Instead, skies were blue, temperatures were just above the 50-degree mark. The winds were so calm that I was able to do some ultralight flying at a grass strip in Issaquah—just east of Seattle. Meanwhile, the rest of the northern tier of the nation was experiencing snow, ice, or rain. The reason for this weather contrast? Washington was under a high pressure ridge. The central and eastern parts of the United States was beneath a weather-making trough aloft.

Ridging happens often enough that ballooning has become popular in the region, a sure sign of stable, benign flying weather. And let's not forget all the seaplane activity in the Pacific Northwest. When good VFR happens, hundreds of the region's indigenous seaplane pilots leave their docks for their much-coveted fishing, camping, or sightseeing trips.

But alas, these kinds of conditions are all too rare. The Pacific Northwest's geography and air flows work for, not against, instrument flying weather.

The most important dynamic here is the close proximity of one of the semipermanent weather features mentioned in the previous chapter on Alaskan weather. This is the Aleutian low,

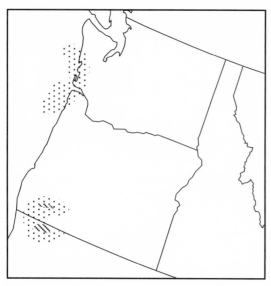

*Percentage of hours in **Spring** when ceiling is below 1,000 feet and visibility is less than 3 miles*

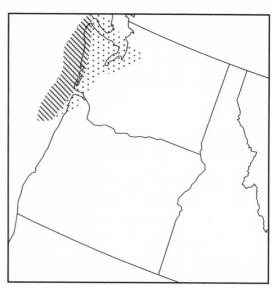

*Percentage of hours in **Summer** when ceiling is below 1,000 feet and visibility is less than 3 miles*

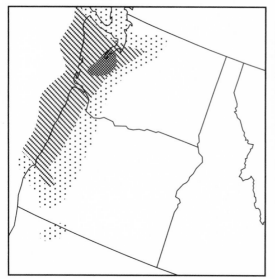

*Percentage of hours in **Autumn** when ceiling is below 1,000 feet and visibility is less than 3 miles*

*Percentage of hours in **Winter** when ceiling is below 1,000 feet and visibility is less than 3 miles*

50% or more **40-49%** **30-39%** **20-29%** **10-19%** **Less than 9%**

or rather, series of Aleutian and Gulf of Alaska low-pressure centers that continually traipse along the Aleutian chain, then dive for the Pacific Northwest, having a relatively short distance to travel before making landfall on Washington and Oregon. In the fall and winter months, the fronts they spawn are more vigorous, and the resultant precipitation is much heavier than at other times of the year. Ceilings come down, and visibilities plunge in fog and rain. And they can stay there for days.

Geostationary Operational Environmental Satellite (GOES) imagery shows Aleutian and Gulf of Alaska lows very distinctly. Just look for a spiral band of clouds near the Aleutians. Often there are a string of lows stretching along the Aleutians, each one signaled by a spiral band of clouds or large blot of cloudiness. If you see one and plan to fly in the Pacific Northwest within the next week or so, be prepared. You'd better have an instrument rating, and you'd better be prepared to use it. That's because Aleutian and Gulf of Alaska lows make a bee-line for Washington and Oregon.

Sometimes, the low-pressure systems will be simple affairs. On surface analysis charts, you'll see a single low, and a cold front arcing from it to the southwest. Other times, the lows can sprout many fronts. Often, occluded fronts—referred to as simply "occlusions"—may form as frontal systems come on-shore in the Northwest. **Occlusions** are created when a surface cold front "catches up" and overtakes a warm front ahead of it. What happens next determines the type of occluded front that's formed. Cold-type occlusions occur when the advancing cold air slides beneath the warm front ahead of it. Warm-type occlusions occur when the advancing cold air rides up over the warm front ahead of it. Either way, occlusions are really two fronts in one. There's a surface front—the one shown on surface charts—and a front aloft. The front aloft is either behind the surface front's position (cold-type occlusion) or ahead of it (warm-type occlusion). Many times, the front aloft contains more in the way of clouds and precipitation than the surface front.

GOES. Geostationary Operational Environmental Satellite. Orbiting at altitudes of approximately 22,300 statute miles with the earth's rotation, this satellite system gives continuous, overlapping coverage of the cloud cover, surface temperatures, and vertical distributions of the atmospheric temperatures and humidities below. (*See* Glossary, Page 313.)

occlusion. A composite of two fronts, formed as a cold front overtakes a warm front (*see* illustration in the Appendix, Page 303, for an example.)

How Low Can It Go?

You'll know when they arrive. There will be instrument meteorological conditions galore, along with vast areas affected by drizzle and rain. Be ready for low IFR conditions (abbreviated as LIFR in aviation area forecasts and terminal aerodrome forecasts, indicating ceilings and/or visibilities below 500 feet and one statute mile, respectively.)

How much IFR is there in the Pacific Northwest? Well, let's put it this way: The Olympic Peninsula and Puget Sound lowlands have the highest annual precipitation amounts of any location in the continental United States. There is even a rain forest on the windward slopes of the Olympic Mountains, one of the very few rain forests in the world located outside tropi-

Figure 3-1. Here's a common sight on winter surface charts in the Pacific Northwest—a low pressure system from the Aleutians and the Gulf of Alaska coming on shore. This system, drawn from weather maps of January 17, 1997, contains a cold front running to the south of the low, a warm front to the south-southeast, and an occluded front to the north. Coasts, valleys, and other low-lying areas were hit with low clouds that day. Hatched lines indicate areas affected by precipitation. As with most storms and fronts affecting the western half of the United States in the colder months, precipitation often occurs as rain at lower altitudes, and snow above 2,000 to 3,000 feet MSL. Icing in clouds and precipitation, of course, can also be expected.

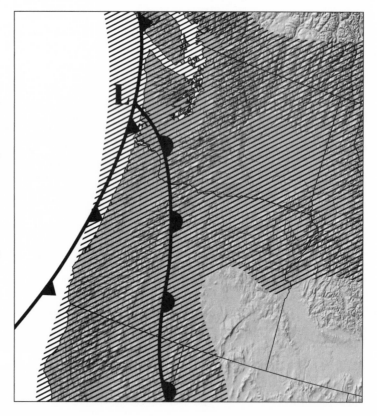

cal latitudes. The northwest corner of the state of Washington receives about 150 inches of precipitation a year. Seattle's average annual precipitation is 48 inches; 80 to 90 inches a year is the average for the bulk of coastal Washington and Oregon. Compare those figures with the normal annual precipitation levels in Hawaii, which range from 32 to 300 inches on the windward coastal areas, or southern Alaska, with its 64 to 150 inches, and it's simple to gauge the impact of the wind flows coming from the northerly sectors of the Pacific high.

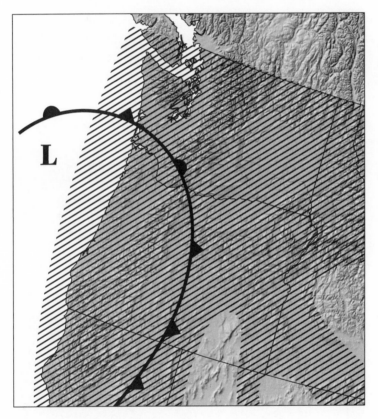

Figure 3-2. Another low-IFR winter weather situation in the Northwest can involve a Pacific low arriving from the west, and trailing an occluded front. Occluded fronts— sometimes referred to as simply "occlusions"—are usually created when a cold front "catches up" and overtakes a warm front. In this situation, which took place on November 19, 1997, a warm-type occlusion formed to the northeast of an Aleutian low when colder Pacific air moved over the slightly warmer air mass ahead of it. Farther south, over central Oregon, cold-front characteristics prevailed. After causing marginal VFR and IFR conditions in rain all along the west coast as far south as Los Angeles, by the following day the front dissipated and changed into a surface trough over eastern Washington.

Regional Effects

So much for precipitation. As for ceilings and visibilities, we know that the Pacific Northwest also experiences lower values than any other part of the nation—especially in the winter months. IFR ceilings and visibilities can be expected at least 50 percent of the time in any one winter month in the following regions:

> Vancouver Island;

> the Olympic Peninsula;

> the Puget Sound lowlands;

> the southeast portion of Washington, in the vicinity of Walla Walla and Colfax, and the Palouse–Blue Mountains region;

> Northeast Washington, near Spokane, Colville, and Newport;

> Oregon's Willamette Valley;

Figure 3-3. Annual precipitation totals for the Pacific Northwest show that the most precipitation and low clouds happen in the band between the coast and the Cascade Mountain ranges to the east. The northwest corner of Washington, with 150 inches per year, takes the precipitation prize. Once east of the Cascades, precipitation totals drop to approximately one-third the coastal levels.

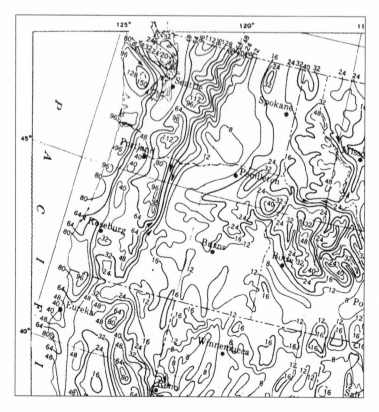

➤ the Coastal and Cascade mountain ranges, which run through both Washington and Oregon;

➤ the coastal inlets of Washington and Oregon.

Nearly all these regions have one thing in common: they're located on the windward slopes of mountain ranges. The rest are lowlands surrounding large bodies of water. The IFR-plagued Pacific Northwest, then, illustrates not just the effects of proximate lows, but also how orographic lifting can amplify the moisture that already exists in marine air masses. As the prevailing winds send marine air up the western slopes of the Cascade Range, condensation is given a boost, and the hillsides and nearby lowlands are drenched. Low-lying stratus decks are the rule.

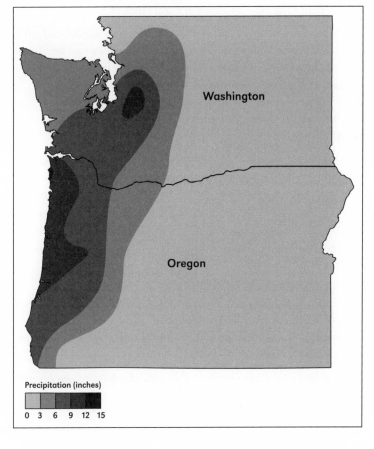

Precipitation (inches)

0 3 6 9 12 15

Figure 3-4. Winter storms from February 3-9, 1996 caused unusually heavy rains and lousy flying weather, as evidenced by this rainfall chart for those seven days from Storm Data. *The problem was a series of Pacific lows, some of them coming ashore with cold fronts pushing huge areas of precipitation ahead of them. (*Storm Data, *February 1996; NOAA)*

Move east, and the Pacific Northwest's climate changes dramatically. The lee slopes of the Cascades and the interior portions of Washington and Oregon have much drier air. As air flows over the Cascades, then descends their lee terrain, compressional heating squeezes moisture out of the air. This creates a "rain shadow" effect, a more or less permanent condition seen in the lee portions of many of the world's mountain ranges oriented perpendicular to prevailing wind flows. Upwind, it's soggy; the lee side of the slopes is comparatively rain- (but not cloud-) free.

Even in the inclement winter months, the east slopes of the Cascades have IFR conditions less than 20 percent of the time. South central Oregon's weather is IFR less than 10 percent of the time in winter. In fact, meteorologists often refer to central Oregon as a desert and, in fact, there is a desert of sorts—The Great Sandy Desert—in south central Oregon.

While the Pacific Northwest's coastal zones are loaded with precipitation in the fall and winter, temperatures can be much milder than those of other states in the same latitudes. High pressure ridges and northward-skirting jet streams explain this, but so does the influence of the ocean, which behaves like a giant radiator when it comes to influencing atmospheric temperature.

insolation. Total solar radiation received at the Earth's surface; the rate of delivery of direct solar radiation per unit of horizontal surface area.

Oceans are slow to heat and just as slow to dissipate heat once water temperatures have been elevated by **insolation**, or solar radiation received at the earth's surface. This gives coastal land masses colder temperatures in the summer months as sea surface temperatures linger, then slowly rise from their winter levels, and warmer temperatures during the winter when the residual heat built up over the summer is released.

The interior portions of Washington and Oregon have continental climates. We already talked about the rain shadow effect that occurs east of the Cascades and other mountain ranges. But three additional factors give these states' interiors their drier climate.

The first one is proximity to Canada, which often sends cold, dry air southward when a jet stream's trough bulges over the northwestern states. The second is a Chinook wind effect. Chinooks are periodic, short-duration events that are rather like more intense versions of the continuous rain-shadow flows. Once strong westerlies have traveled up the west slopes of the

Cascades and other coastal ranges, then dumped their moisture, they can flow down the easterly slopes. As this air descends, it heats by the compression of its molecules, as mentioned earlier. This leaves the areas east of the Cascades with a much warmer, drier climate than the coastal areas just 150 or so miles to the west. In the lee of the Cascades and the Okanogan, Wenatchee, Umtanum and other ridges in west central Washington, there is only 8 to 12 inches of precipitation a year. Hence the reason for calling these lee areas climatological deserts, even though they may not exactly fit the Saharan model.

The third strong influence on the weather of the interior sections of Washington and Oregon is the heating and cooling of their land surfaces. Unlike oceans and lakes, land masses are quick to heat up, and just as quick to lose that heat once given a chance to radiate it back into the surrounding air.

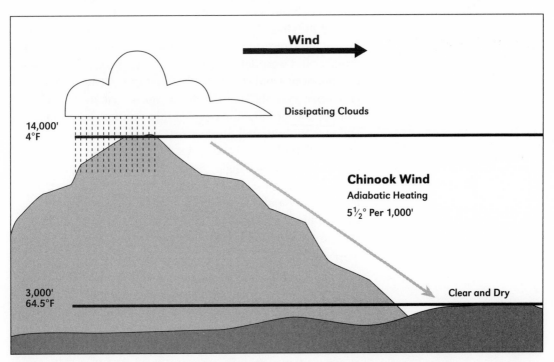

Wind

Dissipating Clouds

14,000'
4°F

Chinook Wind
Adiabatic Heating
$5\frac{1}{2}°$ Per 1,000'

3,000'
64.5°F

Clear and Dry

Figure 3-5. When fronts and storms hit the western United States, why do areas to the east of the Cascades and other mountain ranges often have higher ceilings and visibilities? One reason is the adiabatic heating that takes place as downslope winds, often called Chinooks, drop to lower terrain. This kind of heating is a reversal of the dynamics of air rising, cooling, and condensing into moisture, which is the case on the western slopes of the representative western mountains shown here. With Chinooks, air is heated and moisture is squeezed out of the descending air mass. The result is good VFR weather with warmer temperatures and higher cloud bases.

The net effect of all these influences is a more volatile temperature profile in the inland regions. Summers in the interior are warmer than those of the coast, and winters are colder. These rapid diurnal temperature swings of Washington's and Oregon's interiors also promote thunderstorms in the summer months. On average, thunderstorms occur on 20 days a year east of the Cascades. Closer to the Pacific coast, where temperature extremes are much less, there are only about 10 thunderstorm days a year.

Spring and summer bring the best flying weather to the Northwest. The Pacific high returns, bring sunny skies and drier air. Statistically speaking, IFR conditions then occur only 10 to 20 percent of the time.

Just watch out from fall to spring. Washington and Oregon can have horrendous icing conditions, some of the worst in the world—right up there with the North Atlantic and the regions around the Great Lakes and the Appalachians. That onshore flow of moisture-laden ocean air makes for huge supercooled droplets and legendary ice accretions. This is true all through the mountains and valleys of Washington and Oregon, particularly when a strong Aleutian storm comes onshore. Strong winds, blowing snow and freezing rain—both in low-lying areas and in mountains and their passes are other common features of instrument flying in the Pacific Northwest. It's best to fly an airplane certified for flight in known icing, have experience flying in icing, have an awareness that even ice-protected airplanes can't handle severe icing (by the FAA's own definition), and a willingness to turn around, land, or otherwise throw in the towel when ice accretions become too much for comfort.

If any place does, the Pacific Northwest emphasizes that every pilot should be a student of geography—simply because the earth's physical features have such an immense influence on weather. Buy a high-quality topographic map of the United States, hang it in a prominent place, and take a good look at the routes you plan to fly, whether it's in Washington, Oregon, or any place else. It's very easy to discern general weather trends just by learning a little about prevailing winds, orographic effects, and large- and small-scale pressure systems. Apply your knowledge and intuitions, learn from old hands who've flown in the area, and you'll have a definite edge when you receive your preflight briefing from flight service.

Accidents

On May 5, 1995 the pilot of a Cessna 152 took off into IMC weather from Monroe, Washington without a flight plan and, apparently, no preflight weather briefing. The destination was Tonasket, Washington, well to the east of the intervening Cascades. Witnesses in Snoqualmie Pass reported seeing the airplane flying east into the pass at about 300 feet AGL, and just under the cloud ceiling. They said there was fog and low clouds all through the pass. The airplane collided with trees at about 11:45 A.M., killing the pilot and a passenger. Lows at both the surface and at upper levels had been teaming up since the previous day, producing rain and low ceilings all over Washington and Oregon. Seattle, just to the west of Monroe, reported 400-foot ceilings, rain, and a temperature and dew point of 50 degrees at 7:00 A.M.

A pilot and passenger in a Mooney M20E were on a flight from Friday Harbor, Washington to Medford, Oregon on August 2, 1996 when the airplane crashed in a residential area in Purdy, Washington at 1:19 A.M. Both were killed. Night IMC prevailed, but the pilot was on a VFR flight plan. The pilot contacted ATC and asked for a lower altitude (he was at 2,500 feet), but was told to maintain a VFR altitude at his discretion. The airplane climbed to 3,200 feet, then descended to 2,700 feet before being lost on radar. At one point, the pilot radioed Seattle approach, asking for "...some help right..." The area was under the influence of a cold front passing through at roughly the same time as the accident, plus an upper-level trough draped smack-dab over Puget Sound. Another cold front, to the west of Vancouver Island, was on the way. Low IFR ceilings and visibilities were along the Washington coast, although conditions in Oregon and Medford were well above VFR minima.

Two Cessna 172s, part of a five-airplane flight, crashed southeast of Bellingham, Washington at 7:45 P.M. on March 5, 1991 after encountering IMC in the form of clouds and snow showers. The pilots received a weather briefing prior to their last departure from Everett, Washington, at 7:08 P.M. Two of the other airplanes reversed course and landed at an alternate airport after entering the weather. One airplane turned to the west, then navigated north and landed at Abbotsford, British Columbia, where the airplanes were based. A northwest–southeast cold front was over extreme southern British Columbia, and a surface low with a trailing coastal trough was forming off the Washington coast. IFR weather had been in the Seattle area for the past three days, thanks to support from a trough aloft at 500 millibars. The accident area was also affected by virtue of it being in the northeast corner of the developing surface low.

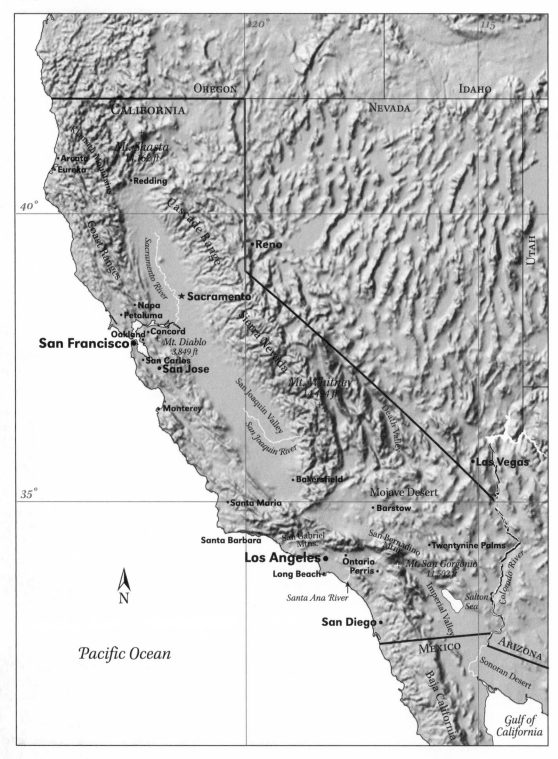

California
Fog in the North, Smog in the South

For pilots or any other student of meteorology, the state of California represents one of the most interesting weather regions in the United States. It is a state with an abundance of different climatological areas in close proximity to each other, a condition made possible by a unique combination of widely disparate geographic features. This is especially true of southern California, where the Pacific Ocean, coastal lowlands, mountain ranges, valleys, and a desert adjoin each other in a strip of land hardly more than 100 miles wide.

As might be expected of a state with 1,340 miles of coastline, California owes a great deal of its weather to the Pacific Ocean, and the air circulating above it. This oceanic circulation has some seasonal aspects central to the nature of California's summers and winters—especially in southern California. Like the Atlantic Ocean, the Pacific is the site of a large, semipermanent high pressure system. And just as the Atlantic's Bermuda high affects so much of the eastern United States' weather, so the Pacific high influences the western coastal areas.

But the differences are great. The clockwise circulation around the "back side" of the Bermuda high sends warm, moist air from the Caribbean and Gulf of Mexico inland. In California, it's the high's "front side" that's at work. Here, the clockwise flow sends air of more moderate temperature from the central Pacific to Californian shores.

In the summer months, the Pacific high is situated more or less due west of central California. There, it exercises a blocking function, preventing low pressure areas from traveling to the southern regions of the state. The flow of air is nearly always from the west, both at the surface and aloft, and wind speeds are moderate—seldom exceeding 40 knots even at

Where ocean, valleys, deserts, and mountains meet in deceptive tranquility

45

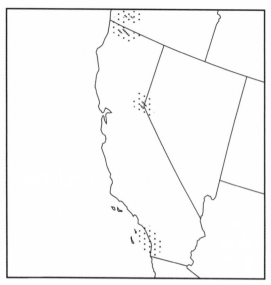
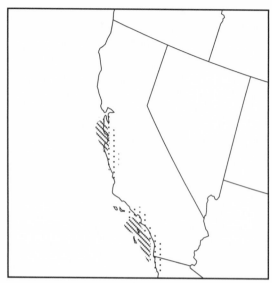

Percentage of hours in **Spring** *when ceiling is below 1,000 feet and visibility is less than 3 miles*

Percentage of hours in **Summer** *when ceiling is below 1,000 feet and visibility is less than 3 miles*

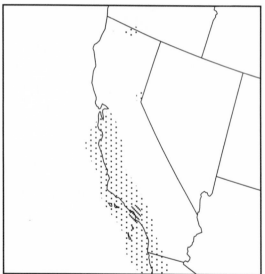
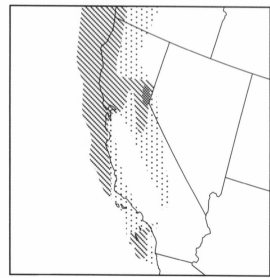

Percentage of hours in **Autumn** *when ceiling is below 1,000 feet and visibility is less than 3 miles*

Percentage of hours in **Winter** *when ceiling is below 1,000 feet and visibility is less than 3 miles*

50% or more   **40-49%**   **30-39%**   **20-29%**   **10-19%**   **Less than 9%**

altitudes as high as 10,000 feet. In the fall and winter, the Pacific high drops to the south, and this permits low pressure and/or cold fronts to strike California as they are pushed through by the northernmost segment of the high's flows.

It's useful to break California up into two basic climatological divisions—northern and southern. As an arbitrary point of reference, let's use 36 degrees North latitude as our dividing line. This would run roughly from a point south of Monterey across to Las Vegas, Nevada, well to the east of Death Valley.

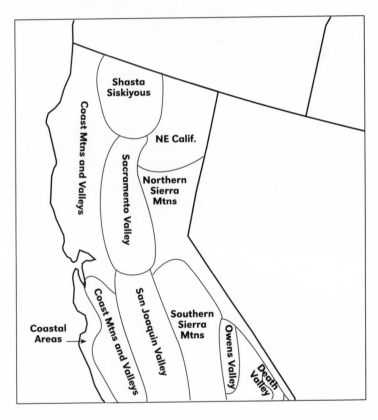

Figure 4-1. In northern California, a super-flat Central Valley is surrounded by soggy coastal mountains, and the turbulent Siskiyou and Sierra Nevada ranges. The San Francisco Bay area is a major passageway for damp marine air to flow inland to the often fog-shrouded Valley. The geographic areas and descriptors used here are the same as those used in area forecasts and other aviation weather reports.

The North

Northern California is a fascinating climatological region, because it has the same basic geographic features as those to the south of our dividing line—cool waters offshore, coastal lowlands, and a system of mountains and valleys extending to the east.

But the northern California coast ranges from five to fifteen degrees farther north in latitude, just enough to lower average temperatures by a few critical degrees. In January, for example, San Francisco's normal daily average temperature is 49°F; in Los Angeles, it's 54°, just five degrees warmer. But northern California's mean **dew point** temperatures average around 40°F, and normal daily minimum temperatures in January average 42°F. That's a 2° temperature–dewpoint spread, and you know what that means: Fog.

In southern California, the average temperature–dewpoint spreads are a few degrees farther apart. Just three to four degrees, mind you, but enough to give the Los Angeles basin far more VFR weather.

As in southern California, it's the clash between land and ocean air masses that give northern California its distinctive climate. However, its slightly lower temperature profile makes all the difference in the world. Together with the immense size of the Sacramento and San Joaquin valleys in the center of the state, this conspires to make much of northern California an extremely efficient fog machine.

The Pacific high—a semipermanent high-pressure region centered some 1,000 NM west of central California—begins setting the fog machine in motion. Its clockwise flow sends northwesterly winds to the entire California coast, especially in the spring and summer months. But northern California's cooler temperatures create unique effects. Air temperatures are cooler, and so is the temperature of the offshore waters. Add in the **upwelling** effect of the onshore winds on coastal current flows, and sea temperatures averaging in the low 50s are dredged to the ocean surface. That's why swimming from Alcatraz has proven such a disappointment to so many escaped prisoners (with perhaps a single exception). In southern California, offshore ocean temperatures are about ten degrees warmer.

dew point. The temperature to which a parcel of air must be cooled in order for saturation to occur.

fog. A cloud on the ground; formed when temperature and dew point are within a few degrees of each other.

upwelling. The rising of water toward the surface from subsurface layers of a body of water.

The combination of cool, moist air, cold waters, and a very close temperature–dewpoint spread are reasons enough for widespread IFR conditions in northern California's coastal areas. Just ask any of the pilots who flew into Arcata, California's airport in the 1940s. Arcata's fog was so thick, so persistent, that the government used the Arcata airport as a testbed for fog dispersion equipment. The first ceilometers were also reportedly tested at Arcata. The government reasoned that the fogs of northern California were the closest the United States could come to duplicating the dense fogs that plague England. In an effort to develop a means of ensuring that bomber crews returning from Nazi Germany would not miss their approaches to their home fields, scientists at Arcata took to burning diesel oil and 60-octane gasoline under pressure to quite literally burn off the fog. They even tried burning fuel in trenches along the sides of the runways.

The flames were 15 feet high, and these experiments worked. In fact, the original Southwest Airlines used the flaming trenches of Arcata to allow their DC-3s to land in WOXOF (Indefinite ceiling, sky obscured, visibility zero in fog), or zero-zero, conditions as long as the flames were dialed up. The captain would call the tower at the outer marker, the fuel was ignited, the fog "burned off" and the ceiling rose to a legal 200 feet. The subsequent landing was made between two rows of burning fuel—a sight that must have startled the passengers.

That's dramatic enough, but it's California's immense Central Valley that really helps augment this fog scenario. The Central Valley—more properly called the Great Central Valley—is a huge, low-lying flatland that stretches from the foothills of the Klamath and Cascade ranges in northernmost California to Bakersfield in the south, at the foot of the Tehachapi Range. At 350 miles long and 50 miles wide, containing the Sacramento and San Joaquin rivers, flat as a board, and surrounded on all sides by mountains, the Central Valley is a unique geographic oddity. There is quite literally nothing else on earth that matches its features. Longitudinal valleys in Chile and Pakistan come the closest in comparison.

At any rate, this is a lot of land surface, isolated from winds aloft by the mountainous circumference. Land heats up more quickly than large bodies of water, so when the summer sun bakes the Valley, the heated air rising from the Valley floor creates semipermanent low pressure centers. Air always flows from high to low pressure, so the fog-laden marine air is quickly drawn inland through gaps in the coastal terrain. The Golden Gate Bridge marks one of the biggest of these fog gaps. Smaller passes in the coastal range offer other fog passageways to the Central Valley.

See Appendix Page 297 for an inflight photograph of marine fog in San Francisco Bay.

(Incidentally, if you were ever uncertain about the term "advection fog," this is a great illustration. Advection fog occurs as a result of the horizontal movements of saturated air masses.)

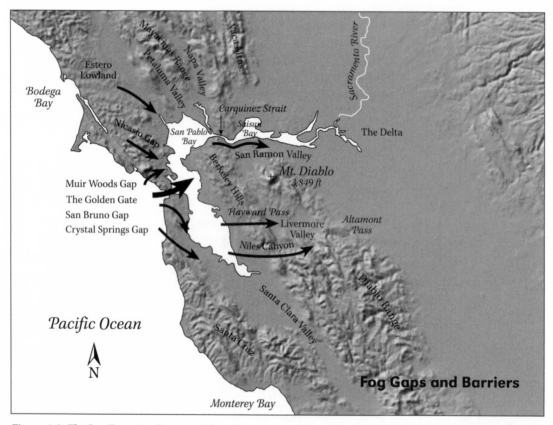

Figure 4-2. The San Francisco Bay area is home to numerous geographical gaps acting as pathways that allow fog to migrate inland from the coast. When low pressure over California's Central Valley draws coastal air inland, fog can move inland through the Bay area's many passes and valleys. On the other hand, the mountains and ridges around the Bay can block fog from moving any farther, causing it to deepen so much it can literally spill over high terrain to the Sacramento and San Joaquin Valleys to the east. It's times like this, when Bay area visibilities can go to Low IFR (ceiling below 500 feet, visibilities below one mile).

As summer wears on, the Valley reaches its maximum heating—produces its maximum levels of turbulence—and the inland flow of saturated air increases. As the Valley fills with this marine air, its air and surface temperatures stabilize at a cool, dewpoint-hugging level. With no more heat in the Valley, its low pressure subsides and the inland flow of air ceases.

After a few days, the sun eventually heats the Valley floor and burns off the fog. Low pressure reforms, and the fog machine's flow of air starts up anew. This activity follows weekly as well as daily cycles.

Because the air in northern California is so often close to the saturation point, be prepared for sudden fog and cloud formation. Anything that can lower air temperatures by a few degrees can do it—air passing over a lake or marsh, for example, or the shadows cast by clouds. The cool waters of an incoming tide often trigger fog near San Francisco's Golden Gate Bridge.

The Golden Gate also demonstrates how the San Francisco Bay area can fill with a deepening fog during the summer months. The warm air above the bay forms a temperature inversion over the air cooled just above the ocean's surface. This reversal of the usual lapse rate puts a cap on vertical motions at lower altitudes, and traps fog, clouds, and pollutants at low levels.

In the spring, that inversion layer is often marked by a fog bank that extends from the surface to the deck of the Golden Gate—about 200 feet AGL. By July and August, when the fog season is at its height, the inversion layer can rise to 2,000 feet AGL, covering the highest portions of the bridge in fog and cloud. Ceilings can hover in the 500- to 1,500-foot range, making VFR flight in the Bay area inadvisable. Often, ceilings go to low IFR levels—low enough to envelop the bridge and other obstacles, and virtually stop all flying due to zero-zero ceilings and visibilities. This is when the airlines frequently make use of their Category II, III, and IIIa approach privileges.

The Bay area is home to microclimates—zones where weather conditions vary greatly in short horizontal distances. This is important to know because when these fog events set in it's possible for Concord, for example, to be in the clear while nearby Oakland or Napa can be locked in the grips of a pea-soup fog.

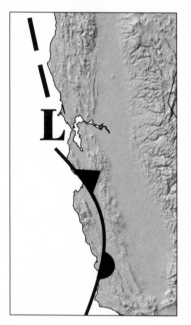

Figure 4-3. *Sunny California? Not always, and certainly not always in the winter months, when typical oceanic lows and weather systems such as the one depicted here can affect the entire western half of the state.*

tule fog. *See* Appendix Page 297 for a satellite view of a fog-filled Central Valley.

With autumn, the Pacific high moves south and the sun's elevation decreases. The temperature difference between the land and sea becomes less dramatic, and the onshore winds subside, along with the bay's foggy inversion. Fog season is essentially over, and it's during the autumn months that central and northern California can offer the best flying weather.

Winter brings the nearly complete breakdown of the Pacific high. This allows low pressure storm systems from Alaska and Hawaii to make their way to California. Both can bring copious amounts of moisture, and create widespread areas of aggressive turbulence and severe icing conditions. Typically, storms of Alaskan origin bring snows that cover the Sierra Nevada mountains from the 3,000-foot elevation. Hawaiian storms are known for their propensity to dump an abundance of rain. If they bring snow, it is likely to cover the Sierras beginning at the 8,000- to 10,000-foot level.

These storms affect central and northern California much more than the sunnier south. Want proof? Los Angeles' mean annual precipitation is 17.7 inches. San Francisco receives 21 inches a year. Northwestern California has a whopping 41.5 inches.

Winter also brings on episodes of very dense fog—called tule fogs—in the Central Valley. These are shallow, low-lying radiation fogs that can build slowly over several days, merge, literally fill up the Central Valley, then spill through the passes in the coastal ranges as they make their way west and north. These fog events often commence with buildups at the southern end of the Central Valley, which then advance northward and fill the Valley to the brim in the process.

By the third day after it first formed in the south end of the Valley, the fog can make its way as far north as San Francisco. Tule fogs tend to move to the west because in the winter months, Valley temperatures are cool relative to sea temperatures, and cool air is drawn to warmer, rising air. This means that the winter months are characterized by fog forming over land; in summer, the fog migrates from the sea. It also means that strong easterly winds can blast from the Valley through the East San Francisco Bay hills about five to ten times per winter, causing low-level wind shear as well as low ceilings for pilots flying in Bay airspace.

Pilots in northern California should be especially alert. In the spring and summer months, keep track of the onshore flow by watching the surface observations and terminal forecasts of coastal stations. Likewise, remember that a hot, dry central valley dominated by high pressure very often coincides with instrument conditions along the coast. Remember, too, that radiation fog is a very common early-morning phenomenon in the valley at this time of year, and that summer thunderstorms (and wicked turbulence) often form in lines along the Sierra Nevadas when conditions (high temperatures, high dew points, and unstable air) are ripe.

In the winter months, watch the areas around Hawaii and the Aleutian Islands. Satellite views can be very helpful in spotting storms that can bear down on California in a few days' time. Central and northern California have generally good weather, to be sure, but it's certainly a different climate than that of its southern portions. Expect more IFR, and expect fog to crop up at any time.

The South

South of our arbitrary, 36-degree-North latitude line, the weather of southern California features more moderate temperatures, and infrequent easterly blasts of hot, desert air—Santa Ana winds—from the regions east of the coastal mountain ranges. However, in the prevalence of coastal fogs, the flying weather of southern California closely resembles that of the northern segment of the state.

As an aside, it's interesting to note that the climate of southern California closely matches that of the Mediterranean coastal zones. It's easy to see the reasons why. Both southern California and the Mediterranean lie at about the same latitude, so solar heating is about the same in each area. Also, most of the Mediterranean's coastal areas face the prevailing westerlies, making them susceptible to fog-producing oceanic air masses. The Mediterranean also has its versions of Santa Ana winds, created by the heating of continental surfaces by high-pressure air masses.

Together with the topography of southern California, the onshore flow of high pressure affecting this area and the rest of the state is directly responsible for the coastal fogs and smog-ridden temperature inversions for which the Los Angeles and other nearby valleys are so notorious. An on-shore flow will always make fog a probability when temperatures drop close to the dew point, but southern California's flow has an added feature that makes fog a semipermanent feature in that area—at least in the early morning hours, when temperatures are lowest. The high's northwesterly onshore flow influences the ocean currents lying just off the coast, by churning colder, deeper waters to the surface. This "upwelling" means that water temperatures at the coast are always some 5°F to 10°F colder than the ocean surfaces 200 to 300 miles farther west. In the winter months, the coastal waters off southern California average 51°F; in summer, it's about 69 degrees—maybe a bit more in the late summer. Meanwhile, the ocean to the west experiences seasonal ranges in average temperature from 60 to 67 degrees.

Figure 4-4. This view of the climatic regions of the southern half of California, like the illustration in Figure 4-1, is taken from AC 00-45D. The 12 regions pack a lot of different weathermakers into the same state. While southern California features predominantly good VFR weather conditions, thanks to the vast deserts to the east and the coast's Mediterranean climate, the chief problems have to do with poor visibilities in the Los Angeles area, thanks to pollutants trapped beneath tenacious inversions, and turbulence over the desert basin.

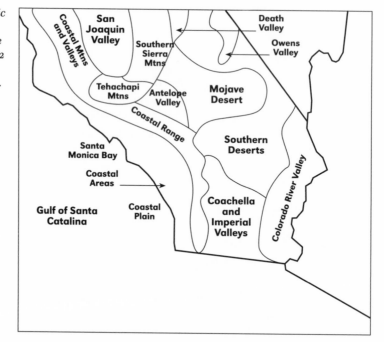

When comparatively warm ocean air flows over this band of cold water, its temperature is reduced, and the result is fog. But while fog is fairly prevalent in the valleys of southern California (Los Angeles International reports an annual average of 53 fog days, Santa Maria has about 88 fog days per year, and San Diego has around 30 days per year—mostly in the winter months), it is seldom long-lasting. Once the fog is carried inland, and the rising sun elevates ambient temperatures, it lifts and usually forms a low stratus deck. Above this cloud layer are cloudless skies and unlimited visibilities.

The air aloft is warmer, too, which creates the L.A. basin's prevalent temperature inversions. In the lowest layers of the atmosphere, air cooled by the Pacific remains stagnant beneath a strong mound of high pressure. Because the air in high pressure weighs more, it descends, and thus warms by the compression of its molecules. Where the high's descending, warm air meets the cooler, oceanic air mass, there will be the top of the inversion—at about 2,000 feet—marked by the sharp edge of a haze or smog layer. Fly above it, and you'll be in the clear. But when flying VFR down low, keep a sharp eye out for traffic, terrain, and obstructions.

Smog can be a greater danger to pilots flying in the Los Angeles area than even the most dense pea-soupers of the northern coastal areas. Southern California's fogs generally lift or burn off by late morning, but smog has become a nearly permanent fact of life in the Los Angeles area and the nearby intermountain valleys. With tons of automobile exhaust, an onshore flow, a temperature inversion, and two mountain ranges to trap the free flow of pollutants out of the valleys, the Los Angeles area frequently experiences marginal VFR and IFR visibility conditions. Even on a "good" day, pilots traversing the Los Angeles Class B airspace can have a difficult time picking out traffic in dense smog.

But if you don't believe a temperature inversion can exist over southern California, try flying a balloon, open-cockpit airplane, or ultralight. One early summer morning I took off from from Perris, California's Perris Valley airport, which is southeast of Riverside. I was flying a Quicksilver ultralight, and temperatures were a cool 50 degrees during the preflight and taxi. During the climbout, as I reached about 1,000 feet, there was a startling—and welcome!—change in the temperature.

It had to have risen by at least 20 degrees, and it happened as quickly as if you'd hit a switch. There were no clouds or any turbulence to mark this abrupt inversion, but it was there nonetheless. It made flying over the picturesque landscape even more magical than it usually is. Glass-smooth, warm air, a dynamite view, the sun-washed hills to the east sliding slowly by—and none of Los Angeles' heavy air traffic! It's a great way to experience low-level flying in "SoCal."

The Marine Inversion Layer

We've been talking about coastal fogs and inversion layers in both northern and southern California contexts. This shared phenomenon deserves a little explanation of its own. First of all, the marine inversion layer is another semipermanent feature of California coastal weather. And it's a product of sinking, warmer, high-pressure air aloft interacting with much cooler sea surface temperatures, as we've already mentioned. In southern California, the summertime temperatures aloft can be as high as 80 to 90°F, and sea surface temperatures as low as 60 degrees—so the contrast is great and the fog/cloud layer can be as deep as those of foggy San Francisco latitudes.

How does this relate to pilots flying along California's coasts? In the summer, cloud bases can be as low as 500 to 900 feet MSL, and tops generally max out at 1,000 to 1,500 feet MSL.

In the winter months, the inversion layer in the north can drop to the surface, creating zero-zero conditions. In southern California, the winter cloud bases and tops resemble the summertime altitude values—if a marine layer exists at all at that time of year.

Research indicates that the depth of a marine layer corresponds to a frontal or trough passage. The layer deepens with approach of a front or trough from the west (most often a fall or winter event), then thins out after passage.

A low-level jet stream can also be present at the inversion layer. Not a 100-knot, flight-level brand of jet, but a 50- to 60-knot wind of the strength that can occur in the midwest in advance of a strong summer cold front.

At least one marine inversion study showed that the cloud layers began as stratus layers in the vicinity of 125 degrees west longitude, which progressively merge and descend as they near the coast.

Many marine layer events also seem to operate on a diurnal (day–night) cycle. Starting at 5:00 A.M. or so, and lasting until 10:00 A.M., the marine stratus layers move inland. From 11:00 A.M. to 5:00 P.M., inland surface heating burns the marine layer back to the coast, thinning it out as time passes in the midday heat. Then, between sundown and the next sunrise, the marine layer rebuilds itself at sea before repeating the cycle all over again. The cycle can persist for anywhere between five and 10 days, and occur in either northern or southern California.

With this in mind, pilots should be prepared for early-morning instrument conditions when marine layers affect the coast, and not be surprised if a nearby front or trough causes obscuration of the coastal ranges and an interruption in any diurnal cycle that may have existed prior to the front or trough's arrival. Pilots flying from the dry, higher-elevation, severe-clear, desert-induced VFR regions to the California coast must prepare themselves to execute instrument procedures if they expect to safely and legally reach destinations along the coast or in inland valleys with openings to the coast.

Southern California Winters and the Santa Ana

In the winter months, the Pacific high migrates southward, leaving southern California vulnerable to low-pressure systems and cold fronts invading from the north. The first cold front usually makes its appearance in early October, and brings with it a steady rain that can last for several days. From then until April, southern California experiences most of its rainfall and adverse aviation weather. Rainfall can be intense at times, as evidenced by the mudslides that can occur this time of year.

The most unique feature of southern California's weather is a phenomenon known as the Santa Ana wind. The Santa Ana wind derives its name from the Santa Ana river, which cuts a pass in the San Bernardino mountains to the east. It is through this and other passes that, under certain circumstances, desert air makes its way to the coast. A Santa Ana flow is always warm and dry, with humidities sometimes as low as one-percent. Even more remarkable is the speed of a Santa Ana wind. In mountainous areas wind speeds can reach as high as

100 MPH, especially in passes, where the air is funneled through to the coast in a venturi-like effect.

Santa Ana winds can occur at any time of year. In the winter, a typical Santa Ana episode may occur after a cold front has passed the coast. Post-frontal high pressure then can stall over the Imperial valley and/or the Mojave desert. The descending high pressure air settles over the desert, flowing downhill and to the west as pressure builds.

Contrary to popular belief, it's not the deserts that give Santa Ana winds their relatively high temperatures. The air over the deserts may start out cool, but as it descends to the west, over and through the mountains to the coast, it warms through a **katabatic** process. Think of this as the lapse rate in reverse. If air cools with altitude, then it stands to reason it warms during a descent. The Santa Ana winds are to southern

katabatic wind. Any wind blowing down an incline.

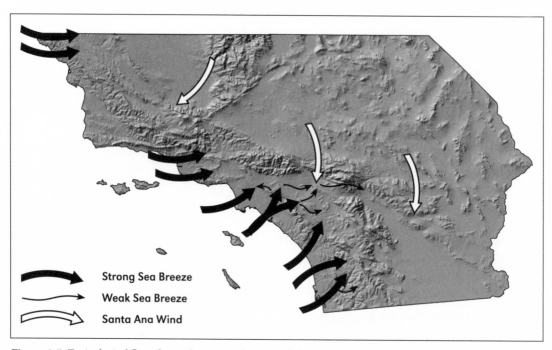

Figure 4-5. *Typical wind flows for sea breeze conditions and those times when Santa Ana winds affect Southern California.*

California what the Chinook winds are to the eastern slopes of the Rockies. For every 1,000 feet of altitude lost, the Santa Ana picks up another 5.5°F or so. With the high desert (the area north and west of Twentynine Palms) at an average elevation of some 2,500 feet, and the low desert (the region surrounding the Salton trough and the Sonoran desert) ranging to about 1,500 feet, the differences between these heights and the coastal areas are just enough to provide a warming effect.

Particularly strong Santa Ana flows often take place in the fall and spring, when a high over the desert clashes with a low at sea. The low intensifies the easterly winds from the desert high, helping to draw it over the Peninsular and Transverse mountain ranges toward the coast line. After a long, dry summer, the occasional thunderstorm often ignites parched foliage. Throw in a hot, dry, and high speed Santa Ana wind this time of year, and you have the makings of a forest fire—another seasonal feature of the L.A. basin, and one that can really cut visibilities when large amounts of smoke accumulate.

Santa Ana winds are rare in the summer months, because this is when **thermal lows** form over the deserts. Thermal lows impart rising motions to the surrounding air because of the intense daily surface heating of the desert. The counterclockwise circulations around these lows help keep the dry air east of the mountains. In the warm months of the year, a semipermanent thermal low will set up over the deserts of southern California, so don't be surprised to see an "L" parked there on a surface analysis chart for days or even weeks at a time. But this low is usually not a weather-maker in the sense of creating its own low ceilings and visibilities. It's caused by the high desert temperatures in this part of the region; the low pressure is the result of all that warm desert air rising in a kind of huge thermal effect. Many times, you'll also see a trough extending to the north-northwest of this thermal low, running up the entire length of the Central Valley. Again, the Valley trough is a summertime, surface-induced heating phenomenon. The Valley's warming causes pressure effects and rising air that closely resemble the dynamics occurring over the deserts to the south. These thermal lows and troughs are signs that turbulence will be likely, and that sailplane pilots will cavort in the abundant rising air.

thermal low. A low-pressure area created by the heated, rising air from a land mass.

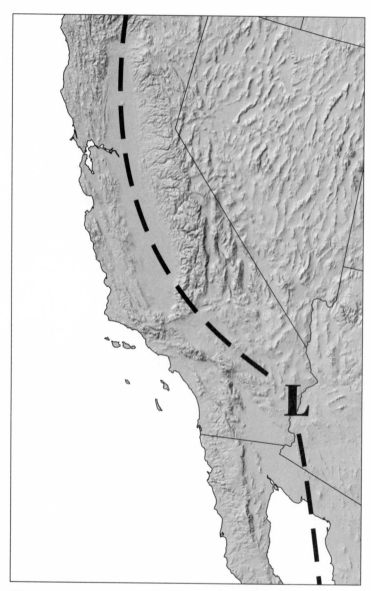

Figure 4-6. *Here's a common sight on many a California surface weather chart, especially in the warmer months of the year. A thermal low sets up somewhere over the Mojave Desert or Imperial Valley, and elongated troughs of low pressure extend to the north and south. The low is the product of the high surface temperatures and rising air coming off the deserts. The troughs, also creatures of surface heating, follow either the floor of the lengthy Central Valley to the north, and/or the Sonoran Desert or Imperial Valley to the south. The main impact to flying weather in this low-and-trough arrangement is twofold: moderate to severe turbulence all along the axes of the troughs, and thunderstorms over desert areas.*

However, those desert lows can be instrumental in drawing rain and storms from the Gulf of California to the interior of the desert southwest. This takes place in the late summer and early autumn, and can include thunderstorms and frequent lightning. Because this moist flow to the interior happens on a more or less regular cycle, meteorologists often call it a **monsoon**—since it resembles the cyclical onshore storms and raininess that hit the Indian and Southeast Asian subcontinents.

monsoon. A seasonal pattern of onshore (summer) and offshore (winter) precipitation movements.

For those flying in the desert areas when there is no "monsoon," IFR conditions will be rare, and confined usually to morning radiation fogs. However, with summer temperatures often higher than 100°F, density altitude calculations should become a part of every preflight. If density altitude erodes your performance too greatly, consider a late afternoon or early morning departure, when temperatures are cooler.

Though the conditions over southern California are usually benign, never forget the potential for extremes. Always, always obtain a thorough preflight weather briefing. The desert can be crystal clear one minute, then alive with sandstorms or dust devils the next. The coastal areas and valleys can experience quick changes in visibility as smog and/or fog builds and dissipates. And in the mountains—the boundary line between the moist oceanic air and the aridity of the deserts—always be prepared for turbulence.

When crossing the mountains, fly high enough to avoid any shear zones and rotors (2,000 feet above the ridge line is a good rule of thumb), and avoid flying too low in the vicinity of passes.

Remember that southern California's weather involves a bit of everything, and prepare accordingly. Most of the time, the weather conforms to the picture-postcard, Hollywood stereotype. But with so many climates packed closely together, it's only natural that conditions deteriorate from time to time.

Accidents

On the morning of January 15, 1991, the pilot of a Cessna 172RG took off from the Concord, California airport, located to the northeast of Oakland in the San Francisco Bay region. He was heard to say that he "flew the route to work over 100 times," which involved flying first to Hayward, California (south of Oakland) on an IFR flight plan, then on to his destination at San Carlos, a short distance across the Bay from Hayward. The day of the accident, the localized areas along the route were affected by radiation fog and a fog-filled flow of air from the Valley to the Bay. The air was further saturated from the rains of the day before. At Hayward, the pilot flew an instrument approach, performed a missed approach, then asked for and received a contact approach to fly over to San Carlos. He crashed into the Bay and was killed. Weather at the time was 200 feet overcast, with one-mile visibility in fog.

A Cessna 182RG pilot with just 158 total hours and only 3 instrument hours crashed during an apparent go-around at the Petaluma, California airport on the night of February 8, 1991. After taking off from the Napa airport—just about 15 miles to the east of Petaluma—the pilot evidently entered instrument meteorological conditions. Conditions at Petaluma were estimated as sky obscured, 150-foot overcast, visibility ½ mile in fog with calm winds. There was no record of a weather briefing. Conditions included localized radiation fog, weak temperature and pressure gradients at the surface and aloft, and an approaching low and cold front off the northern California coast—a typical winter bad-weather setup for instrument flight in the San Francisco Bay region. A dark night didn't help, either; the accident happened at 8:55 P.M.

At 11:50 A.M. on June 6, 1993, the pilot of a PA-23-150 Piper Apache died when he crashed into Mount Diablo (elevation 3,849 feet MSL) while on a flight from Napa to San Jose, California. Hikers on Mt. Diablo—who heard the airplane fly overhead at low altitude—said that the visibility there was "50 to 100 yards," and a park ranger arriving on the scene at 1:20 P.M. said he "couldn't see anything above or below" the crash site. Marine inversion conditions were at work, and there was a cutoff low on the day's 500-millibar chart (representing conditions at approximately 18,000 feet MSL). Precipitation from the day before no doubt helped increase fog density.

A Cessna 340 pilot took off westbound in good VFR conditions at the Big Bear, California airport in the San Bernardino mountains east of Los Angeles on December 7, 1995. The destination was the Brackett Airport near Ontario, in a low-lying, eastern extension of the L.A. basin. No weather briefing was obtained. As he descended into the fog-filled basin, the pilot asked for an instrument approach. At 6:24 A.M. the 340 was cleared for the ILS runway 26L approach to Brackett, but the tower was closed. Personnel preparing to open the tower made a weather observation at the time: it was WOXOF (indefinite ceiling zero, sky obscured, zero visibility in fog). After apparently losing control during a missed approach, the 340 pilot crashed into trees and a building ¼ mile from runway 26L's departure end. The pilot died. A trough at 500 millibars and a surface low in the desert southwest were the main weather features of the day. Dense fog and low ceilings were reported throughout the L.A. basin that morning, with 7:00 A.M. visibility readings of one mile at LAX, along with a temperature of 59°F and a dew point of 58 degrees.

On July 12, 1992 a Beech Musketeer pilot took off from Vacaville (northeast of San Francisco) to show two passengers the sights along the foothills of the Sierra Nevadas. Near Chico, in the northeast of the Central Valley, the pilot ran into building cumulus clouds at 8:00 A.M. while flying at 10,000 feet MSL. He tried to circumnavigate the clouds, but inadvertently flew into one of them. He wound up in a "high-speed dive at roughly 210 knots," according to the NTSB. After "pulling aft with all his power" the pilot regained control of the airplane. Nobody was injured. The incident wasn't reported until 15 days later, when an FAA inspector noticed the airplane parked at Vacaville. Both wings had major buckles, the outer wing panels showed a permanent upward set, and the fuselage was buckled, too. Typical Central Valley summertime convection was at work that day, probably worsened by the proximity to the Sierras.

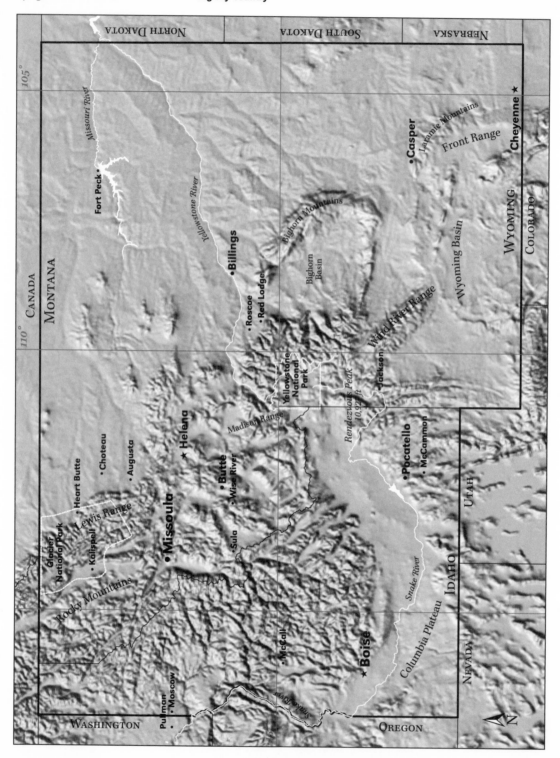

Big Sky Country
Montana, Idaho, and Wyoming

Strong winds, turbulence, and heavy snow mark the flying weather of the northern Rockies.

Ever notice that troublesome flying weather often seems to offer one of two contrasting dilemmas? It's either smooth air, stratus clouds, and low ceilings, or unlimited visibility, high winds, and bone-jarring turbulence. Which would you rather take on?

Well, if you're planning on flying to Montana or elsewhere in the areas affected by the northern Rocky Mountains, you'd better be prepared for a heavy dose of bone-jarring. There are exceptions, of course, and we'll address them shortly. But if you had to use one word to summarize the flying weather of the northern Rocky mountains, it would have to be wind—and lots of it.

This is particularly true of the late fall and winter months, when the progression of low pressure centers and cold fronts through this area increases in frequency. When an Aleutian low, for example, travels down southeast Alaska, through Washington State, and into the northern Rockies it can bring copious amounts of rain or snow, depending on the season. I say "can" because the Rockies have a way of wringing moisture out of Aleutian lows and their associated fronts—or any low or front coming from the west, for that matter. Meteorologists often describe this phenomenon as the Rockies' rain shadow.

Imagine a mass of precipitation heading east, then bumping into the Rockies. As the moisture-laden air rises up the steep terrain, condensation occurs. This means plenty of rain or snow in the mountains. So much that by the time the air flow passes to the east of the Rockies, it is much drier. The "shadow" is the dry area of the high plains, leeward of the prevailing winds. The mechanics that produce this rain shadow are basically the same as those that affect eastern

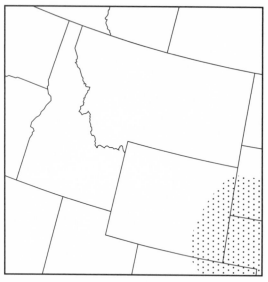

*Percentage of hours in **Spring** when ceiling is below 1,000 feet and visibility is less than 3 miles*

*Percentage of hours in **Summer** when ceiling is below 1,000 feet and visibility is less than 3 miles*

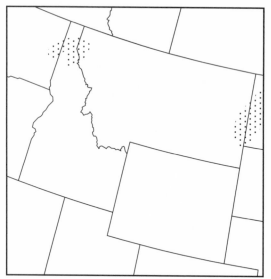

*Percentage of hours in **Autumn** when ceiling is below 1,000 feet and visibility is less than 3 miles*

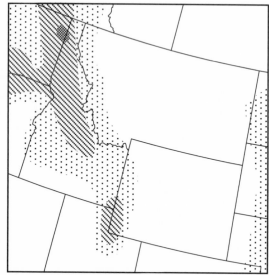

*Percentage of hours in **Winter** when ceiling is below 1,000 feet and visibility is less than 3 miles*

▓ 50% or more	◩ 40-49%	▩ 30-39%	◩ 20-29%	⬚ 10-19%	☐ Less than 9%

Oregon and Washington, where the Cascade Range blocks precipitation to the east.

The other source of weather in the northern Rockies is the eastern slopes of the Canadian Rockies, in British Columbia and Alberta. Lows form in the leeward areas of these slopes, too. But just as an Aleutian low or front reflects its origins, so do systems in western Canada. This is continental polar air, meaning that it's cold and dry. Still, there can on occasion be heavy snow associated with this type of Canadian system.

Pushed and invigorated by jet stream winds, these lows enter the northwest United States in Idaho and Montana, along the storm tracks defined by the jet stream's meanderings. Often, it meanders right past the western border of Montana. Other times, it draws a bead on the Dakotas.

With nothing but flat, nearly featureless terrain ahead of them, these Canadian systems are unimpeded fast-movers, young and full of spirit. The fastest ones are called Alberta Clippers. But the slower ones can be just as violent. All feature steep pressure gradients, which create the fierce winds.

See Pages 132–134 for more on Alberta Clippers.

Blizzard City

How cold and strong are these winter winds? On December 3, 1989 wind gusts to 90 MPH were recorded between Augusta and Choteau, Montana. Remember, these are *surface* winds. As is so typical of these northern Rocky Mountain winter storms, a foot or more of snow accompanied the winds. And that means snow drifts. On the night of the 15th, a Lewiston man died of hypothermia after leaving his car, which had become stuck in the snow. He was lightly dressed, and found within 100 yards of his car.

On January 8, 1990 an intense Pacific storm entered the northwest. It hit northern Idaho with wind gusts up to 78 MPH; at the Moscow-Pullman Airport small airplanes were flipped upside-down in their tiedowns. Near McCammon, Idaho three tractor-trailers and a car were blown off Interstate 15. In southeast Idaho, wind gusts of 59 knots were recorded at the Pocatello Municipal Airport.

In Montana, there were 21 days in January 1990 with surface winds in excess of 53 MPH. A place called Heart Butte—in northwest Montana, just east of the Lewis Range—winds of

100 MPH were recorded. On the 28th, a truck driver was blown off the top of his truck while trying to secure a tarpaulin.

Wyoming was just as rowdy that January. On the seventh and eighth, the entire state felt sustained winds of between 40 and 60 MPH. Rendezvous Mountain received a 120-MPH gust. Out here, they don't give mountain chains names like the Wind River Range for nothing.

I could go on citing fantastic winds and heavy snows, but trust me. All of the events described above represent a typical winter in the northern Rockies. In essence, we're talking about blizzard conditions in the mountains on a bi-weekly basis, and extremely high winds and more moderate snowfalls in the lower terrain to the east of the mountain ranges. These are semipermanent features of the weather in this region— especially in the winter—which is why pilots east of this area should cross off the northern route as an option for reaching the west coast. In winter, fly the southern route.

It can be difficult to fully emphasize the influence that these strong winds have on the northern Rockies. As you travel west from Chicago, the depth of the topsoil becomes progressively thinner. By the time you reach Wyoming, it's almost totally gone; the wind blows it away. Trees in the northern Rockies are permanently bent downwind. Blowing sand will pit and abrade an automobile's (and airplane's) paint and windshield. Old-timers, I've read, used to say that a Wyoming wind gauge was an anvil on a length of chain.

(As a footnote, it's interesting to know that these strong winds have played a large part in the geology of the northern Rockies. Geologists have found ancient rocks scored by windborne particles. Winds of vicious intensity have been a feature of Wyoming ever since the time of the dinosaurs. Evidence shows that large basins, later to become today's lakes, were actually gouged out by millions of years of unrelenting winds. One depression, eleven miles long and four miles wide, is a good example of what geologists call a "blowout.")

For pilots, this kind of wind has several serious implications. Take a strong wind and send it careening through the Rockies—by itself or with a good load of snow—and you've got a recipe for severe turbulence, severe icing, and hostile instrument weather. Minimum enroute altitudes are high, the terrain is as unfriendly as the weather, and well-equipped, paved airports tend to be few and far between. Obviously, many precautions should be taken before flying in the northern Rockies.

In addition to receiving the standard items during a preflight weather briefing, be sure to ask about the jet stream's position, and any weather activity in Alberta or southeastern Alaska. If a system is active in one or both of those regions, it could easily pick up speed and affect your route of flight. Particularly if the jet stream is sending it your way. If a storm threatens, you clearly should cancel the trip until the weather improves.

A knowledge of mountain flying techniques is also essential. Cross mountains at a safe altitude—at least 2,000 feet higher than the highest peaks. Also, cross any ranges at a 45-degree angle to the ridge line. In the event of an engine

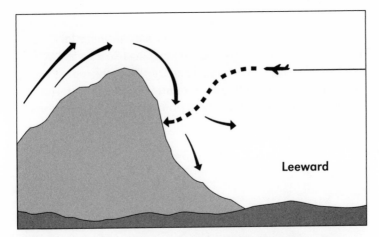

Leeward

Figure 5-1. *Here's an illustration of why you simply have to cross the Rockies with altitude to spare—and the more, the better. Because of the west-to-east airflow that usually prevails over the higher altitudes of the Rockies, downdrafts predominate on the lee (downwind) slopes. The stronger the winds at altitude, the stronger the downdrafts and the more severe the turbulence. On IFR enroute charts, the MEAs published for the routes over mountainous areas are at least 2,000 feet above the highest terrain on a route segment. On sectional charts and world aeronautical charts designed for VFR use, maximum terrain elevation figures (given in an abbreviated form) are published within the blocks defined by lines of latitude and longitude, and it's a good idea to mentally add 2,000 feet to those elevations to come up with a minimum flight altitude for cruising over mountains. But with a piston-powered single or twin, even a 2,000-foot altitude margin may not be safe. It may not be possible to successfully outclimb a lee downdraft.*

failure, this will allow you a quicker, safer turn to what is hopefully lower terrain and a suitable forced-landing site. If you must fly in instrument meteorological conditions, make sure that you have adequate and legal ice protection equipment, and try your best to minimize your exposure to ice by flying VFR-on-top. Finally, carry ample survival gear.

Any time you fly, be prepared for turbulence of the worst sort. Invisible **rotors**, clear air turbulence, and terrain-induced curveballs are commonplace anywhere in the Rockies, but especially up north.

Lest we focus too much on winter weather, let's go through the rest of a typical weather year in Montana, Idaho, and Wyoming.

With spring come moderating temperatures. Ordinarily that would mean good news, and springtime in the Rockies is indeed beautiful. The downside is that the colder, higher elevations are still bearing the winter's heavy snowfall and winter-like icing conditions. Like many other mountainous locales, precipitation amounts (rain or snow) in the Rockies are a function of altitude. The higher the elevation, the more the total precipitation. As all that mountain snow melts during the spring thaw, flooding becomes a problem at lower elevations.

rotors. Intense, localized parcels of air with strong rotating motions.

See the Appendix color photo section, Page 294: circular lenticular clouds in the lee of a mountain peak are an example of some of the turbulence possibilities diagrammed in Figure 5-2 below. *See also* the photograph, Page 79, of "trapped lee wave clouds"—a signal of rotor-type turbulence which can be severe.

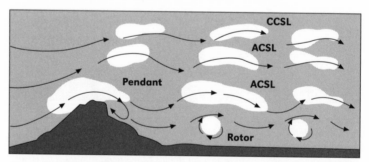

Figure 5-2. Downdrafts are one big problem when crossing the Rockies— violent lee turbulence is another, and this can affect airplanes flying at the flight levels. Cirrocumulus standing lenticular (CCSL) and altocumulus standing lenticular (ACSL) clouds can signal the presence of severe turbulence, although it can just as easily happen with no advance warning, in clear air. At lower altitudes, horizontal rotor clouds have the potential to easily upset even the largest airplanes.

The Jessica Accident

One of the most highly publicized general aviation accidents in recent times—involving 7-year-old Jessica Dubroff, her instructor (the pilot-in-command), and her father—took place in Cheyenne, Wyoming on a spring day in 1996. On April 11, just three minutes after an 8:21 A.M. takeoff from Cheyenne Airport's runway 30, the Dubroff airplane—a 1975 Cessna 177B Cardinal of 180-HP—stalled and crashed, killing all aboard. Much has been said about the causes and factors affecting this crash. First of all, the accident serves as a model of poor decision-making. On top of that was the folly and pretext of the flight as a record-setting event (it was intended that Jessica Dubroff would become the youngest pilot to cross the United States; never mind that she wasn't, owing to her age, a certificated pilot). Add the pressures of attending to media events and meeting the flight schedule, an overloaded airplane, and a

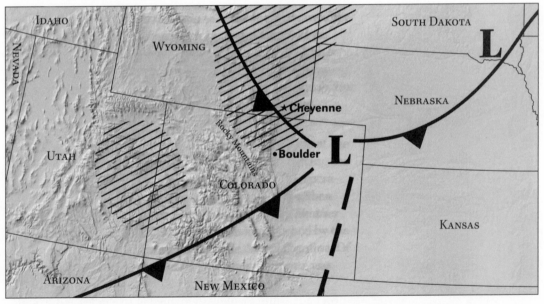

Figure 5-3. The surface situation on the morning of April 11, 1996, the day of the Jessica Dubroff accident near the Cheyenne, Wyoming airport. This is a classic lee-low storm setup of the type that frequents eastern Colorado and can cause a combination of thunderstorms and IMC in either rain or snow. As Dubroff's Cessna 177 Cardinal took off, a post-cold frontal thunderstorm associated with a complex low-pressure system had just moved through Cheyenne. Winds were gusting to 28 knots at the surface. After takeoff, the flight instructor piloting the Dubroff airplane stalled out of a turn intended to clear the storm. Hatched lines indicate areas of precipitation.

grossly inattentive and negligent instructor and you are very close to guaranteeing an accident. Then throw in the weather that so often occurs in the lee of the Rockies and you have really pushed your luck to the limit.

The weather factors affecting that flight serve as great examples of many of the dangers associated with lows and cold fronts anywhere. But in and near the Rockies, some added dangers are present. The Cheyenne Airport's elevation is 6,156 feet; though it's not technically in the Rocky Mountains, Cheyenne, like many other airports to the lee of the Rockies has a very high elevation. For the conditions at the time of the Dubroff airplane's departure, the NTSB calculated the density altitude as being 6,670 feet. That's based on a 40°F surface temperature. Imagine—no, go figure—Cheyenne's density altitude on a 95°F summer day (it would be close to 10,000 feet MSL). But density altitude may have been the least of the problems facing the right-seat pilot-in-command that day.

The surface analysis chart posted an hour-and-a-half before the accident showed a cold front of moderate intensity just south of Cheyenne, accompanied by a center of surface low pressure near Boulder, Colorado. At the 850-millibar level (approximately 5,000 feet MSL) a low was situated over the Nebraska panhandle, and an upper-level trough at 500 millibars (about 18,000 feet) spreading southward over the entire Rocky Mountain chain (with another low right over Cheyenne) completed the synoptic picture. It was a setup for Rocky Mountain weather at its worst.

ASOS (Automated Surface Observation System). *See* Glossary, Page 309.

Cheyenne's **ASOS** observations showed that the weather was changing rapidly. Between 8:15 and 8:23 A.M. the sky conditions went from 2,400 feet scattered, measured ceiling 3,100 feet overcast, to 1,600 feet scattered, 2,400 feet broken and 3,100 feet overcast. Surface wind went from 260 degrees at 15 knots to 250 degrees at 20 gusting to 28 knots. And a thunderstorm had begun. Visibility remained at five miles, but would drop to 2½ miles by 8:30 A.M. A post-frontal storm was moving through just as the airplane took off. The pilot, who had received a satisfactory preflight weather briefing, turned right immediately after takeoff to avoid the worst of the nearby thunderstorm and heavy precipitation, and stalled.

Just before the Dubroff Cardinal took off, a United Express Beech 1900 commuter flight landed at the Cheyenne airport, at 8:20 A.M. The 1900 pilot reported that as he was taxiing to the gate the rain showers became heavier. This pilot also reported hearing the pilot of a just-departed Cessna 414 report to ATC a 30-knot wind shear. After hearing that, the United Express pilot decided to delay his planned takeoff until the weather improved. Oh, and he also remembered seeing lightning within one to two miles of the airport as he pulled into the gate, and stated that the rain changed to what he believed to be small hail. The 1900 next took off at 10:20 A.M. The Dubroff airplane should also have waited as long.

The NTSB found that the Cardinal's right turn "into a tailwind" may have caused the pilot-in-command to misjudge the margin of safety above the airplane's stall speed. He "may have increased the airplane's pitch angle to compensate for the perceived decrease in climb rate, especially if the pilot misperceived the apparent ground speed for airspeed, or if the pilot became disoriented," the NTSB report stated. Further-more, the NTSB said that the airplane "experienced strong crosswinds, moderate turbulence and gusty winds during its takeoff and attempted climb, and that the pilot-in-command was aware of these adverse wind conditions prior to takeoff."

An analysis of Doppler weather radar reflectivity patterns showed that the airplane most likely encountered light to moderate rain as it began its takeoff roll. After takeoff, increas-ing levels of rainfall were encountered, right up to the time of the crash, when the rainfall rate was estimated at 3.146 inches per hour. The density altitude, the overgross condition of the airplane, the rainfall, and the bank angle of the airplane, the NTSB said, would have increased the airplane's stall speed from 59 to 64 MPH, and decreased its V_Y (best rate-of-climb speed) from 84 to 81 MPH.

The airplane should have been able to climb and turn safely, the NTSB said. Why didn't it? The Board speculated that a reduction in power due to carburetor icing or an over-rich fuel–air mixture may have been to blame. That, or wind shear's lift-robbing effects, poor visibility, or the pilot-in-command's "insufficient experience in takeoffs from high density altitudes…"

Outflow Microburst

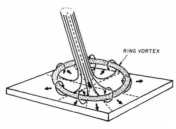

Figure 5-4. One meteorologist's concept of the dynamics at work in what is defined as an "outflow microburst." The powerful, localized downdraft from a thunderstorm violently strikes the surface like a fire hose. At the fringes of the impact zone, a ring vortex created by the outrushing air and its rotational movements can be lethal to any airplanes flying near it. In conditions like these, entire stands of trees have been flattened in a radial pattern. (Excerpted from The Downburst, Microburst and Macroburst, *T. Theodore Fujita; University of Chicago, 1985; p. 73).*

Big Sky Storms

All thunderstorms, of course, should be treated with respect, and the Dubroff accident should remind us that those storms of the northern Rockies are no exception. Furthermore, thunderstorms in this region tend to bear hail more often than not. In August 1995, hail of greater than ¾-inch diameter was mentioned no fewer than 28 times on ten different days in Montana alone; the largest reported hail diameter was three inches, and occurred in Fort Peck, Montana. Funnel clouds and tornadoes infrequently occur when vigorous thunderstorms move through Montana and Wyoming.

As you might suspect, thunderstorm outflow winds and gusts can reach triple digits in Montana, Idaho, and Wyoming. Forested areas show patterns of blown-down timber that indicate frequent microburst activity.

To underscore the importance of avoiding thunderstorms by safe margins, let me give you this terse entry from National Weather Service records for July 30, 1990 in Elmore County, Idaho: "1810 MST, extreme turbulence 10 miles distant from a thunderstorm turned a PA-34 aircraft upside down at 10,000 feet."

Summers in the northern Rockies bring their share of thunderstorms, to be sure, but there's another hazard to watch for. By August and September the region can experience prolonged heat waves. In September, 1990, for example, the area around Boise had fifteen consecutive days with temperatures of 100 or more degrees Fahrenheit. Since even the non-mountainous regions are at relatively high elevations to begin with, density altitude becomes a real factor, as we've seen with the Dubroff example. The Boise airport's elevation is 2,858 feet; at 100 degrees that makes the density altitude 6,028 feet. Helena, Montana is 3,873 feet above sea level; at 100 degrees density altitude is 7,252 feet. Casper, Wyoming, at an elevation of 5,348 feet, has a density altitude of 9,028 feet when the mercury reaches the century mark. Couple this with the need to top the nearby mountain ranges, and you can see that turbocharging can come in very handy. Without it, climb rates could be paltry indeed—and maybe even nonexistent in airplanes with less than 200 horsepower and high gross weights.

Thunderstorms follow these hot spells, and that usually means forest fires. The weather was already hot and dry in the two weeks before the hot spell mentioned above. A complex of severe thunderstorms went through Idaho on September 7, and their lightning ignited fourteen forest fires in the Boise National Forest that burned for four days. Obviously, flight and ground visibilities can suffer around forest fires, and deviations around them are advisable for this and at least one other reason: water-bombing fire-control airplanes may be strafing the area in attempts to extinguish the fires.

Autumn provides the some of the best flying weather in the northern Rockies. Thunderstorm season winds down, the forests put on a great show of color, and the nasty snow, wind, and IFR conditions of winter are not yet a factor. The only problem is that the snows begin in mid-October, and winter really begins to bare its teeth by early November. Consider these excerpts from Montana's weather logs of October 1996: a wind gust of 86 MPH at on October 21 at Heart Butte; 26 to 38 inches of snow on October 26 in Roscoe; whiteout conditions on the 26th in a blizzard at Red Lodge. Winter comes early in the northern Rockies.

Still, the northern Rockies make for one of North America's most scenic and interesting places to fly. Just keep in mind that this beauty comes at a price—keeping a close watch on the weather to the west, and understanding that high winds are almost daily facts of life.

Accidents

On December 8, 1996 the pilot and sole occupant aboard a Beech B36TC Bonanza crashed into a 10,741-foot-high mountain near Jackson, Wyoming during an instrument approach in icing conditions. He was on a flight from Aspen, Colorado to Jackson. Day VMC and IMC prevailed at the time of the crash, but no flight plan was filed. The pilot radioed ATC and asked for the VOR/DME approach to Jackson's runway 36. He said he was picking up moderate rime ice but did not report any problems. The controller advised him of a PIREP from a pilot that just landed at Jackson. He reported a trace of ice during the descent. The Bonanza pilot was cleared for the approach and told to report his arrival time. There were no further communications from the Bonanza, but an ELT signal was detected in the Jackson area. The airplane collided into the southeast side of a mountain, roughly 200 feet below its peak. The collision caused an avalanche and the airplane slid down the mountain another 600 feet before coming to rest. The pilot was killed. At the time, a weak surface low in Idaho formed a cold front that was moving southeast into the Jackson area, pushing clouds and precipitation ahead of it. Conditions at Jackson were 2,200 feet scattered, 3,700 feet overcast, visibility 10 miles, no precipitation, with winds out of 240 degrees at 10 knots.

The pilot of a Cessna 340A apparently lost control during a climb on instruments near Wise River, Montana on September 5, 1996. An IFR flight plan was filed for a cross-country flight from Butte, Montana to McCall, Idaho. At 11:47 A.M. the pilot was cleared to his requested cruise altitude of 16,000 feet MSL. The airplane reached 16,000 feet at 11:50 A.M., but the pilot reported that "the bumps are big time," and asked for a climb to 18,000 feet. The controller then issued the pilot a block altitude clearance of between 17,000 and 19,000 feet. The pilot began his climb, and said that the turbulence was "moderate and sometimes worse." In the next three minutes, ATC radar showed the 340's ground speed decreasing from 173 to 101 knots. Its altitude reached 16,600 feet, then dropped rapidly through 13,600 feet. The pilot radioed that he was "having a problem," and then said "I'm in a dive and I don't..." The wreckage was found in a near-vertical attitude at the 8,500-foot level of a mountain. The pilot was killed. The airplane was equipped with full ice protection equipment. A hiker four miles from the accident site reported a sudden heavy wet snowfall and extreme wind gusts at the time of the crash. At Butte, some 20 miles to the north of the crash site, a thunderstorm, light rain showers, and occasional lightning in clouds were reported 37 minutes after the crash. A trough at 500 millibars prevailed at the time, with winds at 18,000 feet out of the southwest (on the east side of the trough) in the 60-knot range. The trough no doubt helped transform a slow-moving northeast–southwest stationary front over the northern Rockies into a faster-moving cold front running from Manitoba to Arizona, trailing rain showers and towering cumulus. This front evidently blew through western Montana by midday on the 5th, and reached the Great Plains the following day.

A pilot and a passenger aboard a Beech K35 Bonanza received minor injuries after hitting trees while trying to reverse course in a mountain pass near Sula, Montana on June 14, 1992. IMC prevailed , but a VFR flight plan was on file for the trip from Kalispell, Montana to Kremmling, Colorado. The pilot reported that he received two weather briefings prior to departure, and knew that the freezing level was at 9,000 feet and that VFR flight was not recommended through the mountain passes. At about 10:30 A.M., while cruising through a pass at 1,100 to 1,200 feet AGL, the pilot ran into whiteout conditions. He immediately began a climbing left turn to reverse course to return to Kalispell, but hit trees in the process. Though the airplane was substantially damaged, the pilot and passenger escaped with minor injuries.

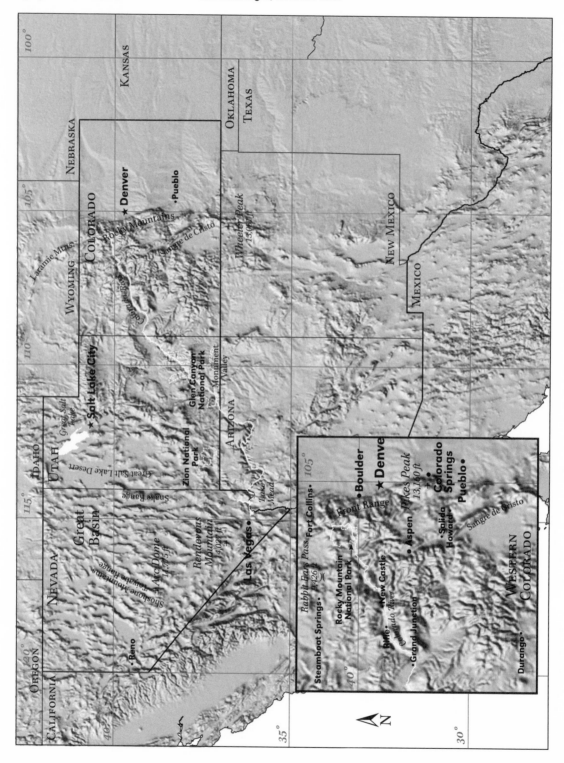

Mountain Highs, Colorado Lows

Colorado, Utah, and Nevada

Low-pressure central, fringed by cumulo-granitis

I n the meteorological world, certain areas of the United States have come to earn reputations as exceptionally good weather-makers. The central Rockies is one of them. This is especially true of the zones on the lee side of the easternmost Rockies, in the region that stretches from Colorado Springs to Fort Collins. This geographic area is prime real estate for **cyclogenesis**, or the formation of low pressure centers. You have to learn respect for this part of the country not just because many, many aggressive low pressure systems form here, but because after forming they and their attendant frontal activity typically move to the east. Want to know what the weather will be like over Texas or the Ohio River Valley in a couple of days? Look at the Front Range—the territory stretching from the Laramie range in Wyoming in the north, to the Sangre de Cristo Mountains in the south—on today's surface analysis chart. If there's a low to the east of this range, expect trouble.

You often hear paeans sung to spring and summer in the Rockies. For the most part, flying weather will most likely be VFR during these times of the year in Nevada, Utah, and Colorado. What data there is indicates that ceilings and visibilities below 1,000 feet and 3 miles occur less than ten percent of the time in the spring and summer months in those three states. Does this mean that the flying weather will be trouble-free? No way. Summer's high surface temperatures and the high airport elevations in this part of the country team up to make density altitude a very real danger for midday and afternoon takeoffs and landings, when diurnal heating reaches a maximum. And turbulence is a factor when flying anywhere near the Rockies, at any time of year. Same thing with the hazards of icing, if you'll be flying in the clouds at or above the freezing level.

cyclogenesis. Any development or strengthening of cyclonic (counterclockwise, in the northern hemisphere) circulation in the atmosphere.

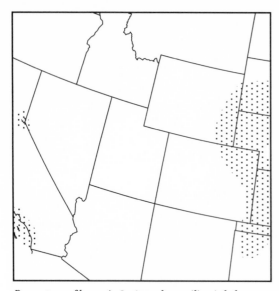

*Percentage of hours in **Spring** when ceiling is below 1,000 feet and visibility is less than 3 miles*

*Percentage of hours in **Summer** when ceiling is below 1,000 feet and visibility is less than 3 miles*

*Percentage of hours in **Autumn** when ceiling is below 1,000 feet and visibility is less than 3 miles*

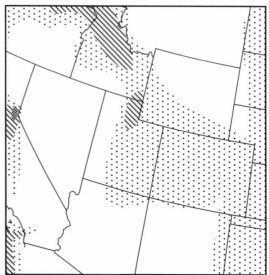

*Percentage of hours in **Winter** when ceiling is below 1,000 feet and visibility is less than 3 miles*

50% or more   **40-49%**   **30-39%**   **20-29%**   **10-19%**   **Less than 9%**

It's in the late fall and winter when more instrument flying weather tends to prevail. The areas around Salt Lake City, northeastern Nevada, and the Front Range of the Rockies lay claim to the most IFR weather. Bear this in mind when flying to Salt Lake City in the winter—where ceilings and visibilities are below 1,000 and 3 at least half the time.

If you wanted to run a quick keyword search for the Colorado and Utah flying weather, I'd suggest the following: mountain waves, altocumulus standing lenticular clouds (abbreviated ACSL in weather reports and forecasts), **orographic turbulence**, strong downslope winds and rotors, mixed icing (a mixture of rime and clear) in clouds, strong low pressure, and blizzards, just for starters. Oh, and severe summer thunderstorms with high cloud bases and well-documented histories of spewing downbursts and microbursts. Downbursts and microbursts—smaller, more intense varieties of downbursts—are localized currents of high-velocity air shooting out the base of mature thunderstorms. After they plunge from the bases of thunderstorms, they strike the ground and spread out, generating sudden, strong head- and tailwind components that can literally force an airplane into the ground.

The first four hazards, of course, are closely linked to the Rockies themselves. With peaks and ridges in the 11,000- to 14,000-foot range, the central Rockies spring up majestically from the terrain to their west and east. In Nevada, where basin-and-range topography prevails, elevations average around 2,000 to 5,000 feet MSL in the basin portions. Peaks of Nevada's many north–south ranges do reach the 11,775-foot (Arc Dome in the Toiyabe Range) and 13,061-foot (Wheeler Peak in the Snake Range) neighborhoods, but these are few and far between, as Nevada's many mini-ranges are spread dozens of miles apart. Most of Nevada's "low" terrain—particularly in the southern half of that state—is well under 5,000 feet MSL.

Approach the eastern border of Nevada, however, and the terrain rises abruptly. Prevailing westerly winds strike this rising terrain and create orographic turbulence. The analogy here is that of water flowing in a boulder-strewn river. Just as water cascades chaotically over and around boulders, so do wind flows become disturbed, creating bone-jarring turbulence. But turbulence alone is not the problem. Severe up- and

orographic turbulence. Turbulence created by wind flowing over terrain.

See illustrations on the next two pages for visualized descriptions of different types of microbursts that can occur in severe thunderstorms.

81

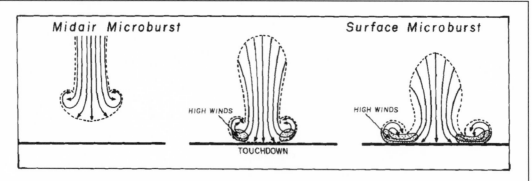

Fig. 5.4 Three stages of a descending microburst. A mid-air microburst may or may not descend to the surface. If it does, the outburst winds develop immediately after its touchdown.

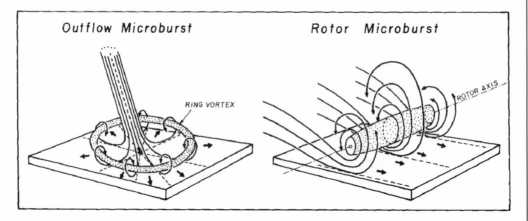

Fig. 5.5 Outflow microbursts are the most commonly observed type of microbursts. Some rotor microbursts develop inside macrobursts behind their gust fronts.

Figure 6-1A. Top illustrations show the progressive stages of a descending microburst. After driving toward the ground at velocities of 700 FPM or greater, the microburst winds strike and fan out from the central impact point. Rotor microbursts can form and travel at the outermost perimeter of a microburst strike zone, just above ground level, as visualized in the lower illustration. (Illustrations on these two pages are excerpted from The Downburst, *Fujita, pages 72-75.)*

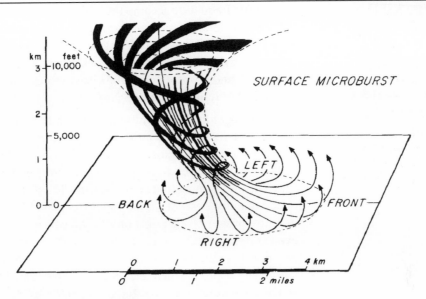

Fig. 5.7 A schematic view of a surface microburst accompanied by a misocyclone aloft. Most misocyclones, less than 4 km in diameter, rotate cyclonically while exceptional ones rotate anticyclonically.

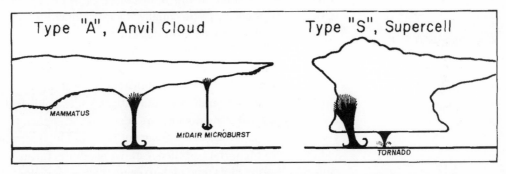

Fig. 5.8 Schematic diagrams showing the formation of microbursts beneath an anvil cloud in dry areas. Supercell thunderstorms are inducers of tornadoes and microbursts.

Figure 6-1B. *Small cyclonic circulations within thunderstorms—called misocyclones by meteorologist T. Theodore Fujita—can also spawn microbursts. While dropping from the 10,000-foot level, these circulations most often rotate cyclonically (counter-clockwise), but anticyclonic (clockwise) circulations occur in rare cases. Locations of anvil-cloud-induced microbursts show that they can strike in dry air, as is often the case in the drier climates of the western United States.*

downdrafts frequently accompany the rough rides that pilots of smaller general aviation airplanes endure while flying through the Rockies at altitudes close to terrain elevations. What exactly is meant by "close"? Well, orographically-induced turbulence and up- and downdrafts can extend as high as 30,000 feet or more in extreme cases.

At the flight levels, updrafts and downdrafts usually mean that pilots have to work a little harder at maintaining their assigned altitudes. But for pilots flying less powerful airplanes VFR, down low (if you consider the 9,000- to 12,000-foot range "low" altitude), downdrafts can send small airplanes into uncommanded descents at rates of up to 4,000 feet per minute—or more. This is just one reason why mountain flying experts recommend that pilots flying amidst the Rockies' (or any other mountain range, for that matter) peaks, ridges, and valleys approach high terrain at a 45-degree angle. This way, if a downdraft is encountered, a turn toward lower terrain—and hopefully away from the downdraft—is more easily accomplished.

The other usual warnings about mountain flying—don't fly into a box, or dead-end, canyon (you probably won't be able to reverse course without hitting a rock face); expect a vigorous updraft to be followed by an equally vigorous downdraft; and carefully calculate density altitude's effects on aircraft performance—hold true in spades for the Rockies. A good general rule for avoiding the worst jolts and downdrafts is to fly at altitudes greater than 2,000 feet above the highest terrain along your route. The minimum enroute altitudes published for airways crossing the Rockies are specifically designed to keep airplanes a safe distance away not just from high terrain, but also from the worst turbulence and downdrafts it can cause. VFR-only pilots who plan to cross the Rockies should look at the low-altitude enroute charts used for IFR flights out west to discover what the government thinks a safe altitude should be. Some texts go even further and say to postpone flying if the winds at mountaintop level are higher than twenty knots, operating on the verified theory that the stronger the wind, the stronger the turbulence and downdrafts.

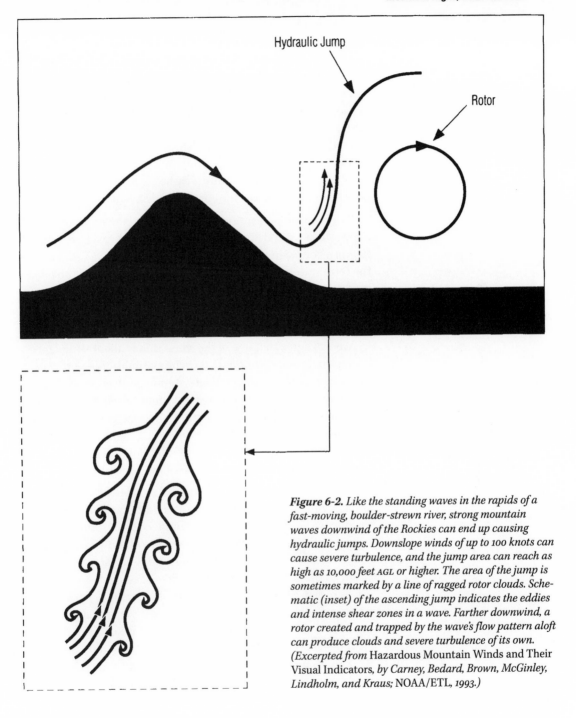

Figure 6-2. *Like the standing waves in the rapids of a fast-moving, boulder-strewn river, strong mountain waves downwind of the Rockies can end up causing hydraulic jumps. Downslope winds of up to 100 knots can cause severe turbulence, and the jump area can reach as high as 10,000 feet AGL or higher. The area of the jump is sometimes marked by a line of ragged rotor clouds. Schematic (inset) of the ascending jump indicates the eddies and intense shear zones in a wave. Farther downwind, a rotor created and trapped by the wave's flow pattern aloft can produce clouds and severe turbulence of its own. (Excerpted from* Hazardous Mountain Winds and Their Visual Indicators, *by Carney, Bedard, Brown, McGinley, Lindholm, and Kraus; NOAA/ETL, 1993.)*

Even following these guidelines, there's no guarantee of a trouble-free ride. Weather observations, be they automated or human, are few and far between in the midst of the Rockies. The resultant dearth of "data points" as the meteorological community is wont to call them, denies us the information needed for truly accurate observations and forecasts of localized weather phenomena. Meteorological computer models starved of data can do little to help us envision how mountain weather really behaves, and this reduces us to relying on tried-and-true, hard-won mountain weather flying strategies that have been developed at the cost of many lives.

Anyone thinking seriously about flying in the mountains of the western United States and Alaska would be well served by taking a course in mountain flying offered by locals who know the terrain well, and who have earned reputations as the most professional flight instructors. This remains the best strategy for minimizing the considerable risks that Rocky Mountain flying can present.

We'd all agree that one of the worst things about turbulence and updrafts and downdrafts is their invisibility. But with lenticular clouds and their attendant standing waves, we do have visible evidence of some of the worst mountain-induced turbulence and aggressive vertical motions. Enter a lenticular, and you can expect severe turbulence, meaning that a loss of control is possible or, to quote the *Aeronautical Information Manual*, "food service and walking are impossible." Ergo, stay away.

See Appendix Page 294 for a photograph and diagram of "circular lenticular clouds."

Standing waves may or may not be signaled by lenticulars, and can provide very smooth flying conditions. If orographic turbulence is water flowing over boulders, then standing waves represent the crests of the rapids—a smooth flow riding high above the chaotic ripples cascading among the smaller rocks closer to the stream bed. Sailplane pilots seek out standing waves because they can make for turbulence-free, elevator-like rides with climb rates of thousands of feet per minute. Learning how to work a powerful standing wave is key to setting altitude records, and many sailplane pilots seek out the Rockies for just this reason. There's a caveat, though. Mountain waves can also carry severe turbulence at their perimeters. Wander too close to the lee edge of a wave, and you can expect strong downdrafts and turbulent air flows.

As for icing, the Rockies are plagued with it during the colder months of the year. As with any mountain range experiencing a traversing flow of moist air bearing clouds with super-cooled water droplets, the Rockies will cause airframe and induction system icing. The worst ice will be found in the areas of rising air flow—the zones analogous to the crests of the waves flowing over the boulder-strewn river mentioned earlier. That's where the largest, coldest droplets usually live.

But turbulence, lenticulars, standing waves, and ice can be found in any mountain range in the United States. The real action that distinguishes the Rockies' weather takes place on the immediate lee side of the mountains, over the uplands east of Colorado's Front Range.

"A Normal Colorado Windy Day"

That's how the captain of a Continental Airlines Boeing 737 described the conditions on his departure from the Colorado Springs Municipal Airport on March 3, 1991, at about 9:54 A.M. He said after taking off from COS's runway 35 there were "gusty winds but no gyrations."

Four minutes earlier another Boeing 737, this one operated by United Airlines as Flight 585, crashed on approach to the same runway at the same airport. While flying the beginning portion of the final leg of a visual approach to runway 35, at 8,500 feet MSL (the airport's elevation is 6,200 feet), the airplane rolled steadily to the right and pitched nose down until it reached a nearly vertical attitude. It crashed 3.47 miles short of the runway threshold, killing all 25 persons aboard.

Two years later, after one of the most exhaustive accident investigations ever conducted by the National Transportation Safety Board (NTSB), that organization failed to come up with a definitive cause or reason for the crash of Flight 585. The evidence, however, pointed to two areas of great suspicion: the weather conditions on the day of the crash, and a possible malfunction of the 737's lateral or directional control system.

"Sounds Adventurous"

The rowdy weather on United 585's approach certainly came as no surprise to the crew. The airplane's cockpit voice recorder (CVR) revealed that the pilots listened to an automated terminal information service (ATIS) broadcast at 9:30 A.M. that mentioned, in part, "...wind 310 at 13, gusts to 35; low-level wind shear advisories are in effect; local aviation wind warning in effect calling for winds out of the northwest, gusts to 40 knots and above..."

At 9:38 A.M.—just five minutes before the crash—the Colorado Springs tower cleared the 737 to land and advised the crew about a pilot report of wind shear on approach. "Any reports lately of loss or, ah, gain of airspeed?" the first officer asked. "Yes, ma'am, ah, at 500 feet a 737-300 series reported a 5—correction—a 15-knot loss at 500 feet. At 400 feet plus 15 knots. And 150 feet a plus 20 knots." The tower replied.

"Sounds adventurous," the first officer replied. The crew then discussed how they would fly the approach so as to minimize the wind shear effects they anticipated would accompany the 15- to 20-knot increases in airspeed they would soon encounter.

"OK, ah, I recommend we hold, what, 120 knots max...is what we can hold to do that and then I'll just...if we get all stable I'll watch that airspeed gauge like it's my mom's last minute," the first officer said. The crew then performed a prelanding check, checked for the location of a nearby Cessna, and selected the 25-degree flap setting during the final descent to the runway.

At 9:42 A.M. the first officer, referring to the airspeed, said, "...a 10-knot change there."

"Yeah, I know...awful lot of power to hold that...airspeed," the captain replied.

"Runway is 11,000 feet long," commented the first officer. Then she said, "another 10-knot gain."

As the airplane neared 1,000 feet AGL, the captain called for a greater flap deflection—"30 flaps"—in preparation for landing. Then things fell apart.

"Oh God," the first officer said.

"15 flaps," commanded the captain, apparently in an effort to reconfigure the airplane for a go-around. The flight data recorder shows that the captain added full power—more evidence that a go-around was being attempted. But the rate of the airplane's heading change increased to five degrees per second to the right—nearly twice that of a standard rate turn. Altitude decreased rapidly, indicated airspeed increased to over 200 knots, and the airplane sustained over 4 Gs.

Both pilots then loudly exclaimed "Oh." A few seconds later, the first officer said "Oh, no," and screamed.

"Oh, no, [expletive deleted]" the captain exclaimed loudly.

One second later, the CVR recorded the sound of impact.

Waves, Fluctuations, and Dented Car Hoods

A meteorological reconstruction of the events affecting Colorado Springs that day reads like a laundry list of some of the worst that Front Range weather can throw at a pilot. All morning, pilots of all types of airplanes had been reporting mountain wave activity, as well as moderate to extreme turbulence, powerful downdrafts, and low-level wind shear.

At 6:28 A.M., a 737 approaching the same runway saw airspeed fluctuations of between plus 20 and minus 30 knots on final approach. Another 737 lost 400 feet in a bout with severe turbulence at FL200, 46 miles south–southwest of Denver at 7:32 A.M. A Beech B36TC Bonanza pilot, at 8:15 A.M. and 30 miles southwest of Denver, said he was in "500 to 1,500 feet-per-minute downdrafts" and that he was "unable to maintain altitude." At 9:16 A.M. several aircraft at 9,000 feet reported moderate to severe turbulence below 9,000 feet. In all, the NTSB investigation of the crash of Flight 585 recorded at least 12 pilot reports of turbulence, mountain wave, and other wind-related chaos that day.

More than 160 witnesses were interviewed as part of the NTSB investigation, and some of them reported rotor activity and tremendous wind gusts at the surface around the time of the accident. Others said that winds were light. One witness, who was 6 miles west of the accident site, reported seeing several rotor clouds in the area of the accident at about 10 to 15 minutes before the crash. He said the clouds were accompanied by thin, wispy condensation.

A glider instructor and 25-year resident of Colorado Springs said that at noon on the day of the accident he observed a rotor hitting the ground with an estimated wind speed of 70 to 80 MPH. He said that on the morning of the accident he observed a rotor system on a line parallel to the Front Range, and that there was "an unusually strong prefrontal weather system and a sky full of rotor clouds."

He said that he was inside a building at a wrecking yard five miles north of the extended centerline of runway 35 when he heard the roar of the wind. He then said he went outside and saw the rotor hit the ground, blowing branches off trees and damaging car hoods. He stated that he believed the rotor was part of a line of rotors extending north to south which would most likely have extended to the area where the accident occurred. This witness also stated that the year's weather activity had been highly unusual, with many days of strong downslope winds and rotors. He also said he personally had experienced rotors with vertical velocities of 5,000 to 6,000 feet per minute, and offered the opinion that rotors can be "as small as a gymnasium" or many miles long.

Inside a Rotor

The NTSB's Meteorology Group held a meeting on March 27, 1991 to discuss orographically-generated weather phenomena that might be pertinent to the 737 accident. Scientists from the National Oceanic and Atmospheric Administration's Forecast Systems Laboratory, the National Center for Atmospheric Research (NCAR), and the University of Wyoming were present. At the meeting, some historical data—some of it present on the day of the accident—were reviewed. Here are a few notes from that meeting:

➢ A representative atmospheric rotor, also called a horizontal axis vortex, has a radius of some 500 meters and an increase in wind velocity from the center to the 500-meter mark. Wind velocity at the 500-meter radius point is 30 meters per second, or about 70 MPH. Outside that radius, velocities fall off. The maximum speed within a rotor is unknown.

➢ Factors in rotor strength include wind speed strength, variation of wind speed with altitude, variability of wind in gusts or surges, angle of wind flow to obstacles/mountains, mountain shape or height, and stability and humidity of the atmosphere. The stronger the wind, the greater the variability of the flow; the more perpendicular to the mountains, and the more stable and dry the air, the more violent the rotor. Small differences in these values produce large differences in atmospheric response.

➤ There are not many measurements of rotors, but it is known that they can form in lines several hundred miles long. The front of the rotor has the most turbulence.

➤ Horizontal gusts of 60 to 80 MPH have occurred at high altitude over mountainous terrain. Based on damage to a sailplane, loads of up to 16 Gs may be encountered.

➤ Rotors can descend and touch the ground.

➤ An instrumented University of Wyoming King Air B200 flew approaches into Colorado Springs the day after the accident. Weather conditions were similar to those of the day of the accident, and these occur about 10 to 15 days per year. Data from the King Air showed a **wind shadow** east of Pike's Peak below 11,000 feet. There were lighter winds and a wind reversal in the shadow. Vortices and turbulence were present at the interface between strong and light winds in the shadow. Above the ground, waves were producing vertical roll, and 800- to 1,000-FPM vertical velocities were recorded.

wind shadow. An abatement of wind speed downwind of high terrain.

➤ Isolated rotors and other vortices caused by Pike's Peak (about 12 miles west of Colorado Springs) are probably more significant than typical mountain wave phenomena.

On March 3—the day of the accident—there was no visible evidence of rotor activity in the Colorado Springs area, according to Geostationary Operational Environmental Satellite (GOES) imagery. However, GOES visible imagery did show an "upper air cloud feature" (the NTSB doesn't say what type of cloud feature) whose southward-extended axis moved across the accident location at about the time of the accident. This feature may have been an area of upward vertical motion containing vortices. Witness statements would seem to corroborate this—especially the testimony of a golfer and a driver of a Chevrolet S-10 Blazer. The golfer, at a course just northwest of the airport, reported gusts of between 50 and 60 miles per hour. The Blazer driver noted that at 9:40 A.M.—just before the time of the accident—he was hit with a brief, strong gust that almost blew his car off the road. At the time, he was three miles northwest of the accident site.

Figure 6-3. The downwind stream-ing of wind flows in the lee of the Rockies was studied as part of the accident investigation stemming from the crash of a United Air Lines Boeing 737 at Colorado Springs, Colorado in March, 1991. These illustrations from the NTSB's accident report show how wind flow reversals can occur downwind of mountains, and progress to compact rotors.
(From NTSB/AAR–92/06.)

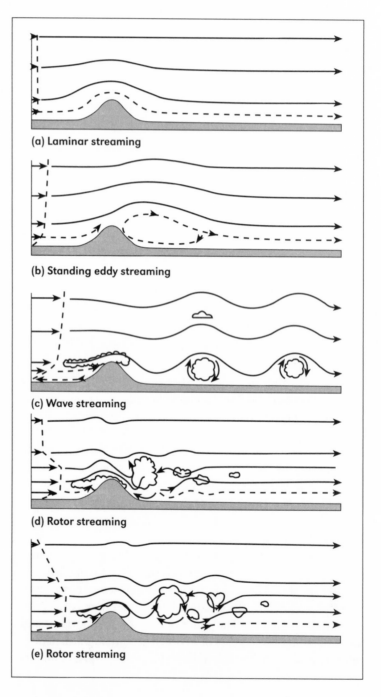

(a) Laminar streaming

(b) Standing eddy streaming

(c) Wave streaming

(d) Rotor streaming

(e) Rotor streaming

Jumps and Gravity Waves

The NTSB report turned up some other information that went into details about how rotors form. The National Center for Atmospheric Research (NCAR), in a February 1992 special study, said that the severe windstorm event on the day of the accident possessed similarities with many other downslope wind events on the Front Range. That is, low-level stable air flowing over the Rockies caused "highly nonlinear breaking gravity waves. Waves result in the generation of severe turbulence, rotors, and hydraulic-type jumps."

This gives us a richer visual metaphor of the wind patterns in the lee of the Rockies than the standard "horizontal tornado" explanation so often used to describe rotors. Under

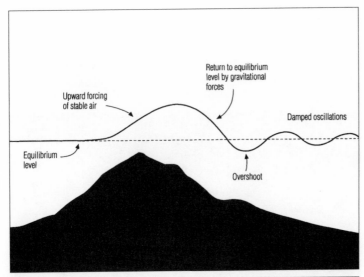

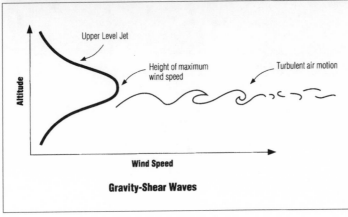

Figure 6-4. Meteorologists refer to some mountain waves as gravity waves, and the oscillations produced by lee gravity wave motions are shown in the top illustration. Gravity waves happen when stable air hits a ridge or mountain range, is displaced upwards by the impact, then returns to its original level once it has cleared the ridge. The deflected air resists its vertical displacement because it is heavier than the surrounding air—it's the force of gravity that returns it to equilibrium, after a few oscillations. The lower illustration depicts how a band of strong winds aloft can interact with air movements in a stable, low-level layer of the atmosphere. Wave motions can be created in the shear zone between the two air masses which overturn, create shear-induced gravity waves, then produce strong turbulence as the waves "break down" and decrease in intensity. (From Hazardous Mountain Winds and Their Visual Indicators, *p. 10-11.)*

NCAR's formulation, air striking mountains shoots upwards, or "jumps," then tumbles downwards under the influence of the restoring force of gravity—hence, gravity waves. The height, extent, and strength of these jumps and waves is highly variable, and unpredictable—hence, nonlinear. NCAR said that the jumps can contain updrafts in the neighborhood of 40 meters per second, or approximately 90 MPH, and that the widths of these jumps are believed to be quite narrow, making for regions of extreme variations in updrafts over small distances. By inference, downdrafts in the descending waves can be equally intense.

NCAR tried to perform a computer simulation of the weather over Colorado Springs, but found the weather too complex for its models to duplicate accurately. Meteorological computer models in use at NCAR at the time assumed a horizontally uniform flow across the Rockies, and used but one atmospheric sounding to describe the basic flow. As it happened, a surface trough and weak upper-level ridge of high pressure prevailed over Colorado Springs on the day of the

Figure 6-5. These are Kelvin-Helmholtz (K-H) wave clouds, and they demonstrate the turbulent, gravity wave motions that can happen when a band of high-speed winds at altitude overlie a slower, more stable flow of air. The mechanism causing this kind of turbulent motion has been compared to that of a flag flapping in a breeze. While K-H waves are common in shear layers near thunderstorms and jet streams, it's rare that clouds like these are present to identify them. Usually, K-H waves occur in clear air, and are the principal cause of clear air turbulence (CAT). (From Hazardous Mountain Winds and Their Visual Indicators.*)*

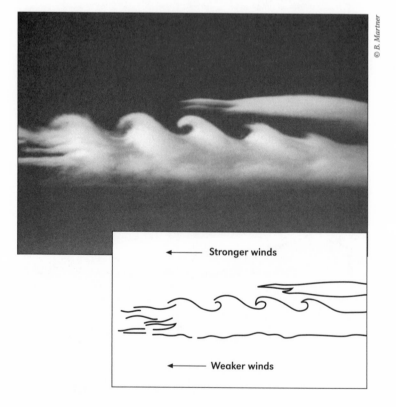

© B. Martner

Stronger winds

Weaker winds

accident—a situation too complex for the NCAR model, or any model for that matter, given the absence of observation sites over the Rockies.

Even so, NCAR believed that the weather events of March 3, 1991 were quite similar to those of January 9, 1989, when they did perform a careful atmospheric case-study simulation of a Front Range windstorm. This simulation used the National Center for Environmental Prediction's "nested grid" computer model. In this model, data points are arranged in grids of 1.11-kilometer-square blocks, which are in turn nested within data grids of 3.33- and 10-KM horizontal resolution. These horizontal grids are then reproduced at altitude, spaced at 500-meter

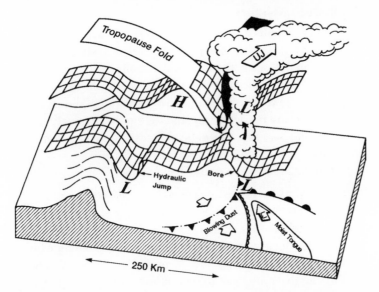

Figure 6-6. *How and why does severe weather form downstream of the Rocky Mountains? A group of meteorologists studying the development of an April 13-14, 1986 storm system blamed a combination of the terrain, downstream low-level lows fed with moisture from the Gulf of Mexico, the wavelike motions of a hydraulic jump and its subsequent drop (bore), and a low with an upper-level jet stream (UJ) at 40,000 feet. At altitude, the two lows interacted with each other to make the storm system a severe one. The illustration shows how high-altitude lows, troughs, and jet streaks (cores of strongest jet stream winds) can intensify the weather below. The surface weather included a warm front ahead of a low-level jet (LJ) that the meteorologists called a "moist tongue" of air, a dryline to its west, and a squall line to the west of that, kicking up blowing dust ahead of it. It was definitely not a time to be flying over the Front Range. (*The Influence of the Rocky Mountains on the 13-14 April 1986 Severe Weather Outbreak. Part I: Mesoscale Lee Cyclogenesis and Its Relationship to Severe Weather and Dust Storms, *by Karyampudi et al; *Monthly Weather Review, *May 1995; AMS.)*

UJ. Upper-level jet
LJ. Low-level jet

vertical intervals. The result is a huge three-dimensional matrix of meteorological values, with the emphasis on the nested grid's core area of highest data density.

NCAR's January 9 nested grid, if it is to be believed, concluded that narrow regions of strong (exceeding 90 MPH) upward motion paralleled the Front Range. These jumps move back and forth relative to the mountains during a windstorm, NCAR said, and some jumps could have moved over Colorado Springs' runway 35 at the time of the crash—though there's no way to tell, from modeling or available observations, if a jump did in fact pass through.

The Rudder Mystery

The rudder systems on a 737 are hydraulically powered and made up of multiple, redundant, independent systems, each of which is capable of safely controlling the airplane. The investigation paid particular attention to the design of the Boeing 737's rudder power control unit servo valve. Could the servo unit malfunction in such a way that the rudder suddenly is slammed and held in a fully deflected position? If so, what could cause this to happen? Has there been a history of uncommanded full-scale rudder excursions?

The answers to the first two questions have yet to be fully confirmed, and while experience to date suggests the answer might be 'yes,' the 737's rudder-deflection issue remains a vexing mystery. The urgency of this mystery was driven home by the crash of yet another Boeing 737 on September 28, 1994 near the Pittsburgh, Pennsylvania International Airport. That airplane crashed under eerily similar conditions: a rapid roll and pitch-down on a visual approach in conditions where extreme turbulence (in this case, the assumption has been the wake turbulence of a preceding airplane) may have been present.

As for a history of uncommanded rudder deflections, the NTSB identified five cases where 737 rudders have jammed.

On July 24, 1974, a 737's rudder moved full right upon touching down. An investigation showed that the primary and secondary rudder control valves were stuck together by a shot peen ball lodged in the valve.

On October 30, 1975 a 737's rudder pedals moved to the right "half way" and then jammed. This action was repeated three times and then corrected by cycling the rudder with the standby rudder system. Further examination indicated that the rudder control system was contaminated by metal particles.

That same day, a jammed main rudder power control unit control valve was found during a routine inspection. The faulty unit was removed, but the United 585 NTSB report said that "the data associated with this report are insufficient to determine the cause of the rudder MPCU [main power control unit] removal." In other words, no reason was given for the control unit's having jammed.

During an approach on August 31, 1982, a 737's rudder "locked up" and the flight crew performed a go-around and activated the airplane's standby rudder system. The subsequent landing was uneventful, but an examination of the MPCU showed internal contamination and worn seals that reduced the control unit's ability to generate enough force to move the rudder.

On November 8, 1990, during another 737's MPCU overhaul, internal corrosion was found and the unit was replaced. There had been no prior reports of rudder malfunctions in this airplane.

Finally, the NTSB report mentions an MPCU anomaly during a July 16, 1992 preflight flight controls check while taxiing for takeoff at Chicago's O'Hare airport. The captain of this United 737 reported that he had moved the rudder pedals more rapidly than he normally would have moved them during a preflight check—at about the same rate that he might have used during engine-out V_1 training.[1] The pedal stopped at about 25 percent left pedal travel.

Tests by United Airlines and Parker Hannifin, the manufacturer of the MPCU, revealed "anomalous" actions when the O'Hare 737's MCPU's input crank was held against its stops while the yaw damper piston was in the extended position. The results ranged from "sluggishness of the actuator piston to a full reversal of piston travel opposite to the direction being commanded," according to the NTSB report. "This condition could only occur if the rudder pedals were moved rapidly to command a maximum rate of rudder travel," the NTSB report continued, "or if the pedal was fully depressed to command full deflection of the rudder."

[1] V_1—Takeoff decision speed. Should an engine fail on the takeoff run prior to this speed, the airplane should be stopped on the remaining runway. Above this speed, the takeoff is continued.

The bottom line: The NTSB concluded that while anomalies (galling on the input shaft and bearing from the standby rudder actuator power control unit) were found with the hydraulic and flight control systems of the accident airplane, there were "none that would explain an uncommanded rolling motion or initial loss of control of the airplane."

A full discussion of the 737's rudder and yaw damper travails and tests falls outside the scope of this text; for that, I'd suggest a reading of the appropriate sections of the NTSB's accident report on Flight 585.[2] Moreover, additional research and findings on the 737 rudder control issue have been published in many venues since the accident report, and the rudder system continues to be a high-priority subject of ongoing efforts to once and for all identify any more specific problem areas—if they exist—and come up with appropriate fixes and procedural advice for pilots. So far, two corrective measures have been mandated. One Airworthiness Directive (AD)—AD 96-23-51—requires a test to verify that MPCU operates properly, and directs that the MPCU be replaced "if necessary." Another—AD 96-26-07—requires revisions to the 737's airplane flight manual, and adds procedures for flight crews to control the airplane during an uncommanded roll or yaw, and to correct a jammed or restricted flight-control condition. But the 1996 ADs may be superseded by others if two more recent Notices of Proposed Rulemaking (NPRMs) are enacted into law. One NPRM recommends a rudder-limiting device be installed to reduce rudder travel. Another would require the installation of a newly designed yaw damper system with fault-monitoring capability. The 737 rudder mystery continues, and it's a safety issue that merits watching.

[2] Full title of this report is "NTSB/AAR-92/06 Aircraft Accident Report: United Airlines Flight 585, Boeing 737-291, N999UA; Uncontrolled Collision with Terrain for Undetermined Reasons—4 miles South of Colorado Springs Municipal Airport, Colorado Springs, Colorado, March 3, 1991"

Did a Rotor Do It?

The NTSB's official probable cause statement for the crash of United 585 mentions rotor activity as the "most likely atmospheric disturbance to produce an uncontrollable rolling moment." But the final sentence of the statement contains both a warning and an admission of ignorance: "However, too little is known about the characteristics of such rotors to conclude decisively whether they were a factor in this accident."

In the recommendations section of the accident report, the NTSB urged the FAA to "develop and implement a meteorological program to observe, document, and analyze potential meteorological aircraft hazards in the area of Colorado Springs, Colorado, with a focus on the approach and departure paths of the Colorado Springs Municipal Airport. This program should be made operational by the winter of 1992." Another recommendation called for developing an educational program on weather hazards for "other airports in or near mountainous terrain, based on the results obtained in the Colorado Springs, Colorado area." The FAA said it agreed with the intent of these recommendations, but as of yet, has done *nada* to implement them, claiming funding difficulties.

To comply with Airworthiness Directive 96-26-07, the airlines have come up with a procedure designed to maximize controllability should a rudder jam occur. Pilot are told to use certain "crossover" airspeeds that should allow aileron control forces to overcome any uncontrollable yawing moments caused by a jammed rudder. Fly at or above the published crossover airspeeds, and you should have enough aileron power to overcome a yaw. Fly below it, and all bets are off.

By now, the implications of this accident should be clear to all pilots flying, or contemplating flying, on the Front Range— and especially near Colorado Springs. Whether it's turbulence, waves, jumps, or rotors, these highly localized, extremely violent events stalk the Rockies and the Front Range to their east. They can be present any time a strong flow crosses the mountains, but tend to be especially intense in the winter months.

Lee Lows

If the Rockies lack weather observations, the same certainly can't be said for the uplands east of the Front Range. As we've seen, NCAR, located in Boulder, Colorado, is on the cutting edge of wind shear research. It's also pioneering super-computer-powered weather displays that allow detailed analysis and presentation of weather observations and forecasts. NOAA's Forecast Systems Laboratory (FSL), also in Boulder, has been very active in identifying a number of Rocky Mountain weather features, and has generated much seminal research.

It was the FSL that identified the presence of the "Denver low," a semi-permanent area of low pressure that hangs around the lee of the Front Range. During a 1981 study known as

PROFS—Program for Regional Observing and Forecasting Services—FSL meteorologists set up a network of 22 automated surface observation stations and noted a 30-by-50-mile semi-permanent, terrain-induced cyclonic vortex, or low pressure center. In the May-to-August time frame, a Denver low exists one-third of the time.

One explanation for this low has to do with the rapid drop in terrain elevation. There's approximately a 10,000-foot difference in elevation from the Rockies to the Denver-Boulder area. Any upper-level low pressure feature, for example, in the form of a trough aloft or a jet stream, would have its **vorticity**—rotational components—reduced as the feature crosses the Rockies. But as upper-level vorticity passes to the east of the Front Range, it's free to intensify over the lower terrain. The applicable theory to this is the "conservation of angular momentum." It's the same theory that lets a spinning ice skater rotate slowly when his or her body is crouched down low, then spin much faster when standing straight. Over the Rockies, our "skater," the upper-air vorticity, is compressed between high terrain and the troposphere—the top of our weather-making atmosphere—and therefore rotates with less intensity. Move east to Denver, however, and the vorticity can extend in height, stretch vertically over the lower terrain, and spin into a full-blown low pressure system. That's one reason low pressure systems form so often in the lee of the Rockies—and in other areas to the east of mountain ranges, as well. Areas east of the Appalachians are also breeding grounds for new low pressure systems, and the Appalachians can intensify any passing lows.

Another theory behind the Denver low involves airflows draining down the canyons of the Front Range and encountering southerly winds blowing more or less parallel to the mountains. The result is a large eddy with a counterclockwise circulation that covers several counties—or a mesoscale vortex, in meteorological parlance. (*See* Figure 6-8 on Page 102.)

Still another theory posits that the winter fronts extending from Front Range lows don't conform to the traditional, Norwegian model of low pressure circulations. In the Norwegian model—so named because it was conceptualized by Norwegian meteorologists during World War I—cold fronts extend to the southwest of a low, and warm fronts extend to the east or southeast. The alternative theory claims that Front Range lows

vorticity. A localized rotation in a fluid flow, in this case the atmosphere.

can have a mixture of drylines (a front-like discontinuity of dew points) and troughs where traditional cold fronts lie, and that the "warm front" to the east is really a misnomer for the leading edge of an Arctic front containing very cold air.

While theories abound, the fact is that much remains unknown about the how's and why's of Rocky Mountain weather. The Front Range will always be fertile ground for research, and for pilots, a place warranting watchfulness and caution—especially in the colder months of the year. Over and near the mountains count on a wild ride, at the very least. In the lee of the Rockies, look for the frontal fireworks that often accompany the clash of drier air from higher elevations with the warmer, wetter air traveling north from the Gulf of Mexico.

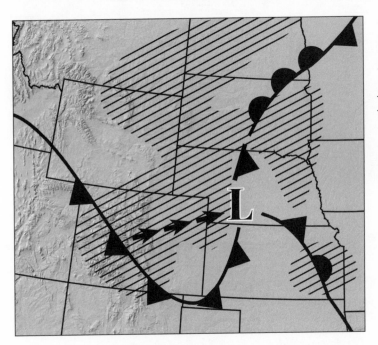

Figure 6-7. A common surface weather pattern downstream of the Rockies can include a frontal complex like the one at left. As the storm center moves east, cold air fills in behind it, creating a cold front. To the north and east of the low, warm fronts and occlusions occur. In the winter months, widespread low ceilings and visibilities in snow will prevail. In the spring, rain to the east, and snow to the west, of the low is likely. Precipitation is usually heaviest to the west at this stage of the storm systems' life cycle. Arrows show the low pressure center's track over the past eighteen hours.

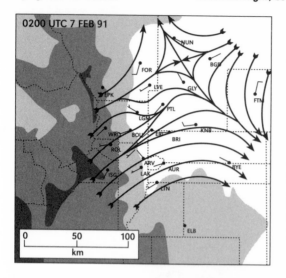
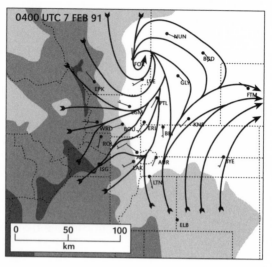
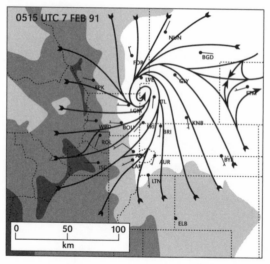

Figure 6-8. *Terrain-induced surface low-pressure systems and vortices, such as the "Denver low" shown here, are semipermanent features of the weather just downwind of the Rockies. This illustration is from a case study of the conditions on February 7, 1991, and its streamlines show how canyon air drainage flows contribute to a convergence zone. First discovered in 1981, the Denver low was identified with the help of numerous automated weather observing stations, linked in what's called a mesonet. The National Oceanic and Atmospheric Administration's Forecast Systems Laboratory (FSL) in Boulder, Colorado pioneered this mesonet, which was later augmented with the addition of Doppler lidar (light detection and ranging equipment, which directs lasers into the atmosphere from ground stations) to study motions higher in the atmosphere. (*Observations of a Terrain-forced Mesoscale Vortex and Canyon Drainage Flows along the Front Range of Colorado, *by Levinson and Banta;* Monthly Weather Review, *July 1995; AMS.*)

Accidents

The pilot of a Piper PA-32-300 Cherokee Six crashed into terrain during a forced landing near Howard, Colorado on February 8, 1995, at about 3:45 P.M. IMC prevailed but no flight plan was filed. The passenger survived and was rescued two days later. The passenger said that the pilot was trying to climb to clear the mountains south of Salida, Colorado, but that "severe winds" made the airplane descend at 2,500 FPM. The pilot tried to land on a frozen lake at the 12,500-foot level, but the engine and right wing broke off at touchdown. The right main landing gear came through the cockpit and injured the pilot and the passenger. Both spent the night in the airplane, and started to walk out the following day. Progress was slow because of the deep snow—only about 100 feet in 45 minutes. At one point the pilot lost a shoe and became disoriented. A decision was made that the passenger should go ahead and bring back rescuers, but the pilot died some time during the second day. A strong low and trough with 60-knot winds at 18,000 feet had passed through the area the previous two days, dragging behind it a stationary front at the surface. The accident took place in an area to the west of the front, and in conditions estimated at, at their worst, 900 feet overcast and 1½-mile visibility.

A Mitsubishi MU-2B-60 Marquise crashed into mountains near New Castle, Colorado in a nose-low, high-velocity condition during an instrument approach to Rifle, Colorado on March 5, 1992 at 10:02 A.M. The IFR flight plan listed Aspen, Colorado as the destination, but Aspen was below landing minimums. The pilot diverted to Rifle, and was instructed to hold at 16,000 feet while another airplane was cleared for an approach. The pilot was then cleared for the Localizer/DME-A approach to Rifle and told to contact Rifle tower for advisories. The call was never made. The airplane reportedly crashed at 10.5 DME from the airport, killing the pilot and his five passengers. Weather at the time was estimated as 500 feet scattered, 1,700 feet broken with an 8-mile visibility. A cutoff low at 18,000 feet had been affecting the area for two days, causing widespread low ceilings and visibilities. The day of the accident, the cutoff low was over southeastern Colorado and a surface low was parked south of it, in northern Texas.

On September 4, 1992 a Beech E55 Baron crashed at Rabbit Ears Pass, about 14 miles southeast of Steamboat Springs, Colorado, at 7:30 P.M., killing the pilot and his sole passenger. The pilot obtained a preflight weather briefing warning him of an approaching front and numerous flight precautions. IMC prevailed but no flight plan was filed for the flight. Witnesses saw a twin-engine airplane circling the pass and reported low ceilings and visibility along with high winds and rain mixed with snow. Near the time of the crash, Steamboat Springs reported the weather as 150 feet overcast and a visibility of two miles, with precipitation and winds at 25, gusting to 40 knots. A fast-moving surface low, boosted by a trough at 500 millibars (approximately 18,000 feet), was moving through the area, with an accompanying north-south cold front to its south and a stationary front to its north.

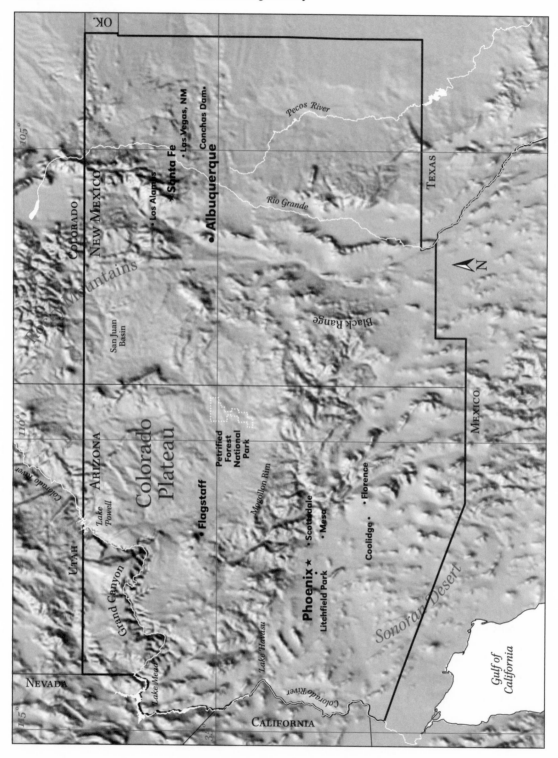

Southwest: High and Dry
Arizona and New Mexico

C ompared to most of the United States, the southwest might at first glance seem to be a climatological bore. With the uniformly warm and dry conditions you'd expect from an area that's largely desert, the weather in Arizona and New Mexico is, for flying purposes, quite unremarkable. Most of the time the weather is VFR and that, coupled with the low humidities and very mild winters characteristic of the area, makes these two states very popular with pilots.

However, this region does have its meteorological drawbacks. Severe weather can be very common in the desert southwest, especially in the summer months. In addition, those 100-degree-plus summer temperatures can make for some chart-busting density altitudes. As a matter of fact, on one day in July, 1990, temperatures rose to 122°F (50°C) at Phoenix's Sky Harbor Airport. That was enough to stop all airline operations. While the density altitude at that time was a respectable 5,201 feet (Sky Harbor's elevation is 1,112 feet MSL), it wasn't the density altitude that kept the heavy iron on the ground. It was that airframe and powerplant manufacturers had never determined their products' abilities to perform at such high temperatures. Their charts didn't go that high. By the way, when was the last time you checked your aircraft's performance charts? It's a safe bet that they call it quits at temperatures substantially lower than 122 degrees. It's something to remember when flying in the southwest in the summer months.

Plenty of VFR—with a few quirks—is the rule in the southwestern United States.

Percentage of hours in **Spring** *when ceiling is below 1,000 feet and visibility is less than 3 miles*

Percentage of hours in **Summer** *when ceiling is below 1,000 feet and visibility is less than 3 miles*

Percentage of hours in **Autumn** *when ceiling is below 1,000 feet and visibility is less than 3 miles*

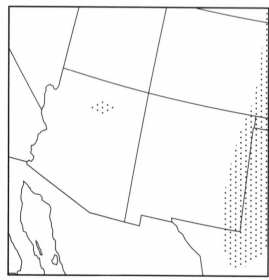

Percentage of hours in **Winter** *when ceiling is below 1,000 feet and visibility is less than 3 miles*

50% or more   **40-49%**   **30-39%**   **20-29%**   **10-19%**   **Less than 9%**

Danger Potential

While density altitude can be a major factor affecting any flight in the southwest, it's especially dangerous in high terrain. The southwest has plenty of that. Albuquerque, Flagstaff, Santa Fe, Las Vegas (New Mexico), and many, many other airports have a potentially dangerous combination of features. They have high elevations, and they are ringed with mountainous terrain. In the heat of the day, it's not at all unlikely to find density altitudes of 10,000 feet—well beyond many piston-powered airplanes' abilities to climb safely enough to clear nearby terrain.

Density altitude affects phases of flight other than takeoff, too. A twin flying on a single engine might not be able to maintain altitude. Climb rates are heavily compromised, so reaching a high minimum enroute altitude (MEAs often reach 14,000 feet in mountainous areas of the southwest) may be impossible. Takeoff runs and landing rolls take far more runway than usual because high density altitudes increase true airspeeds and, consequently, ground speeds.

Fortunately, there is a remedy. The southwest has very wide diurnal temperature ranges. It may be 100 degrees during the day, but near sunrise or sunset temperatures may drop by 50 degrees or more. So, if density altitude is a concern, wait it out for cooler temperatures.

Thunderstorms, many of them quite severe, are another feature of Arizona and New Mexico. A large portion of northeastern New Mexico, for example, experiences 70 thunderstorms per summer. Only Florida beats this level of thunderstorm activity.

Because of the drier climate, thunderstorms in the southwest—and in the lee of the Rockies—tend to have higher cloud bases. This can make it tempting to fly beneath a southwestern thunderstorm. Don't do it. Flying beneath any thunderstorm can be a dangerous experience, but with high terrain all around, the deck is stacked even more against you. Here's another interesting fact: southwestern thunderstorms frequently have lots of lightning and carry a lot of hail. The area near Los Alamos, New Mexico has a very high frequency of hail.

virga. Wisps or streaks of rain or ice particles falling out of a cloud but evaporating before reaching the earth's surface.

For an inflight photo of a desert microburst, *see* Appendix Page 295.

A good deal of research has been done on microbursts at Denver's (now-closed) Stapleton Airport, near the home of NCAR, and another high-elevation, dry-climate station. Researchers have found that in dry climates, microbursts very often coincide with **virga**. Virga is rain that evaporates before it reaches the ground. The downbursts that produce virga shafts can be violent, so if you see virga, avoid it. Particularly if it happens to be over or near your departure or destination airport.

With many mountains in the 12,000-foot range, turbulence of varying intensities is commonplace in the southwest. As high-speed, high-altitude winds stream across mountain ridges and passes, they can create powerful rotors as well as turbulence of the severe variety. Throw a hot day, a high elevation airport, and high terrain together and you've got a recipe not just for a dangerously poor climb rate, but the chance of encountering severe or extreme turbulence as well.

Clearing mountainous terrain in this part of the country also implies the threat of icing. Icing conditions over a desert may sound incongruous, but when you consider the altitudes required to safely traverse the southwest's mountains, it's easy to see how temperatures aloft can drop below freezing.

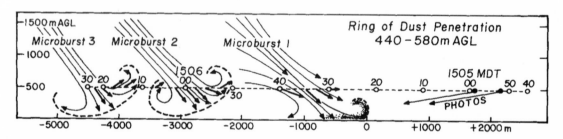

Figure 7-1. *A series of microbursts 17 miles east of the old Denver–Stapleton Airport were studied in July 1982. In one case, a sequence of microbursts set up surface gust fronts made visible by rings of dust. These so-called "dry microbursts" can issue from cloud bases as high as 12,000 feet AGL; and sometimes rain shafts or virga can pinpoint their locations. "Wet microbursts," of the kind that descend from supercell thunderstorms, take place in the wetter climates of the Gulf of Mexico rim, evolve from cloud bases lower than 1,000 feet AGL, and are nearly always marked by a dense rain shaft. (Excerpted from* The Downburst, *Fujita, p. 95.)*

Desert Rains

While the southwest is a desert, there is precipitation. Apart from thunderstorms, the southwest has two sources of moisture that run in seasonal patterns. Lows and even hurricanes can move in from the southwest. Monsoon-like precipitation is another visitor to the area, and so are Pacific-bred cold fronts.

In the summer months, rain often travels to Arizona and New Mexico from the Gulf of California and the Gulf of Mexico. Sometimes—though not very often—hurricanes can even make their way to the southwest, dumping several inches of rain before they literally dry up.

The Mogollon Rim lies to the northeast of the Phoenix area, and is a huge butte that stretches along a northwest–southeast arc. It marks the dividing line between the lower terrain of the Sonoran desert in southwest Arizona and the high country of the Colorado Plateau to the northeast. This Rim country is a favorite haunt for all types of thunderstorms and heavy rain. Apparently, on-rim air flows and the lifting forces created by the steeply rising butte are conducive to thunderstorm formation and/or intensification. In July, 1991, thunderstorms formed along the Mogollon Rim, then drifted to the southwest, building in strength as they moved. The storm's outflow winds created a large dust storm and tremendous surface winds. Gusts of up to 60 MPH were recorded at Falcon Field in Mesa, Arizona.

Thermal lows can bring prolonged periods of precipitation. When the summer sun heats the desert, a huge mass of rising air is created. This vast zone of low pressure can draw in precipitation from as far away as the Pacific Ocean and the Gulf of California. Once these dynamics begin, they perpetuate themselves over a week or more. For this reason, some meteorologists call this southwestern phenomenon a monsoon. A monsoon is nothing more than a seasonal flow of air to or from land or sea—really, a large-scale recreation of the mechanics that create land and sea breezes. Monsoons are usually associated with the South- and Southeast Asian subcontinents, where flows of moisture-laden ocean air are drawn inland to create their wet seasons. But the dynamics are just the same as those at work in the southwestern United States; the only difference is that the ocean is much farther away from Arizona and New Mexico.

Figure 7-2. Winter storms, complete with snow or rain at lower altitudes and frozen precipitation at higher levels, can and do strike the desert southwest. In this chart, we see the surface conditions for December 22, 1997, when a winter low in the Sonoran desert moved east, creating widespread instrument weather.

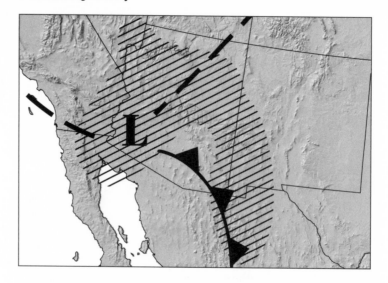

Figure 7-3. Another type of storm frequents the ordinarily-dry southwest in the summer and fall months. In this chart, for September 25, 1997, Hurricane Nora comes on shore in Baja California. The following day, Nora moved to southwest Arizona.

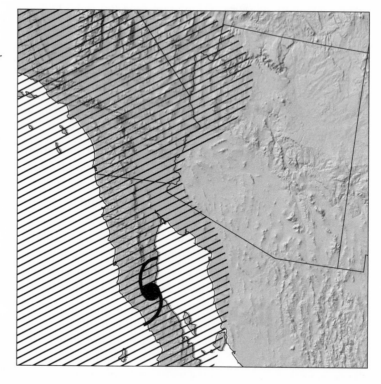

In the winter, cold fronts can pass through the southwest. Usually, these are extensions of strong Pacific lows that push their way inland from the west and northwest. In the mountains, the precipitation brought by these fronts falls as snow; 100 inches per year is typical. At lower elevations rainfall is more common.

The mountains of the southwest frequently do great jobs of slowing down frontal motion, so it's very common for some passing fronts to stall and die in the northern portions of Arizona and New Mexico.

There's no doubt that the southwest is a Mecca for general aviation. Many flight schools call this area home because nearly every day is ideal for training in superb visual weather. Lufthansa has even set up a permanent training facility at the Goodyear Airport in Litchfield, just west of Phoenix. *Ab initio*

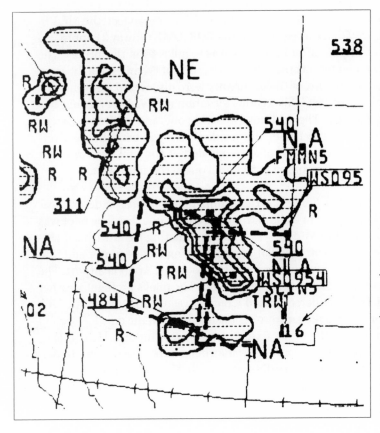

Figure 7-4. This excerpt from a radar summary chart for 5:35 P.M. on August 14, 1996 portrays a typical summer, Mogollon Rim convective situation. Rain showers and thunderstorm cells with tops as high as 54,000 feet formed over the Rim country as moist air from the Gulf of California and Pacific Ocean moved inland, beneath upper-level, cool, dry air. The resultant instability, aided in large part by surface temperatures of 105°F and dew points in the high 60s, caused two severe thunderstorm watches and Convective SIGMETs (areas within dashed boxes). After the storms formed, intense outflows from downbursts and microbursts converged over the Phoenix area, causing a new thunderstorm cell to form. One downburst with 100-knot winds hit the Deer Valley Municipal Airport near Phoenix—a new wind gust record for Arizona. Once storms begin over the Rim, they tend to move to the south and west, toward the Sonoran Desert. (Storm Data, August 1996; NOAA)

pilot candidates are selected in IMC-plagued Germany, then sent to sunny Goodyear for primary training in Beech Bonanzas and Barons.

If you've ever visited the area you know why so many pilots from northerly climates pack up and head for the southwest when winter comes. It's a place where very, very good VFR, triple-digit visibilities, and light winds reign; but the weather hazards, when they appear, stand out in shocking contrast.

Accidents

A Piper PA-32-300 Cherokee Six crashed during an instrument approach to the Flagstaff, Arizona airport at 11:00 A.M. on November 18, 1994. Icing conditions were forecast along the route of flight, which originated in Grand Canyon, Arizona and was to land at Albuquerque, New Mexico. After receiving a weather briefing and filing an IFR flight plan, the pilot and his single passenger took off at 9:58 A.M. and reported "picking up a little bit of ice" at 10:32 A.M. About half a minute later the pilot said he was "picking up, uh, static is iced over right now," and advised controllers he couldn't climb to 11,000 feet, the MEA in the area. He diverted to Flagstaff and was cleared for the VOR/DME runway 21 approach. Radio contact was lost with the pilot after he said he was 13 miles from the airport. The current Flagstaff weather was 600 feet overcast, with a visibility of 1¾ miles in light snow and fog. The wreckage and the remains of the occupants were discovered eight months later about 15 miles north of the airport. This weather situation involved the passage of a cold front through the Flagstaff area. The cold front was a big one, and ran from a parent low pressure center in Wyoming. Furthermore, the accident area was beneath the divergent, storm-producing flow of air to the east of a trough aloft at 500 millibars, or about 18,000 feet. At that level, winds were recorded at 70 knots out of the southwest.

At 7:52 P.M. on November 14, 1993, a Beech A36TC Bonanza crashed in the desert near Florence, Arizona after picking up ice in a climb from 9,500 to 12,000 feet. The pilot was cleared to descend to 11,000 feet, but said he was still accumulating ice at the new altitude. After being cleared to 10,000 feet, the pilot reported losing engine power and said his rudder was frozen. ATC gave him radar vectors to the Coolidge, Arizona airport. The pilot's last radio transmission was that his engine had quit. The pilot's preflight weather briefing mentioned AIRMETs for moderate mixed icing between 6,000 and 17,000 feet. The pilot and the right front seat passenger were seriously injured in the crash. A second passenger had minor injuries, but the other six passengers were unhurt. Here, a fast-moving surface low that formed over the southern California desert moved east into Arizona, intensified by the circulations present to the east of a cutoff low aloft at 500 millibars, or about 18,000 feet.

The pilot and passenger of a Glasair III were killed in a 9:09 A.M. crash on October 27, 1991 east of Scottsdale, Arizona. The airplane was being vectored onto an airway while climbing to 13,000 feet when the comment "losing control of the aircraft" was heard over the frequency. At Mesa, Arizona, 20 miles southwest of the accident site, the weather report for the time six minutes before the crash was: estimated ceiling 6,000 feet overcast, visibility six miles in rain showers, and lightning in all quadrants. A cold front trailing from a surface low in Wyoming appears responsible for this weather. This front contained two other, smaller surface lows along its leading edge, and a trough aloft—again, at 500 millibars—played a part in strengthening the front.

After encountering hail at about 6:30 P.M. on August 30, 1996, a Cessna 421 crashed in the desert near Conchas, New Mexico. The pilot reported level at 21,000 feet at about 6:05 P.M., and ATC cleared the airplane to descend to 19,000 feet a few minutes later. A convective SIGMET for an area of severe thunderstorms 20 miles in diameter and tops above 45,000 feet was issued at 5:55 P.M. The SIGMET covered the 421's route of flight, but ATC did not relay this to the pilot. The pilot said he saw clouds 50 to 60 miles ahead of the airplane, turned on his radar, and saw precipitation to the left and right of his intended route. He said he saw a 20-mile-wide clear area on his radar screen, and flew toward it. Some 10 miles before reaching the clouds, the airplane ran into hail that broke the windshield. The next thing the pilot or either of the two passengers remembered, the airplane was on the ground, broken into several pieces. The pilot and one passenger were seriously injured; the other passenger received minor injuries. This storm system appears to have been associated with dryline convection augmented by a north–south trough of low pressure at the surface.

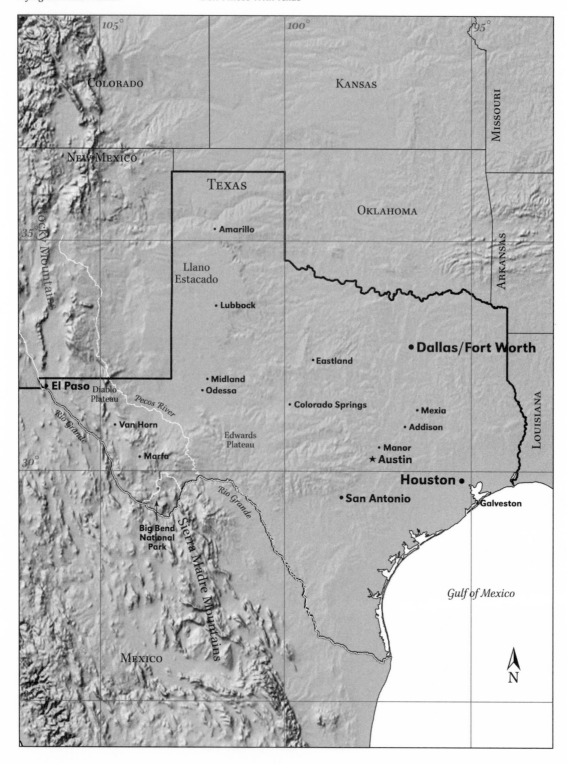

COLORADO

KANSAS

MISSOURI

NEW MEXICO

TEXAS

OKLAHOMA

• Amarillo

ARKANSAS

Llano
Estacado

• Lubbock

•Dallas/Fort Worth

• Eastland

LOUISIANA

•El Paso Diablo
Plateau

Pecos River

• Midland
• Odessa

• Colorado Springs

• Mexia

• Van Horn

Edwards
Plateau

• Addison

• Marfa

• Manor
★Austin

Houston •

Rio Grande

Rio Grande

San Antonio

Galveston

Big Bend
National
Park

Sierra Madre Mountains

Rocky Mountains

MEXICO

Gulf of Mexico

N

Don't Mess With Texas

The Dryline Headquarters

It's a well-known fact that many Texans are given to—let's see, how can I put this diplomatically—boastful exaggeration. Some might assert that this kind of bravado is unjustified, but in terms of its weather, Texas does indeed have a great deal of everything. Part of Texas' weather personality can be attributed to its sheer size, but its geographic location plays an even bigger role.

First, the size. Texas, at its biggest, runs 773 miles east to west, and 801 miles north to south. Most of the state is relatively flat, but in the Pecos region there are over 90 mountains higher than 5,000 feet MSL. Of the 50 United States, 15 could fit inside its borders. From north to south, Texas stretches over 10 degrees in latitude. This is comparable to the distance from North Carolina to southern Canada. With all this territory, you would expect Texas to have a variety of weather, and it does. In fact, the National Weather Service divides Texas into ten climatic zones.

Some other superlatives have greater relevance to Texan weather. The state's 624-mile-long coastline along the Gulf of Mexico is testimony to the great influence the Gulf's moist, tropical air mass brings to bear. The entire eastern third of the state has what climatologists call a maritime tropical climate, which means hot, humid summers and warm winters.

Traveling northwestward from the Gulf, the Texas terrain gradually slopes upward. By the time you've reached the New Mexico border, surface elevations average about 4,000 feet MSL. In the western half of the state, the southwest desert and semi-arid climate east of the central Rockies have the greatest influence. The NWS may divide Texas into ten zones, but for the sake of simplicity, we can divide it into two broad regions— a moist half and a dry half.

Texas fits a continent's worth of weather into just one state: the Gulf Coast, desert, and high plains combine to produce violent and highly changeable weather.

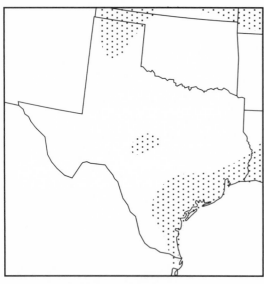

*Percentage of hours in **Spring** when ceiling is below
1,000 feet and visibility is less than 3 miles*

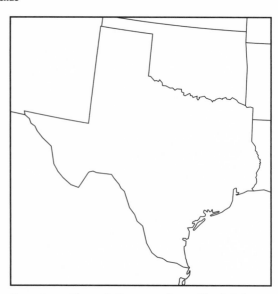

*Percentage of hours in **Summer** when ceiling is below
1,000 feet and visibility is less than 3 miles*

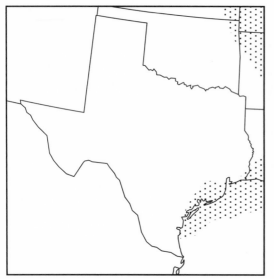

*Percentage of hours in **Autumn** when ceiling is below
1,000 feet and visibility is less than 3 miles*

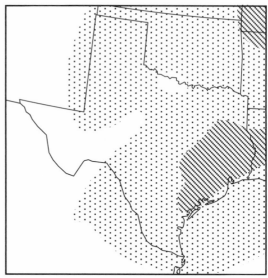

*Percentage of hours in **Winter** when ceiling is below
1,000 feet and visibility is less than 3 miles*

50% or more **40-49%** **30-39%** **20-29%** **10-19%** **Less than 9%**

Keep this picture in mind: a huge expanse of warm, moist, Gulf air to the south and east, and warm, dry, desert conditions to the west. And in between these two very different types of air masses we have—nothing. No mountain ranges, no large bodies of water, no peninsulas, nothing to create any natural barriers between these two air masses. That's the Texas weather setting at the surface.

Now let's look at the large-scale synoptics and identify some wind flows. Once again, we can roughly divide the state in half. The southeastern half usually experiences a southerly flow of air, especially in the summer months. This is the result of the clockwise flow of air around the "back side" of the Bermuda high, a semipermanent feature of summer weather in the central and eastern United States. In the dry half of the state, winds are also most often southerly or southwesterly, and sometimes products of the dry, thermally-induced low-pressure systems of the desert southwest.

The Gulf's southerly flow can travel unimpeded all the way to west Texas, where it encounters the dry desert air. Gulf air can and does fan northward into the entire United States east of the Rockies, and it's an essential ingredient in nearly all strong fronts and storms in the eastern half of the nation. It would be no exaggeration to say that southerly flows of Gulf air define almost all weather events east of the Rockies.

In west Texas, a collision of Gulf air with desert air would ordinarily be a classic setup for frontal development. But these two different air masses share one common feature: both are relatively warm. There's not enough of a temperature contrast between the air masses to create a traditional front.

Drylines

But there is one major contrast between these air masses: their dew points. The Gulf air can have dew points as high as 70° or more; it's packed with moisture, and as such it's convective nitroglycerin. If you're looking at a DUATs briefing, scanning a surface analysis chart, or listening to a flight service station briefer and find out that dew points are 50° along your route of flight, don't be surprised if thunderstorms crop up in the heat of the day. If dew points are 60°, expect them. And if dew points

Figure 8-1. *The 13 climatological regions of Texas. In aviation weather reports and forecasts—as well as public weather information and NOAA weather radio—these identifiers and regions are used to define areas of significant weather.*

are 70° or higher, you can almost bet on severe thunderstorms—if the air is unstable enough, and if frontal or orographic lifting forces are strong enough. Then again, with 70-plus dew points it won't take much instability at all to trigger a nice batch of towering cumulus by noon and multi-county-sized (*mesoscale*, in meteorology-speak) supercells by 5:00 or 6:00 P.M., when daytime temperatures reach their peak.

Conversely, it won't take much of a temperature drop to create fog or condense moisture in the high dew points of a Gulf air mass. This means that when temperatures drop after nightfall, visibilities can be reduced in fog.

In desert air, dew points typically run in the 20° to 30° range; this means that temperatures must drop a great deal before fog, moisture, or any type of condensation can occur. In mid-summer, it's a long way from triple-digit daytime high temperatures to the rock-bottom dew points of dry desert air.

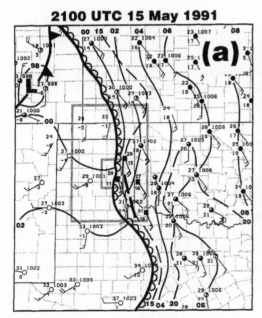

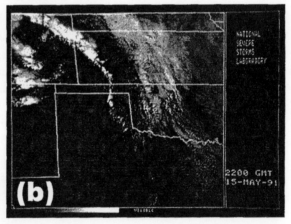

Figure 8-2. The spring and early summer are times when many drylines—"fronts" consisting of boundaries between air masses of differing dew points—form in eastern New Mexico and West Texas. With humid air from the Gulf of Mexico to the east, and dry air from the high, arid country to the west, drylines can bring about intense thunderstorms, as shown above. The north-south dryline snaking through the Texas panhandle in (a), produced lines of thunderstorms, as shown in the GOES visible spectrum imagery in (b). (Convective Initiation at the Dryline: A Modeling Study, *by Ziegler et al;* Monthly Weather Review, *June 1997; AMS.*)

To see a GOES image of a dryline defined over east Texas, turn to Appendix Page 296.

So when Gulf and desert air meet in central and west Texas, there is a front of sorts. It's just not called a front. Instead, meteorologists call the boundary between the moist and dry air a *dryline*. Sometimes, it's called a dewpoint front, and sometimes it's called a "Marfa front," after a west Texas town where the phenomenon is common.

Early in the day, visual evidence of a dryline may be completely absent. But as afternoon heat encroaches, the instability caused by the clashing of the two air masses can turn a fair-weather cumulus into a huge cumulonimbus cell in thirty minutes or less.

The odd thing about drylines is that they migrate from west to east in a fairly regular daily pattern. (In the spring and early summer months, drylines affect west Texas on more than 40 percent of the days.) Early in the morning, drylines are typically situated in eastern New Mexico. By late afternoon, they will have migrated to positions along a line from, say, Amarillo, through Midland, and down to the hill country near the Big Bend area of the Rio Grande River. (That's where Marfa is located.)

As drylines pass by, several things occur—things that pilots traversing west Texas should always watch closely. The first is a wind shift. With dryline passage, winds often shift from the south to the southwest, or even take up a westerly tack. It's an unmistakable signal that the southerly Gulf flow has been replaced by the northwesterly breezes from the desert. In this sense, drylines exhibit the characteristics of troughs, extensions of low atmospheric pressure that show counterclockwise flows. (On surface analysis charts, drylines are indicated by a scalloped line.)

Next is a drop in the dew point. Dewpoint temperatures can fall as much as 28°F in a matter of moments. Ground observers would certainly notice a dryline's passage as a dramatic drop in relative humidity.

Now that the desert air is in place and the sun begins to heat the earth's surface in earnest, temperatures begin soaring. When a dryline passed through Big Bend National Park on May 3, 1983, the temperature rose from a morning low of 53°F to an afternoon high of 108°F. With post-dryline highs commonly of 100 or more degrees, it's easy to see how much lifting force can be exerted on the retreating, moisture-packed Gulf air.

Presto, instant convective SIGMET. And the whole process may have taken as little as one-half hour.

Back to Marfa for an example. On May 17, 1990, a dryline thunderstorm went through Marfa—in style. Golf ball-sized hail accumulated in drifts up to ten inches deep. Winds of 80 MPH were recorded, along with torrential rains. Several aircraft were damaged at the Marfa airport, along with some hangars. In town, three buildings were completely uprooted.

Come nightfall, dryline thunderstorms usually peter out— but only after traveling some 200 miles into central Texas. After midnight, the southerly flow resumes and the dryline retreats to New Mexico, waiting for another day's action.

Drylines are New Mexico and Texas idiosyncrasies, but can also be found in Oklahoma, Colorado, and Kansas—other states where dry air from the west runs into the juiciest of Gulf air. A dryline will ruin your day, but there are plenty of other ways that Texas weather can take a bad turn.

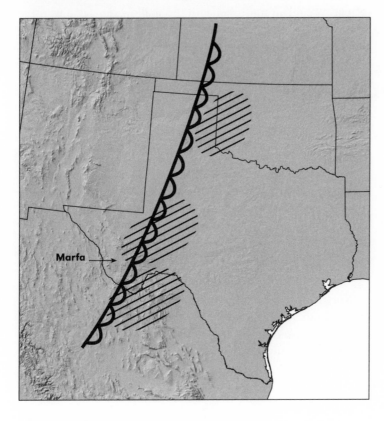

Figure 8-3. Sometimes, drylines can extend all across the western half of Texas. This weather chart is an example of the "Marfa front" dryline situation that can run through the trans-Pecos region, the Big Bend region where the town of Marfa is located.

Texas-Sized Weather

In the spring and fall months, lows have a habit of migrating from their breeding grounds in Colorado. Most often, they track east. But sometimes they draw a bead on Texas. Either way, Texas can come under the influence of violent, sometimes fast-moving, cold fronts and their attendant severe thunderstorms. Dryline thunderstorms are bad enough, but Texas' frontal thunderstorms are in a separate category altogether. The extra heat of a typical, high-90-degree Texas summer day combined with the atmospheric organization provided by a low or front—and all that Gulf moisture—makes, well, *Texas-sized* thunderstorms. **Squall lines** in advance of cold fronts are another aviation hazard common to Texas.

squall line. A narrow band of extremely active thunderstorms, which often precede the passage of a fast-moving or otherwise violent frontal zone.

If a low-pressure center moves into Texas, watch out. There can be cold and warm fronts and high cloud tops trailing from it, and sometimes severe weather can last for days. In the colder months of the year, episodes of freezing rain are not unknown. Freezing rain is most often found in the cold air of a retreating cold air mass, beneath the shallow slope of a warm air mass producing rain aloft. The rain falls into the cold air below, becomes supercooled (a condition where moisture is below freezing temperature, but still in liquid form) then adheres to airframes as clear ice. It's the worst kind of clear ice because it forms so suddenly, builds accretions rapidly, and can happen with little warning. Freezing rain can even occur in VMC, as you can discover if you fly into a light rain shower while traversing the cold sector beneath a warm front.

Be especially aware of the danger of tornadoes and hail shafts, both of which accompany a large number of Texas summer thunderstorms. Remember that parts of north Texas are in "Tornado Alley" (*see* Page 137), and that well over 350 documented tornadoes have struck northeast Texas over the past thirty years. In eastern Texas, some 60 days per year bring severe thunderstorms.

North Texas can also be considered as part of a "Hail Alley" that extends southward from Wyoming and Colorado. (Trivia item: the first recorded hail death occurred on May 13, 1939 near Lubbock, Texas, when a farmer was caught in the open during a severe hail storm.)

Gulf Coast Extremes

Wait, there's more. The Texas Gulf Coast has its own share of special weather attributes. With all that water nearby, and narrow temperature-dewpoint spreads in the morning hours, fog frequently lowers visibilities to IMC levels. In an average year, fog creates IFR weather over one-third of the time at stations along the Gulf Coast. Compared to the Gulf Coast, the rest of Texas is virtually free of persistent IFR conditions.

Moreover, the Texas Gulf Coast can serve as a highway for Gulf rains and moisture to penetrate deeper into the northern reaches of the state. You can pretty much count on this to happen when a strong Colorado low's counterclockwise flow extends to southern Texas, drawing heavy rains as far north as the Dallas–Fort Worth area, and perhaps beyond—to Oklahoma.

Finally, there's the hurricane threat. From June through October, sea temperatures in the Gulf of Mexico are conducive to hurricane formation. Depending on jet stream locations and other upper-air movements, hurricanes that form over the Gulf head for the Texas coast. A hurricane that struck Galveston on September 8-9, 1900 remains the single most destructive natural disaster in United States history—an estimated 6,000 to 8,000 persons died.

More recently, hurricane Camille devastated the Texas coast on August 17, 1969. Camille's top winds were recorded at 201.5 miles per hour, and the barometric pressure in its eye fell to 26.61 in. Hg. This was the second lowest pressure reading of all recorded hurricanes. So next time you think of hurricanes, don't limit your thinking to Florida and the Caribbean.

Big Blue Skies

Now that I've documented all this adverse weather, I can see where some pilots might view Texas as some sort of perpetual convective nightmare. But those familiar with the state know otherwise. Except in the depths of summer, temperatures across most of the state are mild, and don't present too many difficulties in terms of density altitude considerations. And all Texas-based pilots long for the much-vaunted "blue northers"— cold fronts from the north that dip into Texas, bringing clear blue skies, crisp temperatures, and the type of severe clear conditions you'd expect from a system that was born and grew up in the northern plains and southern Canada.

The best offense against an encounter with Texan convection and IMC is to follow the usual rules for safe flying anywhere in the summer months. Plan your flights for early in the day. Wait for objectionable morning coastal fogs to burn off as daytime temperatures rise. Obtain a complete preflight weather briefing. Enroute, contact flight watch often for weather updates. If in doubt, turn back.

Above all, keep in mind that Texas weather can be complex, can change quickly, and be extremely deceptive. In a 15-minute span on August 2, 1985, the DFW weather went from good VFR to microbursts that downed an L-1011 in 70-knot gusts (*see* Page 158 for details).

During your preflight briefings, be alert to any mention of a north-south cold front or an east-west warm front along your route of flight. These are the producers of the mammoth severe thunderstorm complexes. Also, listen up if the briefer describes a north–south trough in west Texas. This is a tip-off for dryline activity, and if the briefer doesn't say so, be sure to ask if a dryline situation is in the works. Remember Marfa.

Accidents

The pilot and three passengers aboard a Beech V35B Bonanza were killed after apparently suffering severe turbulence and airframe failure over Manor, Texas at 10:20 A.M. on May 16, 1991. The Bonanza was flying on an IFR flight plan from Addison to Austin, Texas, and was originally assigned a cruising altitude of 8,000 feet. After reporting severe turbulence, the pilot requested a higher altitude and was assigned 10,000 feet. He reported no more turbulence and was eventually cleared for descent to 5,000, then 3,000 feet and given vectors for an instrument approach to Austin's ILS runway 31 approach. Shortly after reporting passing through 7,000 feet, radio and radar contact with the airplane were lost. The fuselage wreckage was found in one location, but the wings and ruddervator were discovered well away from the site. Weather at the time was 1,700 feet broken, visibility five miles, with light winds and no precipitation.

A Cessna 177RG with a non-instrument rated private pilot and two passengers aboard crashed on December 29, 1993 near Van Horn, Texas after an apparent loss of control in cruise flight. IMC existed along the pilot's route from a fuel stop at San Angelo to El Paso, but after a weather briefing earlier in the day—obtained from Mexia, Texas, the flight's original departure point—the pilot departed without filing any flight plan. At 2:00 P.M. the pilot radioed the Van Horn, Texas airport (about 90 miles east of El Paso) UNICOM, asking for the current weather. He was told it was 500 feet overcast with freezing rain. The pilot replied that he would continue to El Paso. The flight was reported missing the next day, and searchers found the wreckage in the mountains some 46 miles north of Van Horn. All aboard were fatally injured. A weak trough was present over central and west Texas that day, bearing high clouds that likely prevented lower cloud layers from burning off.

In another apparent VFR-into-IMC situation, a Cessna 182 flying from Eastland to Odessa crashed at about 9:50 A.M. on November 12, 1996. Though the pilot was instrument-rated, no flight plan was filed. A witness said he saw the Cessna descend from an overcast at Colorado Springs, Texas in a nose-low attitude and in a right turn. The airplane flew that way until hitting the ground. Ceilings in that area were estimated at 300 to 900 feet AGL. The pilot—the sole occupant—was killed in the crash. A northwest–southeast-oriented stationary front had persisted on a line from Colorado to Louisiana since the day before the crash. It caused marginal VFR and IFR ceilings and visibilities across central Texas from the 11th through the 13th of November.

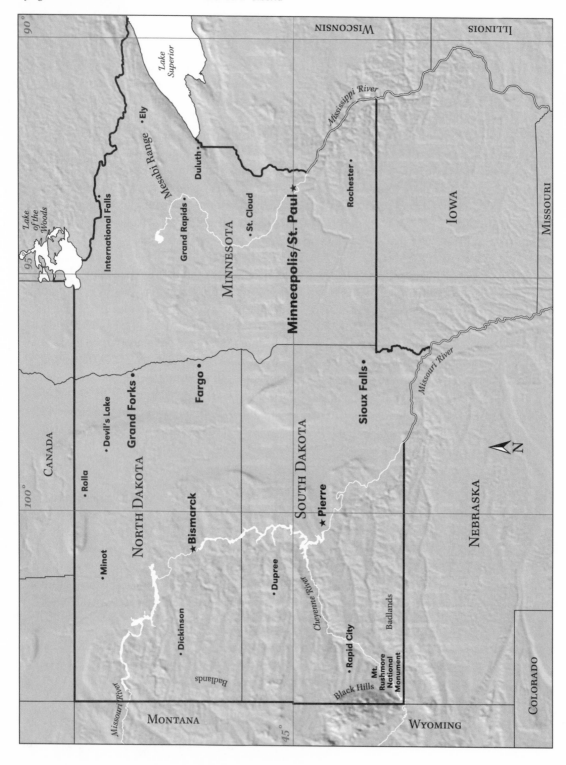

America's "Siberia"

Minnesota and the Dakotas

Whenever winter approaches, it's only natural that our thoughts turn to a part of the United States that bears some of the worst of winter's onslaughts. This dubious distinction belongs to the northern plains states—more specifically, North and South Dakota, and Minnesota. Statistics show that these states have the most consistently cold temperatures during the winter months. Mean surface high temperatures for December, January, and February hardly ever go higher than freezing; in most locations the mid-20s is an average high. Mean low temperatures are in the single-digits.

This kind of cold implies some serious operational considerations. Preheating becomes an absolute essential prior to any cold start in a northern plains winter. Engines must have the proper grade of oil, and batteries must be religiously maintained, and kept charged. If it's too cold, engine starts may even be prohibited per some manufacturers' recommendations. For example, the AlliedSignal (formerly Garrett) TPE-331 series of turboprop engines carry a cold-temperature starting limit of −28.9°C (about −20°F). At or below that temperature, you're technically prohibited from starting these engines, primarily because the lubrication of the TPE-331's many gears and other internal components can be compromised by oils that can turn less viscous under extremely low ambient temperatures. In addition, battery starts can be fatal to battery life in super-cold temperatures of the kind found in a northern winter—and not just in airplanes with TPE-331s. The cranking power of any battery plummets with the mercury, and if you have any chance at all of a successful battery start, it had better be on the first try. Compounding the winter starting problem is the fact that Avgas vaporizes poorly in very cold temperatures, making a start on that first try even more of a dubious proposition.

Extremes in temperature, rain, wind, and snow mark the flying weather of the northern plains and Minnesota.

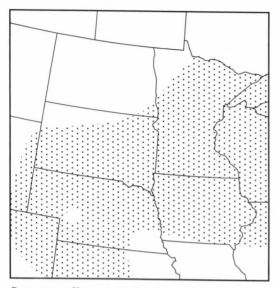

Percentage of hours in **Spring** *when ceiling is below 1,000 feet and visibility is less than 3 miles*

Percentage of hours in **Summer** *when ceiling is below 1,000 feet and visibility is less than 3 miles*

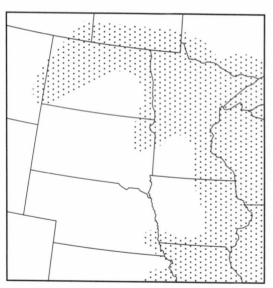

Percentage of hours in **Autumn** *when ceiling is below 1,000 feet and visibility is less than 3 miles*

Percentage of hours in **Winter** *when ceiling is below 1,000 feet and visibility is less than 3 miles*

50% or more   **40-49%**   **30-39%**   **20-29%**   **10-19%**   **Less than 9%**

Subzero to Triple Digits

This type of cold is very understandable, given the northern plains' geographic setting. First of all, this area's latitude is relatively high, which means close proximity to the even colder subarctic regions of Canada, and very short winter days. Large bodies of water are a long way away, and as you've see in other chapters, oceans and lakes exert a moderating effect on temperature. Without them nearby, land masses become very cold when arctic air invades, stay cold longer, and are slower to respond to any warming trends. Worse, any snow that falls has a slim chance of rapidly melting. Once snow is on the ground, a vicious cycle can begin. The whiteness of the snow reflects most of the sun's rays back into the atmosphere, shielding the earth from its customary source of heat. The earth remains frozen, and thus reinforces the impact of any additional movements of cold air from Canada. In other words, snow brings more snow.

On the other hand, it's interesting to note that the plains can have soaring summer highs—to 100°F and beyond. Only one other area in the northern hemisphere can boast of such extremes between summer highs and winter lows: Siberia.

Blizzards and Cold, Cold, Cold

Let's look at some synoptic features affecting the northern plains. Apart from its latitude and the cold this brings, two semipermanent highs set this area up for a nonstop series of traveling lows in the winter. The Pacific high, located west of central California, shunts low pressure northward, intensifying the semipermanent low pressure zone that already exists in the area of the Aleutian Islands.

In the Atlantic Ocean, the Bermuda high—another semi-permanent feature—traditionally moves eastward, to a position off the African coast, where it will stay for the winter. This allows a semipermanent low, akin to that in the Aleutians, to form between Iceland and Greenland, with a December mean pressure of 29.46 inches of mercury. This is not the time to plan a flight to Europe in a small airplane via the usual stops at Goose Bay or St. John's in Canada; Sondestrom, Narsarssuaq, or Kulusuk in Greenland; or Reykjavik, Iceland. Icing levels will extend to the surface, and ice accretions will come swift, heavy, and strange.

By December, mean barometric pressure in the Aleutians is 29.53 inches of mercury.

So with two highs over either ocean, and lows in the Aleutians, the stage is set. There's nowhere else for the huge dome of polar high pressure over central Canada to go but south. The prevailing westerlies make sure that any strong Aleutian lows will track eastward, toward the Canadian Rockies. There, the strongest of these storms often reorganize their counterclockwise flow, then head southeast, riding the dip in the jet stream that is so common over the central United States in winter.

As these lows travel south, moisture from the Gulf of Mexico can feed them. With nothing but a few fence posts between the Dakotas and the North Pole, wind speeds can reach spectacular levels. Combine the two, and you have the potential for a snowstorm—or a blizzard. Blizzards are defined as snow storms with surface temperatures at or below 20°F, wind speeds at or above 32 MPH, and visibilities less than 500 feet. Severe blizzards are defined as having wind speeds higher than 45 MPH, temperatures near or below 10°F, and visibilities near zero. It should be noted that much of the snow in a blizzard is fine in texture, and blown from snow accumulations already on the ground.

© S. Albers

"Street-light pillars" in North Dakota on a February night. This strange phenomenon is caused by refraction of light through ice crystals in the atmosphere.

In terms of aviation weather, this obviously represents very dangerous IFR. Blizzards can mean zero visibility in blowing snow, severe turbulence, whiteout conditions, and missed approaches. Because of the electrical charges generated by the widespread collision of snow and ice crystals, blizzards can also contain thunderstorms with some surprisingly intense displays of lightning. On average, two blizzards per year affect the northern plains states. The Front Range of the Rockies is another popular staging area for blizzards. (*See* the inset map on Page 78 in the chapter on Colorado, for the location of the Front Range.)

Blizzards are bad enough, but the sheer cold and snow of more "moderate" northern plains winter weather extracts its fair share of penalties on the aviation community. Each winter takes its toll in terms of frozen control surfaces, snowbound runways (and airplanes), and numbing preflight inspections.

Turbocharged aircraft face a special threat from operations in extreme cold. The dense air that accompanies a polar high makes it easy for the unwary to overboost turbocharged engines on takeoff. Careful preflight calculations are necessary to determine the proper manifold pressure settings for both takeoff and cruise.

How cold can it get? On December 21, 1990 the mercury dropped to –33°F at the Dickinson, North Dakota airport. The wind was blowing at 21 MPH, so the wind chill was –86°F. Fly-in breakfast, anyone?

Two days later, most of North Dakota woke up to freezing rain as a low moved in from the northwest. After the previous cold spell, the ground was frozen rock-hard, and the freezing rain—which lasted for eight hours—covered everything with a sheet of ice.

Minnesota was also true to form in December 1990. On December 2, winds with gusts up to 56 MPH hit the Rochester airport when a strong Canadian cold front passed through. On the 14th, wind chills of –50°F to –70°F were recorded all over the state. Minneapolis reported subzero temperatures for 116 consecutive hours.

Northern Plains IMC

However, this region does have its advantages when lows are away. Because humidities and dew points are so low, there is little in the way of atmospheric moisture. In the winter and spring months, less than 20 percent of the time is spent in instrument meteorological conditions. In the summer and fall, IMC prevails only 10 percent of the time. When there are icing conditions, the comparative dearth of atmospheric moisture that usually prevails in this region means generally smaller water droplets in cloud, and so ice buildups tend to be of the rime variety. Dangerous, but not as dangerous as the large-droplet ice accumulations so common in the Pacific Northwest and Great Lakes regions.

Once winter has passed, the chief hazards to flight become thunderstorms. These can be particularly severe in the early spring, as frontally-induced thunderstorms in this part of the country involve the clash of air masses with widely divergent properties. When a strong jet stream moves over the Dakotas, the cool, dry air north of the jet collides with the warm, moist air from the Gulf, and severe thunderstorms soon follow. Severe thunderstorms have one or more of the following: surface winds in excess of 50 knots, ¾-inch hail, and tornadoes.

On average, the northernmost portions of the Dakotas and Minnesota experience 30 thunderstorm days per year; the southern areas have 45. May, June, and July are the big tornado months, and South Dakota and southern Minnesota have an average of 23 tornadoes per year. North Dakota's average is 15 per year. This means roughly half of North Dakota's thunderstorms spawn tornadoes. This alone is more than enough reason to always ask your flight service station briefer for the Convective Outlook (AC) before deciding to fly in the Dakotas during thunderstorm season.

The "Alberta Clipper"

But hey, that's summer. For winter flying, anyone wanting to fly in the northern plains would be better served by keeping an eye on the areas to the lee of the Canadian Rockies. If a strong low is on its way to the northern plains, you'll see it first in Alberta. You'll see a tightly-wound surface low on surface analysis charts, trailing a mean-looking cold front with a southerly bow in it. These "Alberta clippers" are fast-moving cold fronts that typically contain more cold, turbulence, and strong winds than snow, but are still cause for caution. Once the low's cold front passes through, get ready. Hook up your airplane's battery charger and set it to trickle-charge. Plug in your engine block and cylinder head heaters. Don't have any? Then drain the oil from the airplane's crankcase and store it indoors. Put covers on the wings and tail so the snow and ice can be more easily removed. Even better, put the airplane in a hangar. A heated hangar. While you're at it, put your car in there, too.

Checklist complete? Then find a couch and hit the remote for some quality televised entertainment. Try The Weather Channel. Chances are, flying conditions will improve in the next day or so. A call to flight service will probably back up that prediction. For added kicks, ask for any PIREPs in the areas affected by the Clipper. If anyone's flying, they're getting kicked around fairly well, and should have provided some interesting reports.

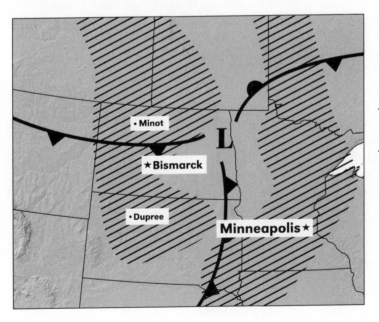

Figure 9-1. The Alberta Clipper of December 21, 1993. This system was involved in the crash of a Comanche 250, described in the accident section on Page 134. The pilot crashed while attempting to fly from Colorado Springs to Minot, North Dakota. An FSS briefer suggested that if the pilot postpone his flight he'd be able to fly in the improving conditions expected behind the cold front, which at the time of the crash was extending westward through central North Dakota.

Accidents

On December 21, 1993 the pilot of a Piper PA-24-250 Comanche planned a flight from Colorado Springs, Colorado to Minot, North Dakota. Before departing on a VFR flight plan, the pilot received four weather briefings. During the first briefing, he was told of scattered to broken clouds between 5,000 and 7,000 feet in South Dakota, with visibilities of 20 miles. In North Dakota, however, the briefer said that some stations were IFR in fog and stratus. In the second briefing, the pilot was told that no big changes were anticipated in the forecasts. On the third briefing he was told that a weak cold front would be coming through about midnight, with some snow shower activity through the Dakotas, with less than 50 percent coverage. Minot, he was told, had an outlook of marginal VFR or IFR conditions. The briefer suggested that if the pilot waited an extra day he could probably fly around the back side of the weather system. During the fourth briefing, a briefer said that a fast-moving cold front was headed for Minot, and that it "might be best for you to get underway shortly." "I'm leaving right now," the pilot said, and took off. En route, he received two more briefings. In the first, he learned that there weren't any precautions yet, but that four miles in light snow was expected. In the second, he was told that satellite imagery showed moisture entering western North Dakota. He then asked for, and received, flight following from the Denver Air Route Traffic Control Center, saying he was at 8,250 feet and 48 miles southwest of Dupree, South Dakota. After a transfer to the Minneapolis ARTCC, the pilot asked for a descent to 6,500 feet, saying he wanted to keep sight of the lights on the ground, and that "it looks kinda cloudy." Radar contact was lost, but the pilot asked what his position was. He was told he was 93 miles south of the Bismarck VOR. While en route to Bismarck, the pilot was advised that Pierre, South Dakota had VFR weather. A minute later, the controller said that the Bismarck weather was 1,100 feet broken with 12 miles visibility in light snow. The pilot acknowledged the transmission, and there were no further communications. At about 7:30 P.M. the Comanche crashed into a hill; the pilot was killed. He flew into a classic Alberta Clipper—a fast-moving low out of the lee side of the Canadian Rockies, containing two or more fronts, snow of varying intensity, and localized pockets of instrument weather. By the following morning, the Clipper was over central Illinois. (*See* Figure 9-1.)

On February 24, 1994 at 9:49 A.M. a Cessna 401 crashed in IMC during an ILS approach to runway 31 at Minot, North Dakota's International Airport. The flight originated at Devil's Lake, North Dakota, with an intended destination of Rolla, North Dakota. Conditions at Rolla were below VFR minima, so the flight diverted to Minot. The pilot had received an outlook weather briefing the day before the flight, but there was no record of a briefing on the day of the accident. The pilot made one attempt at a visual approach to the Rolla airport, but abandoned it, saying he encountered whiteout conditions at 400 feet. He received an IFR clearance to Minot, and was vectored for an approach. On the first try, the pilot declared a missed approach, saying to the approach controller, "that was my mistake…I've got to get this thing a little slower on final." Then the pilot called a missed approach on the second approach. The airplane then crashed, killing all four aboard. Conditions near the time of the accident were: indefinite ceiling 600 overcast; sky obscured, visibility ½-mile variable in snow; temperature 6°F; dew point 3°F; with visibility variable from ¼ to ¾ mile. Other pilots reported heavy snow at Minot at the time. A pilot on approach behind the accident airplane reported the conditions as almost at whiteout, and also missed his first approach. He said he caught sight of the ground at 300 feet AGL, that the horizontal visibility was poor, and that he saw the sequential approach lights at the time he initiated his missed approach. A low-pressure trough bearing a weak center of low pressure, pushed to the southeast by high pressure in Alberta, caused the heavy snow that day. There had been snow in North Dakota the previous three days—all due to trough activity. The low eventually tracked to central Minnesota the following day, but its trailing trough still caused snow in the Dakotas.

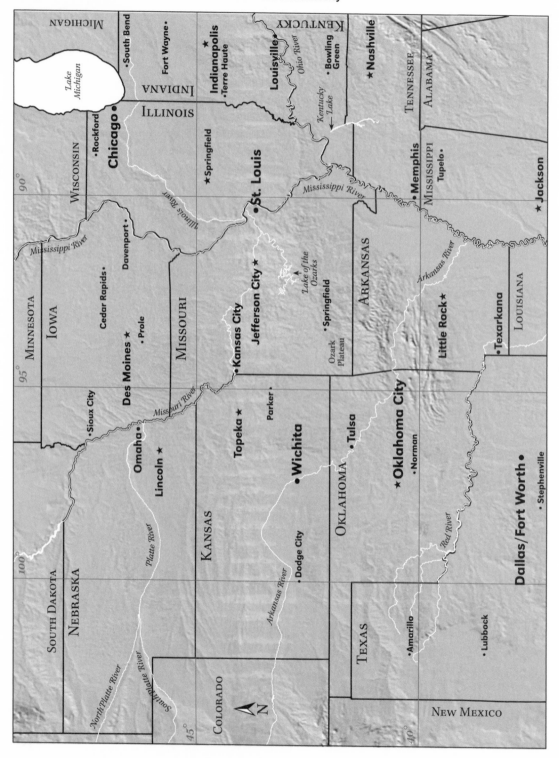

Storm Central and Tornado Alley

MCCs, LLJs, and F-Scales

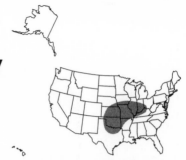

Visiting the zones with the most severe convective activity

Visit any well-stocked curio shop in Kansas and you're bound to find T-shirts bearing tornadoes and the slogan "I don't think we're in Kansas anymore, Toto." On a shelf nearby will be the miniature cylinders dubbed "pet tornadoes." These soapsuds-filled containers, with a flick of the wrist, make tiny tornadic vortices inside. Welcome to the heartland. And welcome to storm central, the region we all see so well-decorated with thunderstorm, tornado, winter weather watch and warning boxes on The Weather Channel.

What we're calling "storm central" includes several states other than Kansas. It's just that Kansas achieved prominence as an exceptionally stormy place—thanks to the 1939 film *The Wizard of Oz*—and ever since seems to get all the press attention whenever tornadoes touch down there. "Storm central" takes in a region bounded by Iowa, Nebraska, Missouri, and Illinois to the north; Indiana, western Kentucky, western Tennessee, and northern Mississippi to the east; and Texas, Oklahoma and Arkansas to the south. That's where a whole lot of nasty warm-weather convection has found a home.

Storm Brew

Why do so many strong and persistent thunderstorm—and snowstorm—complexes form over and traverse this area of the central United States? Part of the answer lies in Colorado, where low-pressure systems form in the lee of the Rockies (*see* Page 99), and head east to the central United States, growing as they move. Another reason is that low-level (at approximately 5,000 feet MSL) jet streams often shoot up from Texas or Louisiana and drive as far north as the Great Lakes. These warm, wet winds—creatures essentially born of the Gulf of Mexico—

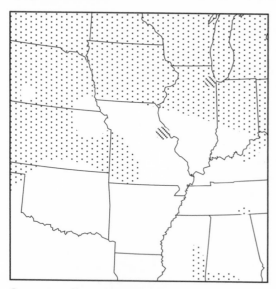

Percentage of hours in **Spring** when ceiling is below
1,000 feet and visibility is less than 3 miles

Percentage of hours in **Summer** when ceiling is below
1,000 feet and visibility is less than 3 miles

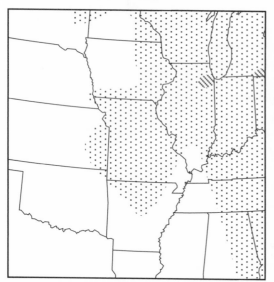

Percentage of hours in **Autumn** when ceiling is below
1,000 feet and visibility is less than 3 miles

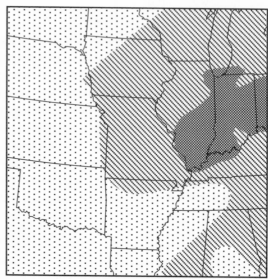

Percentage of hours in **Winter** when ceiling is below
1,000 feet and visibility is less than 3 miles

50% or more   **40-49%**   **30-39%**   **20-29%**   **10-19%**   **Less than 9%**

can blow as fast as 70 knots, and seem to be important elements in intensifying daytime thunderstorms and in forming and perpetuating nocturnal thunderstorms over the central United States. They can also be unwelcome surprises to southbound pilots who count on the light winds and smooth air they may have come to expect from night flying. This low-level jet (or LLJ, to use meteorological jargon) is most evident in advance of a north–south cold front—the kind that so often traipse from west to east across the center of the country.

Last, but by no means least, is the high-altitude jet stream. When large troughs aloft settle over the central United States, the core winds in jet streams that cycle around the perimeters of these troughs can impart lifting and destabilizing forces to the air parcels beneath them. This is especially true for high-speed jet cores located at the southeast fringes of troughs aloft. That's because this is the region with the greatest temperature and moisture contrasts. The cold air aloft is parked over the warmest, wettest, Gulf-fed temperatures in the lower levels of the atmosphere. That right there is a setup for instability, lifting and thunderstorms.

Next, factor in the **ageostrophic flows** within the jet's core of strongest winds. What in the world is an ageostrophic flow, I hear you ask, and why should you care? Good questions. Normally, air flows with isobars (seen on surface analysis charts) and height contours (on constant pressure charts)—facts we learn so well in ground school. Those are examples of geostrophic flows. Ageostrophic flows cross height contours at jet stream altitudes, and in so doing cause divergence aloft—which supports and intensifies surface lows. Also, at the surface, they help create squall lines and fast-moving cold fronts. Figure 10-1 goes into more detail about the exact locations, whys and wherefores of the diverging and converging sectors of a jet stream's core of highest winds.

Then there's the low-level jet stream mentioned earlier—add it to this brew and you can see why spring and summer are so volatile in the central United States, and why winter snowstorms can be so widespread.

Why should you care about this rarefied meteorology? Because by calling up a 500-millibar chart you can do some of your own, homegrown forecasting. Should you see a large

ageostrophic flows. Air flows that move across isobars or height contours at an angle toward either high or low pressure.

For a discussion of height contours and constant pressure charts, *see* Appendix Pages 306, 307.

trough, find its southeasternmost portion. If the height contours there are diverging—fanning out—downwind, you're on to something. Now find a surface analysis chart for roughly the same time frame and look where the southeast corner of the trough aloft was. Chances are, you'll find a fairly well-developed surface low beneath that target area of the trough. Congratulations: You've just learned one rule of thumb in a forecast meteorologist's bag of tricks—surface lows and fronts tend to intensify beneath the leading edges of troughs aloft. It's a trick meteorologists didn't thoroughly convince themselves of until World War II.

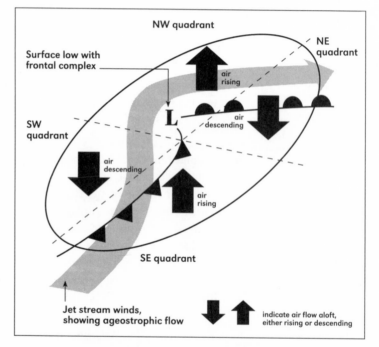

Figure 10-1A. In weather-making, the jet stream winds at 30,000 feet or so have a lot of influence. In a jet stream's core of strongest winds—represented by the oval in this illustration—vertical air movements create and influence the weather below. These movements occur when a jet core's ageostrophic winds—winds that cross isobars or height contours (the lines that depict pressure patterns on constant pressure charts)—cause rising and descending columns of air below. As pulsing, high-speed winds enter the core's southeast quadrant, they bend toward the low pressure center in the trough aloft, in effect sliding down the descending height contours. As this air exits the southeast quadrant, it creates diverging air aloft, which in turn causes the air below it to rise and condense into clouds and precipitation. The same thing happens when air exits the northwest quadrant. At this location, divergence aloft often creates and/or intensifies a surface low pressure system. The areas below the quadrants with converging air aloft—the southwest and northeast—*have converging, descending air, which discourages cloudiness. The "clear slot" of cloud-free skies that shows up on some satellite shots of low-pressure systems is frequently caused by* these motions in the southwest quadrant. Convergence aloft in the northeast quadrant causes divergence near the surface, which in turn can generate squall lines and thunderstorms.

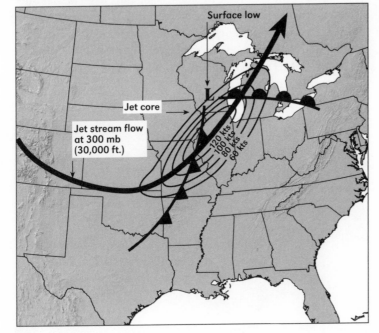

Figure 10-1B. (top) *Air flowing around a trough aloft follows the patterns made by height contours— lines depicting the altitudes of a sloping constant pressure surface. Surface lows form to the southeast of the trough aloft.*

(bottom) *Jet stream air enters the chart from the northwest, then makes a bend to the northeast after crossing the trough's axis. The pressure surface aloft is sloping from higher altitudes to the south to the center of lowest pressure over the North Dakota/Minnesota border, as shown in the top view. Surface lows and fronts usually set up in zones of diffluence—where height contours begin to fan out. On the top chart, that spot is right over Tornado Alley. In the bottom chart example, the jet core is superimposed on a surface weather system. This shows the typical geographic relationship between jet cores aloft and the surface weather below them.*

Mesoscale Convective Complexes (MCCs)

For a satellite view of an MCC, turn to Appendix Page 293.

Another, even more recently-discovered weather phenomenon that lives in storm central is the Mesoscale Convective Complex, or MCC for short. MCCs are large, roundish thunderstorm formations that can cover 60,000 square miles—and sometimes, an entire state. Meteorologists first discovered and elaborated on these huge, long-lived complexes in 1980 after identifying them in satellite imagery.

It's their long lifetimes, heavy rainfall amounts, and nocturnal persistence that distinguish MCCs from the other brands of thunderstorms. Like supercells and other severe thunderstorms, MCCs can produce tornadoes, hail, strong winds, and vivid lightning. Unlike isolated air mass cells and frontal thunderstorms, however, MCCs seem to result from mergers and interactions between storm cells that develop in different locations. Some MCCs start out at the southern end of squall lines, where their associated cold fronts can weaken and slow down.

At other times, MCCs appear to form out of a parent storm coming from the lee of the Rockies. One study asserts that one-fourth of MCCs have their origins in thunderstorm activity first detected over the Rockies or their eastern slopes. Another theory holds that MCCs form ahead of troughs aloft, in processes described above—just like so many other convective and frontal weather events.

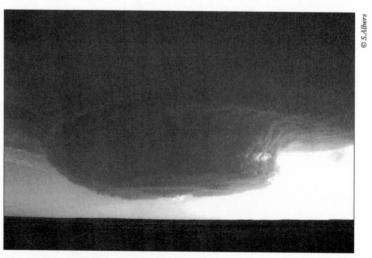

© S.Albers

Mesocyclone near Akron, Colorado, June 1990

Another convincing explanation connects MCCs with stationary fronts and ridges of high pressure. This theory is backed up by the fact that so many MCCs seem to form to the north and east of stationary fronts, and west of high pressure ridges. Here, the stationary front acts as a repository of LLJ-fed moisture. Once the MCC forms, the theory goes, it moves to the east–northeast, toward the back side of the high pressure ridge to the east.

See meteorological data that exemplifies this MCC theory, in Figure 10-2A and 10-2B on the next pages.

Whatever their origin, MCCs form in the late afternoon and reach their maximum sizes in the hours just after local midnight. Coincidentally, the LLJ also reaches its maximum strength at about the same time. This intersection of events argues for the LLJ's importance as an ingredient in the formation not just of MCCs, but of any nocturnal thunderstorms in the midwest. The LLJ's transport of warm, moist air must in some way feed nocturnal storms, and serve as heat "engines" in much the same way solar heating drives the convective process in diurnal thunderstorms.

MCCs have also been linked to a newly defined phenomenon known as **derechoes**. Derechoes are widespread, convectively induced windstorms that often precede squall lines and can generate surface wind gusts up to 60 knots, although most derechoes run in the 45- to 49-knot range.

derechoes. Families of strong downbursts, embedded in thunderstorm lines or clusters.

Pilots receiving weather briefings mentioning nighttime thunderstorms, consider yourself forewarned. Though aviation forecasts may not use the term "MCC" in their verbiage, you should know that such complexes may come together during your flight. If you find yourself in the middle of a growing complex, the safest option is probably to land at the earliest opportunity. MCCs are usually too large to circumnavigate in general aviation airplanes with low power and four-hour endurances (excluding IFR reserves).

Turbulence at the LLJ altitude is another problem. As night falls, surface winds may die off, but the LLJ is still up there, and still cranking up to its maximum velocity. This separation of surface air flow from low-level flows aloft is called decoupling, and a pilot who encounters an abrupt decoupling of winds— and notices it—should be alert to the chance of thunderstorms, particularly if he or she enters an area of strong southerly winds aloft. Those winds might be feeding a growing

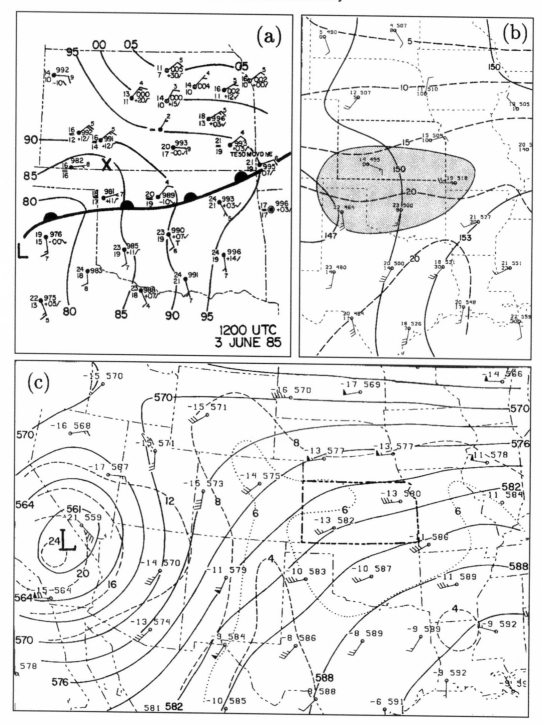

Figures 10-2A and 10-2B

Excerpts from a case study of the Oklahoma/southern Kansas MCC of June 3, 1985 show the usual synoptic situation seen with these complexes.

At left: *The surface analysis chart shows a warm front in (a) that is oriented east–west (it would become a stationary front later in the day), and on the 850 millibars/500 feet chart (b), the shaded area shows where dew points are a moist 57°F or better. On the 500 millibars/18,000 feet chart (c), Tornado Alley is to the east of an upper-level low, a place where lifting motions prevail.*

At right: *Later in the day on June 3, radar plots show how MCC precipitation echoes and storm cells moved from west to east, following the northern edge of the stationary front. This imagery is from the Wichita, Kansas radar site. From top to bottom, the times of the radar plots are 10:40 A.M., 12:10 P.M., and 1:00 P.M.*

(An Observational Analysis of a Developing Mesoscale Convective Complex, *by Nachamkin, et al; Monthly Weather Review, June 1994; AMS. Some illustrations from earlier MWR papers: (a) Stumpf, et al (1991), and (c) Fortune, et al (1992).)*

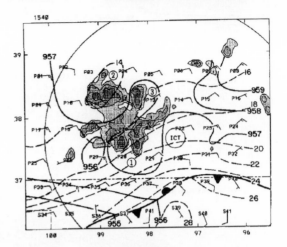

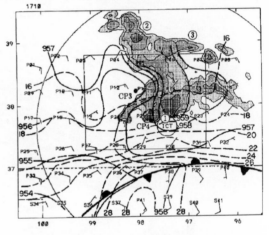

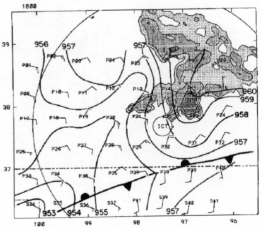

storm cell somewhere up ahead. Also, it stands to reason that as you climb from still air and make the sudden passage to air tooling along at 60 or more knots, you'll encounter some bumps. So there's another warning.

Bear these MCC clues in mind when planning night flights in the midwest. Flight service may mention a chance of thunderstorms and southerly winds aloft ahead of a dying cold front. If you hit turbulence at 5,000 feet or so on the climbout, then see terrific southerly winds aloft, you've got reason enough to expect that the "chance" of thunderstorms is fairly solid.

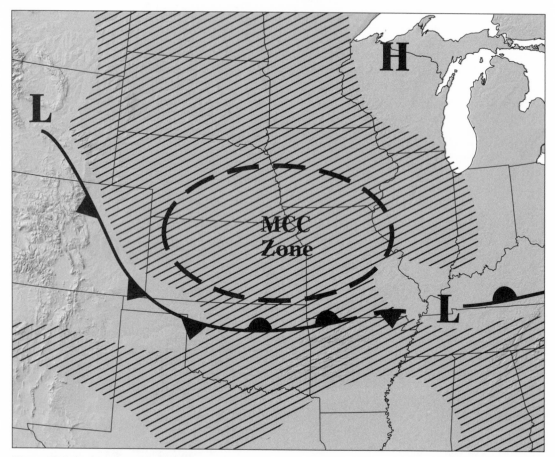

Figure 10-3. *Looking for MCCs? Find a surface chart that looks like the one above, and then keep a close eye on the zone where MCCs usually form.*

Tornadoes

By definition, a severe thunderstorm is accompanied by one or more of the following: surface winds at or greater than 50 knots, hail ¾-inch or more in diameter, and tornado activity. Mind you, no thunderstorm should ever be treated casually, but the severe variety deserve the highest degree of a pilot's attention and respect. Pilots flying in or near the nation's midwest in the spring and summer months should be especially aware of the high frequency of severe thunderstorms and tornadoes that occur in these areas. Luckily, most of us have this awareness, and the good sense to stay on the ground when conditions are prime. That's probably why there are so few aviation accidents involving pilots knowingly flying into severe storms in the midwest.

Because of the central United States' tornado awareness, local and federal authorities have kept a reasonably good count of tornadoes over the years. So we have very reliable information on where to expect severe thunderstorms. Figure 10-4 shows maps of tornado and hail frequency, based on counts between 1955 and 1967. As you can see, central Oklahoma, eastern Kansas, and northern Texas take the prize for the highest tornado counts. You can also see that the states north and east of Kansas are by no means shabby when it comes to tornado frequency. And while Oklahoma is also the winner for hailstorm frequency, it's obvious that portions of the mountainous west are also subject to hail—probably more often than the chart shows. One of the problems with the remote areas around the Rockies is a lack of observations. Areas of these charts marked "less than ten" or "less than five" may actually experience more tornadoes or hail. It's just that no one was around to count them.

Tornadoes are of great interest to meteorologists not just because of their destructive potential, but because so little is known about the dynamics of their formation, their structure within a cumulonimbus complex, or their life cycles. Forecasters can do a very good job of identifying large-scale areas likely to experience severe thunderstorms and tornadoes, but have a hard time when it comes to pinpointing exactly when and where tornadoes will form or touch down. They are simply too small-scale a phenomenon, and too short-lived, to permit adequate study—even with the best Doppler radars. So

See Appendix Pages 304–305 for charts of yearly thunderstorm frequency. (Hail and tornado frequency is charted in Figure 10-4 on the next page.)

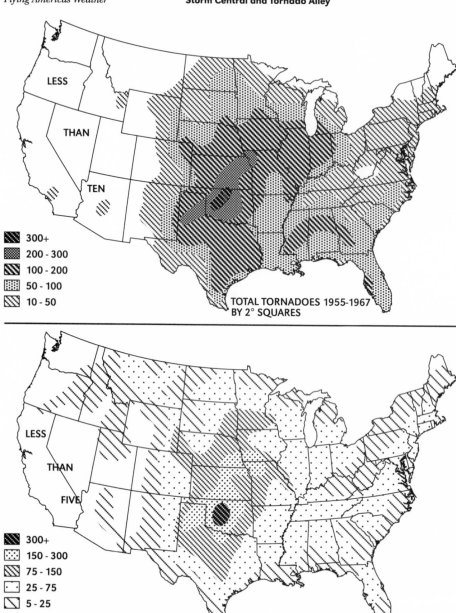

LESS
THAN
TEN

300+
200 - 300
100 - 200
50 - 100
10 - 50

TOTAL TORNADOES 1955-1967
BY 2° SQUARES

LESS
THAN
FIVE

300+
150 - 300
75 - 150
25 - 75
5 - 25

Distribution of Major Hailstorm Frequency, 1955-1967

Figure 10-4. *There's a reason why they call it Tornado Alley, as the climatological record for a 12-year period shows. With 300-plus tornadoes, central Oklahoma wins the prize for being most tornado-prone, as well as the winner for hailstorm frequency.*

tornado meteorology remains basically a descriptive science rather than a predictive one. One theory holds that tornadoes begin to form as horizontal rotors, created by vicious lateral wind shears within strong convective cells. As vertical currents strengthen within the thunderstorm, the horizontal rotor becomes a vertical one, descending to the ground as its rotation strengthens.

What do we know for sure? First, they tend to form between four and eight P.M.; not surprising, since this is the time of maximum solar heating of the earth. It's this vertical boost that intensifies any cumulus development, no matter where it may be. According to data, most tornadoes form when surface temperatures are between 65 and 84°F, and when dew points are 50°F or higher. That 50° figure should be considered a low-ball number. A 50° dew point can be likened to a convective hand grenade; moisture content is sufficient to feed growing cumulus cells, but not as likely to help create, for example, a 50-mile diameter supercell. When dew points climb to 60 degrees, that's the equivalent of a convective napalm bomb— more than enough sticky, humid air to contribute to potentially large areas of thunderstorms. Dew points of 70°—well, that would be the equivalent of a convective nuclear weapon. At this dewpoint level, it doesn't take much to break a sweat as you preflight your airplane, and when temperatures rise in the heat of the day the vast moisture content implied by that 70° dew point is easily enough to spawn thunderstorms with VIP Level 4, 5, and 6 radar returns—not to mention tornadoes.

See Page 194 for a table that shows how to decipher "VIP Level" storm intensities on radar returns.

Second, we know that the United States experiences about 700 tornadoes each year. The number is probably higher than

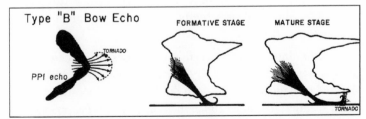

*Figure 10-5. When checking radar summary charts, Nexrad, Nowrad, and on-board weather radar, be on the lookout for bow echoes. When supercells and bow echoes are fully developed, they can generate both tornadoes and microbursts. Drawing at left refers to the imagery on a ground-based radar's scope, or plan position indicator (PPI). (*The Downburst, *Fujita, pages 75-76.)*

that, because a large number go unobserved in isolated regions. The climatological record shows that well over half of these tornadoes happen in Tornado Alley. Surprise, surprise.

It's also well known that tornadic winds can go as high as 250 to 300 MPH. Because they are small—but very, very intense—low pressure centers, tornadoes usually rotate counterclockwise. Pressure falls of .76 in. Hg have been recorded in the space of a ten-minute tornado passage. Contrary to popular belief, it's not the pressure drop itself that causes such great destruction. Buildings don't explode or collapse because the pressure trapped inside them cannot equalize quickly enough with the low-pressure air outside it. Instead, tornadic winds destroy houses by lifting their roofs (which have shapes that act like airfoils in triple-digit winds). After the roof is gone, the structural integrity of the house is done for. The windward wall is free to fall in, the side walls blow out, the downwind wall falls down and out, and the roof then falls in on top of the whole mess—or the next county. Obviously, any airplane caught in a tornado, on the ground or in the air, would suffer catastrophic structural failure—if not from the pressure drop, then from the effects of those three-digit winds.

The average duration of tornadoes is about a half-hour, and their average ground tracks run about six miles. But there have been some notable exceptions. In May 1917, a tornado lasting seven hours, twenty minutes passed through Illinois and Indiana. Ground tracks as long as thirty miles have also been recorded.

Once their funnel clouds have formed and touched down, tornadoes usually move along at 25-45 MPH. The average width of the funnel cloud is 400 yards; at the surface, its width can be much less. Almost always, their direction of movement is southwest–northeast.

Another interesting fact is that tornadoes often occur in groups, some of them very large. One especially well-documented tornado series has been dubbed the "Superoutbreak" of April 3-4, 1974 (*see* Page 208 in the "Ohio Valley" chapter), when 148 tornadoes struck an area bounded by Alabama, Illinois, Ohio, and Virginia; 315 people were killed, and 5,484 were injured. Where did this outbreak of tornadoes occur, synoptically speaking? In the warm sector just ahead of a cold front, and no doubt fed by a strong low-level flow of warm, wet air, and per-

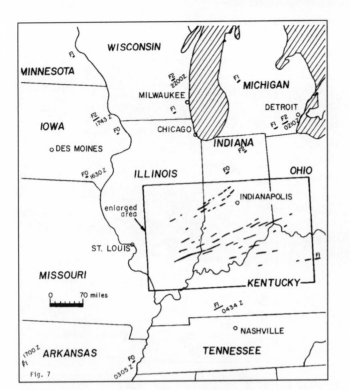

Figure 10-6A. The tornado outbreak of June 2-3, 1990, with 64 tornadoes in the Midwest, Great Lakes, and Ohio River Valley, was the biggest spate of tornadoes since the infamous "Superoutbreak" of April 3-4, 1974. These charts plot the locations, paths, and intensities (based on the F-scale*). One F4 tornado had an unusually long track, stretching from eastern Illinois to central Indiana.

On the next page, Figure 10-6B shows surface weather charts for the days in question, with a cold front bulling its way through the region, accompanied by a squall line ahead of the front (shown on the 1800 UTC chart for June 2). (Storm Data, *June 1990; NOAA.)*

* *See* explanation of the F-scale of tornado intensity, Page 161.

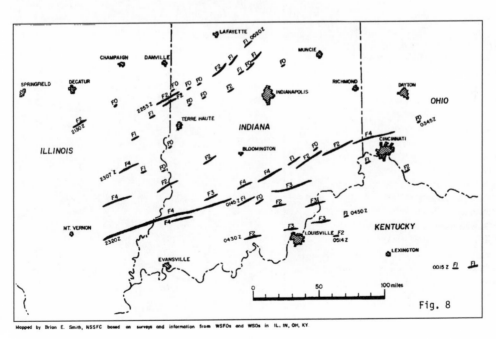

Mapped by Brian E. Smith, NSSFC based on surveys and information from WSFOs and WSOs in IL, IN, OH, KY

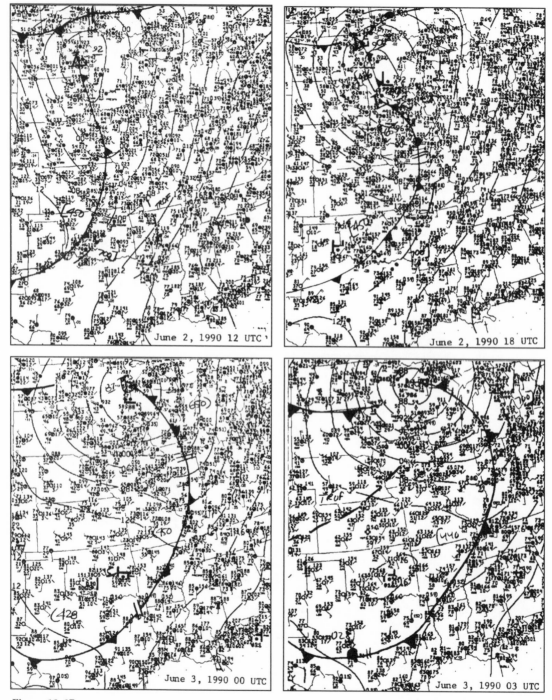

June 2, 1990 12 UTC

June 2, 1990 18 UTC

June 3, 1990 00 UTC

June 3, 1990 03 UTC

Figure 10-6B

haps even a low-level jet stream. Another outbreak of 60 tornadoes occurred on April 7 and 8, 1980, in an area ranging from Texas to Ohio. Yet another outbreak came in 1990.

Figure 10-6A shows the ground tracks of an outbreak of 64 tornadoes that took place on June 2-3, 1990, ranging from parts of the Midwest and Great Lakes, to the Ohio River Valley. This was the record-breaking largest since the Superoutbreak of 1974. The state of Indiana took the biggest hit, breaking their own state record of 37 tornadoes in a day, and 44 in a month (they also had the highest death toll—eight of the nine reported tornado-causing deaths).

Severe thunderstorms and tornadoes can occur anywhere east of the Rocky Mountains. But Texas, Oklahoma, Kansas and other portions of the midwest are most susceptible, for a number of reasons that every pilot should understand well.

Texas, Oklahoma, Kansas, and other midwestern flatlands are the battlegrounds where cold, polar air masses continually fight it out with the warm, moist air flowing northward from the Gulf of Mexico. This is especially true in the late spring, when the jet stream retreats northward, and Gulf air penetrates the heartland in earnest. The result is often a violent, fast-moving cold front, complete with squall lines. This alone is enough to create tornadoes. The terrain's flatness is also conducive to tornado formation, because there is less frictional drag to impede the flow of air into the base of a thunderstorm, or to break up a tornado once it's begun.

Here's a typical setup. At the 500-millibar level (about 18,000 feet MSL) the constant pressure chart shows a deep trough of low pressure containing very cold air over the central United States. The core of the jet stream's strongest winds are over Texas and Oklahoma, giving strong lift to the air below, and intensifying any low pressure centers or cold frontal activity at the surface. *See* Figure 10-6B for the surface analysis charts corresponding to the tornado activity shown in Figure 10-6A; this is a good example of a textbook situation.

Surface activity perks up by late afternoon, as the warm air ahead of the cold front rises with the heat of the day. It keeps on rising, right into that very cold air aloft. Now we have a classic illustration of absolute instability. Warm air always rises, but when a parcel of warm, moist air rises into colder and colder air, it really rises. In a matter of minutes, a Texas (or

153

Oklahoma, take your pick)-size thunderstorm complex can go to 50,000 feet or more, and cover several counties. The tornadoes soon follow, as the complex enters its updraft and mature stages. (Another theory explaining a tornado's initial spin says that it begins when strong, converging winds collide at the base of a cumulonimbus cloud. The resultant shear zones create low pressure, and the rush of incoming air helps to perpetuate the funnel cloud as rotational velocities increase and the funnel eventually touches down.)

That's a spring scenario. Severe thunderstorms and tornadoes haunt the southernmost portions of the southeast United States in late winter, when the jet stream lies farther south. As the jet makes its summer retreat northward, the belt of tornadic activity migrates with it, bringing a spate of tornadoes to the northern plains. So really there are many "tornado alleys." It just depends on the season.

Apart from the thunderstorms and tornadoes (which, admittedly, is saying a lot), the traditional tornado alley provides good flying weather. Days-long periods of IFR conditions seldom prevail in the spring and summer months in northern Texas, central Oklahoma, and eastern Kansas. Even in the fall and winter, IFR ceilings and visibilities are problems only 30 percent of the time. But surface winds can be fierce. Just look at all the "Kansas wind socks" (wire hoops, trailing shreds of ragged, erstwhile sock) at airports all over Tornado Alley.

Weather Briefing in Tornado Alley

Pilots can obtain information about severe thunderstorms and tornadoes from a variety of sources. Flight service should convey any convective SIGMETs as part of any standard or abbreviated briefing. Tornadoes will surely be mentioned if any are reported or suspected. Area forecasts mention them, as well as any convective activity, as part of their "significant weather" segments. On radar summary charts, boxes are used to outline areas under severe thunderstorm or tornado watches (abbreviated WS and WT, respectively, and coded with numerals identifying their recency)—but remember, these can be up to three hours old by the time you see them. A watch means that conditions are right for tornadoes and other severe weather. A warning, however, means that actual sightings have been made.

The severe weather outlook (AC) and corresponding charts also describe any areas of potential tornadic activity. On the chart, areas with diagonal lines show where severe thunderstorms are expected. Crosshatched boxes indicate areas forecast for tornadoes. The HIWAS broadcasts, on select VOR frequencies, also broadcast severe weather warnings. Pilots on instrument flight plans are supposed to be informed by ATC of any breaking convective news via Center Weather Advisories (CWAs). Finally, Flight Watch (122.0 MHz) can be a valuable source of inflight weather updates on convective developments.

The National Severe Storms Forecast Center (NSSFC) in Kansas City, Missouri, specializes in the business of predicting severe weather. To help the NSSFC's meteorologists call their shots quickly, the agency has produced two brief internal documents that encapsulate severe weather synoptics, and give forecasters snapshots of what to look for in the severest of storm systems. Excerpts of these documents—"Parameter Patterns and Other Considerations (Forecast Crib Sheet)," and "Watch Checklist" are found in the sidebar on Page 156. Though most of the synoptic scenes in these documents relate to severe weather in Tornado Alley and the rest of the midwest, these setups apply equally well to any territory east of the Rockies.

Another warning sign to look for on a surface analysis chart—and you should look at surface charts when contemplating a flight into areas with promise of strong convection—is the so-called "Larko's Triangle" named for the meteorologist who first came up with this forecast tool. Larko's Triangle is the area between the warm front, the cold front, and the first or second isobars around a surface low-pressure center. This is the area where strong surface convergence, the upper-air divergence caused by a strong jet core, and the cold front often team up to produce tornadoes.

Should any of the precautions, bits of advice, or warnings listed above find their way into your preflight briefing, think twice about flying. Even the most sophisticated airplane, with the most sophisticated weather avoidance systems, cannot penetrate an area experiencing severe thunderstorms—let alone one sprouting tornadoes—without taking on unacceptable risks. If you're on the ground, stay there. If you're in the air, turn around and/or land while—or if—you can.

Forecast Crib Sheets

These thumbnail sketches and descriptions are just a few of those used for quick forecast guidance by the meteorologists in the National Severe Storms Forecast Center. It demonstrates two facts: that severe weather follows certain proven patterns, and that forecasters need to be reminded of them.

Winter and Early Spring

In situations of marginal to moderate instability, the area of severe potential is often closely associated with the upper divergent pattern.

850 MB/5,000 feet

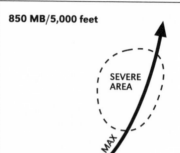

Severe potential is usually greatest along and to the left of the low level jet downstream from a wind maximum.

Summer

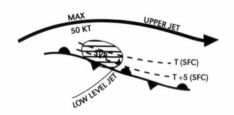

In situations of very strong to extreme instability, the area of severe potential is often closely associated with the low level warm advection pattern.

Surface and Low Level Jet

Severe weather potential is enhanced by low level convergence along a boundary (i.e. cold front, warm front, trough line, dry line activity boundary).

500 MB/18,000 feet

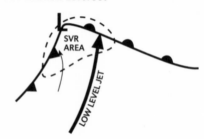

The most massive severe weather outbreaks occur with a 500 MB pattern similar to the one shown above. This pattern usually results from a strongly digging short wave and is characterized by a negatively-tilted trough axis and a pronounced diffluent region between two branches of the 500 MB jet. The severe weather area is generally confined to the area between the two jets. There is usually a massive surface low pressure system associated with this pattern; and, if sufficient low level moisture is available, the severe weather outbreak can cover a large area.

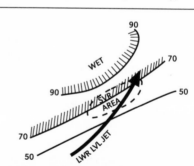

Severe weather sometimes occurs with a mean relative humidity pattern similar to the one depicted above. This pattern is often associated with weak upper short wave troughs, but very strong wind fields.

DFW Microburst Accident

On August 2, 1985 at 6:05 P.M., Delta 191, an L-1011 on approach to runway 17L at the Dallas-Fort Worth International Airport, crashed while trying to fly through a heavy rain shaft beneath a rapidly strengthening, Level 4-thunderstorm with tops of 40,000 feet. A weak, diffuse stationary front was 60 NM north of DFW at the time of the crash, and while forecasts mentioned the probability of thunderstorms that day, no SIGMETs, convective SIGMETs, Severe Weather Warnings or Watches, or Center Weather Advisories were issued for the time and area of the accident.

In terms of meteorological advice and warnings, the Delta 191 crash proved it was possible for even an airline crew to fall through the cracks. The National Weather Service terminal forecast for DFW indicated only a slight chance of a thunderstorm and moderate rain shower for Delta 191's arrival time. Delta's own meteorology and dispatch offices repeated the terminal forecast's warning and gave an enroute forecast that included mention of isolated thunderstorms over Oklahoma and northern and northeastern Texas with a few isolated cloud tops above 45,000 feet.

The Stephenville, Texas ground-based weather radar installation—an old WSR-57 (so named for its inaugural date of 1957) and a unit that obviously lacked the resolution levels and Doppler capabilities of today's ground-based weather radar network—was located 72 nautical miles northeast of the approach end of runway 17L. An examination of the Stephenville radar imagery showed four storm cells were near DFW between 5:28 and 6:13 P.M. The first two cells were small, about 9 to 10 NM northeast of the runway, and disappeared by 5:43 P.M. A third storm cell, called "Cell C," developed 6 NM northeast of the end of the runway at 5:48 P.M.; four minutes later, it intensified to the **VIP** Level 3 intensity. Level 3 is characterized by convective rainfall rates of 1.1 to 2.2 inches per hour, and a Level 3 radar return is termed a "strong" echo.

Also at 5:48 P.M., a fourth cell, Cell D, started out as a pinpoint echo south of Cell C. It began as a VIP Level 1 echo and was 2 NM northeast of the end of runway 17L. But eight minutes later, Cell D was just north of the end of runway 17L, and had grown to a Level 3 storm. By 6:04 P.M., Cell D grew to a Level 4 storm, and hadn't moved. A Level 4 storm is termed a "very

Video Integrator Processor (VIP). A precipitation-contouring feature of weather radar. *(See Page 194 in "The Gulf Coast" chapter for an interpretive table of VIP levels.)*

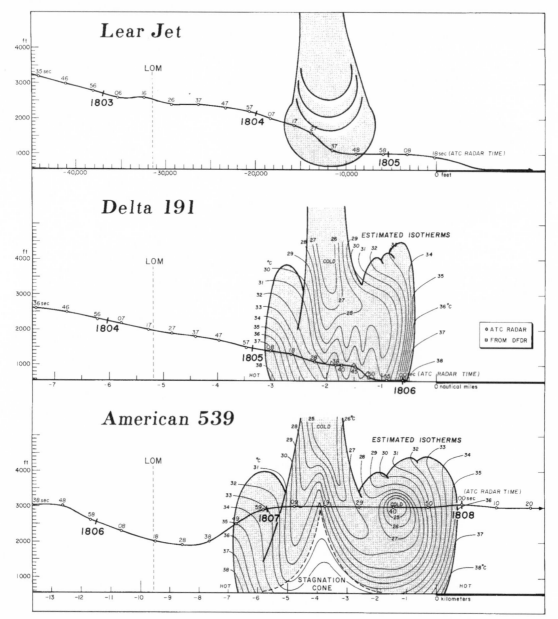

Figure 10-7. *On August 2, 1985, just after 6:00 P.M., three airplanes approached runway 17L at the Dallas-Fort Worth International Airport. A huge microburst was waiting for them. A Learjet hit the descending edge of the microburst, before it struck the ground. Its pilot was able to arrest the subsequent uncommanded descent, then continue to an uneventful landing. Approximately one minute later, Delta 191—a Lockheed L-1011—flew into the now-mature microburst and crashed. A minute after that, American Airlines Flight 539—an MD-80—hit the same microburst as it spread out after ground impact, but its pilot was able to climb and perform a go-around.* (DFW Microburst on August 2, 1985, T. Theodore Fujita; University of Chicago, 1986.)

strong" echo by the NWS, with rainfall rates of 2.2 to 4.4 inches per hour. Severe turbulence is likely, along with lightning.

Also at 6:04 P.M., a Stephenville upper-air radar specialist telephoned the Fort Worth Forecast Office, saying that Cell D had a cloud top of 40,000 feet and was barely a Level 4 intensity storm. The cell was in the vicinity of the airport, the specialist said, but he couldn't give a precise distance because the radar didn't have an internal map overlay. He used a paper overlay that showed geographical features on top of the radar scope, to try to determine the cell's position more precisely, but the overlay didn't have the airport pictured on it. The specialist said Cell D was a very strong echo, but that his observation of the upper structure of the cell didn't indicate any severe weather. The specialist was not a meteorologist and not qualified to issue a forecast as to whether Cell D would continue to grow, or dissipate.

After this conversation, the specialist returned to his scope and looked at other echoes. He didn't redirect his attention to Cell D until about 6:21 P.M. By that time, Cell D had tops of 50,000 feet and was a VIP Level 5 storm. A Level 5 storm is associated with severe turbulence, large hail, lightning, and extensive wind gusts.

Ground witnesses agreed that the storm was north of DFW just before the accident, and moving slowly southward. Rainfall was described as heavy to intense. Witnesses on the highway who saw Delta 191 emerge from the rain described it as coming out of a wall or curtain of water. The wind flowing out from the base of the storm was so strong that highway traffic signs had been uprooted and blown over. A witness 3 to 4 miles north of the airport said a trailer containing 1,200 pounds of fertilizer was overturned when the storm passed.

Flight crews of two landing airplanes ahead of Delta 191 confirmed the presence of wind shear. A Boeing 727, American Airlines Flight 351, after executing a missed approach because a landing airplane ahead of it couldn't clear the runway in time, lost 20 knots on the base leg of its second approach and landed uneventfully at 6:04 P.M. The captain said heavy rain was encountered between the outer marker and about 1,000 feet AGL, but there was no turbulence or wind shear during the final approach leg.

A Learjet sequenced for landing just ahead of Delta 191 had its airspeed drop from 153 to 125 knots after crossing the outer marker and extending the airplane's landing gear and flaps at 6:03 P.M. The captain attributed the speed loss to the added drag of the extending gear and flaps. There was light to moderate turbulence after passing the marker, the captain added, so he decided to maintain 150 knots on the approach instead of the calculated reference airspeed of 125 knots. Then the Learjet entered heavy rain—so heavy that all forward visibility was lost. If he didn't get out of the rain, the captain thought, he might not be able to land, so he decided to fly above the glide slope.

After emerging from the rain, the Learjet captain saw that his airplane was "high and hot," and he wound up landing long.

Delta 191 was next in line. "We're gonna get our airplane washed," the first officer said before the airplane flew into the rain shaft. The crew also commented on the lightning that was occurring along the approach path to runway 17L, Delta 191's arrival runway. The rain shaft contained a strong microburst, and the airplane flew through the microburst's outflow (*see* Figure 10-7). Maximum downdraft intensity reached 49 feet per second, which occurred at 560 feet AGL, and from which the crew was unable to recover.

During the thirty-eight seconds that the L-1011 was in the microburst, horizontal windshears of up to 72 knots were encountered. The airplane hit the ground 6,300 feet north of the approach end of the runway, hit a car on a highway, then hit two water tanks before breaking apart. Of the 163 people aboard, 134 passengers and crewmembers were killed; 26 passengers and 3 cabin attendants survived.

The accident prompted wind shear avoidance and escape training for flight crews, and was central in sustaining the growing initiative to establish a national network of Terminal Doppler Weather Radars at airports around the United States.[1]

[1] NTSB/AAR-86/05 "Delta Air Lines, Inc., Lockheed L-1011-385-1, N726DA; Dallas/Fort Worth International Airport, Texas—August 2, 1985."

The F-Scale (Fujita Scale)

Without question, the world's greatest tornado guru is highly-respected meteorologist T. Theodore Fujita, of the University of Chicago. After years of study, he came up with a scale (the "F" is for Fujita) for measuring tornado intensity—a sort of Beaufort scale for tornadic havoc.

F-0 Gale tornado (40-72 mph)

Some damage to chimneys or TV antennas. Breaks branches off trees. Pushes over shallow-rooted trees. Old trees with hollow trunks break or fall. Signs and billboards damaged.

F-1 Moderate tornado (73-112 mph)

Moderate damage. The lower limit (73 mph) is the beginning of hurricane wind speed. Peels surface off roofs. Windows broken. Trailer homes pushed or overturned. Moving autos pushed off the road.

F-2 Significant tornado (113-157 mph)

Considerable damage. Roofs torn off frame houses. Weak structures and trailer homes demolished. Railroad boxcars pushed over. Large trees snapped or uprooted. Light object missiles generated.

F-3 Severe tornado (158-206 mph)

Severe damage. Roofs and some walls torn off well-constructed frame houses. Steel-framed hangar/warehouse-type structures torn. Heavy cars lifted off the ground and may roll some distance. Most trees uprooted.

F-4 Devastating tornado (207-260 mph)

Devastating damage. Well-constructed houses leveled, leaving piles of debris. Structures with weak foundations lifted and blown some distance. Trees debarked by small flying debris. Sandy soil eroded and gravel flies in high winds. Cars thrown some distance or rolled considerable distance, finally to disintegrate. Large missiles generated.

F-5 Incredible tornado (261-318 mph)

Incredible damage. Strong frame houses lifted clear off foundation and carried considerable distance to disintegrate. Steel-reinforced concrete structures badly damaged. Automobile-sized missiles fly through the air for distances of 100 meters or more. Trees debarked completely. Incredible phenomena will occur.

F-6 to F-12 (319 mph to Mach 1)

The maximum wind speeds of tornadoes are not expected to reach the F-6 wind speeds. Assessment of tornadoes in these categories is feasible only through detailed survey involving engineering and aerodynamic calculations as well as meteorological models of tornadoes.

Accidents

The pilot and three passengers aboard a Beech A36 Bonanza died after crashing just after takeoff from Wichita's Colonel James Jabara Airport on July 7, 1994. IMC existed at the time, with a 500-foot overcast, a 2-mile visibility and a wind speed of 51 MPH, with gusts to 58 MPH. During a 5:37 A.M. telephone briefing, the pilot was warned of a severe thunderstorm watch north of his intended route to Colorado Springs, Colorado. The briefer also mentioned a "pretty severe line of thunderstorm activity" and a convective SIGMET, and said that "...you should—can [sic] slide around the southern edge, south of the Dodge City area, to get around that weather." The pilot filed an IFR flight plan and took off at about 8:30 A.M. Several FBO employees, on the ramp securing airplanes because a severe thunderstorm was approaching from the northwest, and an air ambulance crew witnessed the accident. The airplane took off from runway 18 just as a northerly wind gust arrived at the airport. The airplane's nose reportedly pitched up and its left wing dropped before impact. Doppler weather radar showed a Level 6 thunderstorm next to the airport at the time of the crash. The radar also showed a 90-knot change in wind strength at 500 feet AGL within a few miles of the airport. At 7:50 A.M.—40 minutes before the crash—surface winds were from 120 degrees at 14 knots. One passenger survived the crash with serious injuries.

On December 12, 1995 the pilot of a Piper PA-32 Turbo Saratoga was killed when he crashed near Parker, Kansas. At the approximate time of the crash—2:50 P.M.—instrument weather conditions (400 feet overcast, visibility one mile) prevailed at the nearest reporting station. The flight originated at Dallas, Texas and the destination was to have been Miami, Kansas. No flight plan was filed, but the pilot was talking to an ATC enroute facility. He asked for a descent through the cloud layer below him, but the controller told him to maintain VFR when he learned that the pilot wasn't instrument rated. The pilot then said he saw a hole in the clouds, and began a descent. Witnesses heard an airplane engine going from high to low RPM just before they heard two large "booms." The pilot flew into a stationary front pushed south by Arctic air. The front would eventually reach southern Oklahoma. Conditions deteriorated for the remainder of the day. By the following morning, visibilities in Kansas would fall as low as 3/16-mile in fog, with trace amounts of precipitation.

A homebuilt Tierra II crashed into woods near Prole, Iowa on August 25, 1994. The local flight began at 7:00 P.M. in reportedly good weather, but a fast-moving thunderstorm and gust front overtook the airplane. The airline transport pilot/builder and his single passenger received minor injuries. Dew points that day were in the high 60s throughout Tornado Alley that day. A surface trough was over central Iowa, and air mass thunderstorms kicked in all over Nebraska, South Dakota, and Colorado that day. Iowa wasn't spared, either, having recorded rainfall amounts of up to ¾ inch on August 25.

The Great Lakes
Wet and Wild

I f you ever need a more graphic example of how local geography affects regional weather patterns, look no further than the Great Lakes. These five lakes, formed in the wake of retreating ice-age glaciers, are an important source of moisture that feeds low pressure systems at the surface and aloft. The flying weather in the states that surround them is heavily influenced by lake effects, especially in the winter months. That's when surface low pressure systems of the classic, Norwegian school of air mass analysis race across the Great Lakes region with regularity, bringing with them widespread IMC and, at times, heavy snowfalls.

Side discussion: The "Norwegian school of air mass analysis" is a catchall phrase referring to a group of pioneering meteorologists who forged the rules of modern weathercasting and observation at the Geophysical Institute at the University of Bergen, Norway. During the First World War, meteorologists working under headmaster Vilhelm Bjerknes took a world-class lead in meteorological research. Bjerknes, his son Jakob, Halvor Solberg, Tor Bergeron, Sverre Petterssen, and Carl-Gustaf Rossby came up with several revolutionary concepts—one of them being that cold and warm air masses rotate around low pressure centers. No doubt influenced by the frontal warfare commencing in Europe, the Bergen meteorologists named the zones where the differing air masses clashed "fronts." The name stuck, and the Norwegian frontal analysis model—a low sprouting fronts and/or troughs in a more or less radial pattern—is now taken for granted. Rossby went on to analyze the behavior of large- and small-scale atmospheric circulations, and came up with the concept of the upper-air eddies we now identify with jet stream patterns. In October, 1940 Rossby continued his teaching, this time to U.S. Army Air

Where lows go on vacation —America's biggest lake complex can give you the ride of your life.

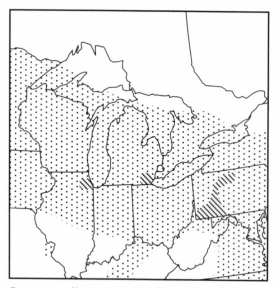

Percentage of hours in **Spring** *when ceiling is below 1,000 feet and visibility is less than 3 miles*

Percentage of hours in **Summer** *when ceiling is below 1,000 feet and visibility is less than 3 miles*

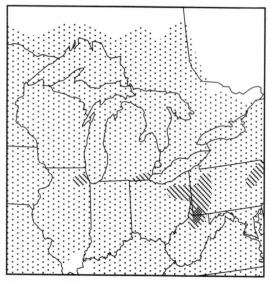

Percentage of hours in **Autumn** *when ceiling is below 1,000 feet and visibility is less than 3 miles*

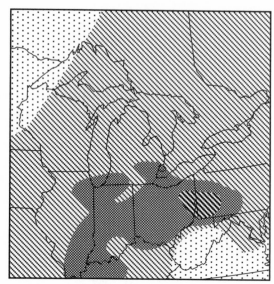

Percentage of hours in **Winter** *when ceiling is below 1,000 feet and visibility is less than 3 miles*

50% or more   **40-49%**   **30-39%**   **20-29%**   **10-19%**   **Less than 9%**

Corps meteorological cadets at the University of Chicago. Before the work at Bergen, the science of meteorology was more conjecture than anything, the only certain rule seeming to be that weather events seemed to move from west to east in the northern hemisphere. Now the names Bjerknes and Rossby are revered in meteorological circles.

Supercooled, Super-sized

Back to the Great Lakes in winter. When there's lifting aloft, and converging low-altitude wind fields out of the south—or blowing over any of the moisture-loaded air over the Lakes, for that matter—the warm sectors of a Great Lakes low pressure system can carry some mighty soggy air. The kind of air that can make for the largest and most dangerous type of super-cooled water droplets and icing conditions in the entire United States. The clouds in these types of air masses can contain droplets estimated to be as large as 2,000 microns in diameter. While that may not sound like a large drop, it's gigantic compared to the droplet sizes typically found in more benign cloud droplet environments.

A cloud with 2,000-micron-diameter water droplets is a cloud with droplets the size of large raindrops. And to be sure, such a cloud may indeed produce moderate rainfall. Now imagine that same cloud with temperatures in the 0°C to -10°C range, the range most conducive to clear icing. If there's rain falling out of that cloud, it's a safe bet that it's freezing rain. Imagine a cloud with droplets less than half that size—only 200 to 400 microns in diameter. When droplets that size hit a wing (or any other forward-facing airframe surface) it splatters and then runs back. It can run back all the way to a wing's mid-chord before it freezes solid, as a layer of clear ice.

This is dangerous—even for airplanes with pneumatic deice boots and certification for flight into known icing. Maybe especially for airplanes with boots. Why? Because a ridge of ice can form just aft of the boots. Cycle the boots a few times through their inflation and deflation sequences in these icing conditions and the ice may be freed from the boot areas all right, but not the areas immediately aft of them. That's because the runback ice continues to accumulate, ruining the airfoil cross-section, destroying lift, increasing stall speed, and adversely affecting the airplane's handling.

167

There's another reason why this type of large-droplet environment, variously called "supercooled drizzle droplet" (SCDD), or "super-large droplet" (SLD) is hazardous. The FAA icing certification envelopes that describe known-icing conditions specify water droplets with diameters between 15 and 50 microns! So a manufacturer could install deice boots and other ice protection equipment on an airplane, fly it in the FAA envelopes successfully, earn known-icing certification, and still put an airplane on the market that just flat can't handle the SLD conditions that are a common fact of life around the vast periphery of the Great Lakes. How could it? An airplane meant to handle 50-micron droplets can't possibly be expected to last long in a 200- to 400-micron droplet environment, let alone one with 2,000-micron droplets. And that's exactly what happened.

The Roselawn Crash

Most of the aviation world didn't even know the SLD environment and its scary ice shapes existed until the October 31, 1994 American Eagle Flight 4148 crash in Roselawn, Indiana. Flight 4148 was a French-built ATR-72, flying four crew and 64 passengers from Indianapolis, Indiana to Chicago's O'Hare Airport. Because of the weather that day, O'Hare was issuing holding instructions to inbound traffic. The idea was to use up time in holding until an arrival slot opened up.

Flight 4148 was told to hold at 10,000 feet at the Lucit intersection, in northwest Indiana and some 50 nautical miles south of O'Hare. The captain reported entering the hold at 3:24 P.M. ATC came back with an expect further clearance time of 3:45 P.M. Nine minutes after entering the hold, the airplane's cockpit voice recorder reported the captain as saying, "Man, this thing gets a high deck angle in these turns, we're just wallowing in the air right now." It was perhaps the first sign that icing was beginning to affect the airplane's handling in a big way. The pilots wouldn't have directly known that, though, because the autopilot was flying the airplane. If there were any ice-related problems—the need to increase angle of attack to maintain altitude and lift, asymmetric wing lift—the autopilot would, and in this case did, automatically compensate and mask the deterioration of the airplane's lift and control.

Five minutes after the captain made his "wallowing" comment, ATC issued an extension of the **EFC** time, to 4:00 P.M. Three minutes after that, a caution alert chime (probably a master caution alert, triggered by ice accumulating on the ice detection system's external probes) was sounded in the cockpit, and then the flight data recorder showed that the crew activated the leading edge deice boots. From here on out, things fell apart quickly.

EFC. Expect further clearance.

In an effort to lower the airplane's deck angle, the ATR's flaps were lowered to the 15-degree setting. "That's much nicer, flaps 15," the first officer said, followed almost immediately by the comment, "I'm showing some ice now." A discussion about the probable flap overspeed warning then took place, with the captain saying, "I'm sure that once they let us out of the hold and [we] forget they're [flaps] down we'll get the overspeed [aural flap overspeed warning when airspeed exceeds 185 knots with flaps set at 15 degrees]."

The captain then went to the airplane's bathroom for five minutes. When he returned to the flight deck the first officer said, "we still got ice."

A minute later, ATC cleared Flight 4148 to descend in the holding pattern to 8,000 feet. As expected, the flap overspeed warning sounded, and the first officer apologized, saying he was trying to hold the airplane at 180 knots. In an apparent attempt to overcome the flap overspeed warning problem, the flaps were raised. Then things went downhill at a shockingly fast pace.

The moment the flaps retracted to their zero setting, the ATR's angle of attack and pitch attitude increased. The ailerons deflected, putting the airplane in a quick, 13-degree bank to the right. The autopilot disconnected automatically. The airplane rolled rapidly to the right once again, this time banking to 77 degrees to the right. The crew started yelling expletives. Someone exerted 22 pounds of up-elevator force. The airplane rolled left, but the airplane responded feebly, coming to a 59-degree right wing down attitude. Meanwhile, the angle of attack kept increasing. Then, almost instantly, the ATR rolled right at a rate of 50 degrees per second.

It kept on rolling, with the nose pointed between 60 and 73 degrees nose down. The flight data recorder showed the airplane pulling anywhere from two to 3.6 Gs—the latter probably reflecting the aft-stick pressures the crew applied when they plunged out of the 1,700-foot estimated overcast and saw the ground filling their windshield.

The Weather at Roselawn

The weather setup for that fateful day gives us textbook illustrations of two fundamental meteorological truisms: That upper-air circulations influence the weather below, and that the quadrant to the northeast of a surface low frequently contains the worst flying weather.

The northeast quadrant of a low-pressure system usually has the worst icing conditions because that's where warmer air runs into colder temperatures and "dams up" as a warm front.

Aloft, the 500-millibar (a pressure level that roughly corresponds to 18,000 feet MSL) circulation showed a pronounced trough of low pressure extending into northern Missouri. The center of low pressure aloft was over northern Iowa. At the 850-millibar level (about 5,000 feet MSL) the upper low had snaked to the southeast, and was situated over central Illinois. This put the zone of maximum lifting and vorticity (rotational) forces aloft directly over the western Great Lakes. One look at that 500-millibar chart and even the greenest, third-string meteorologist could have told you that the Great Lakes was in for some bad flying weather that day.

As for the surface situation, the surface analysis chart for the time closest to the time of the accident showed a low over east-central Illinois. A cold front extended to the south-southwest of the surface low, and a stationary front went to the northeast. Lucit intersection was just north of the stationary front—smack dab in the northeast corner of the surface low pressure's center.

Rime ice is rough in texture, and caused by smaller water droplets at temperatures between about −20°C and −10°C. Clear ice is smooth and transparent; more dangerous and difficult to shed, it usually forms between −10°C and 0°C.

Enough of the synoptics for now. What were the National Weather Service and the FAA's flight service stations issuing for weather advisories? Well, the HIWAS (Hazardous In-flight Weather Advisory Service) broadcast over several VOR frequencies in the area called for light to occasional moderate rime icing in clouds and precipitation from the freezing level to 19,000 feet. Occasional moderate turbulence was forecast for altitudes below 12,000 feet. At the surface, the Gary, Indiana airport (about 32 miles north of Roselawn) at 3:45 P.M. (15 minutes before the accident) reported 800 scattered, 1,700 overcast; visibility seven miles in light rain showers; temperature 44°F/9°C; wind 020 degrees at 13 gusting to 30 knots; and

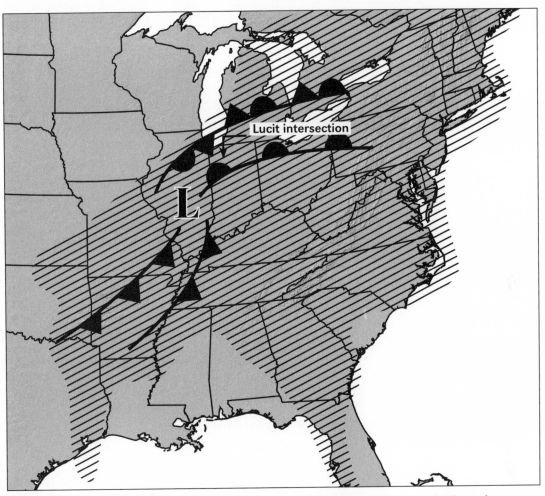

Figure 11-1. *The situation on October 31, 1994—the day of the American Eagle ATR-72 crash. The airplane was to the northeast of a surface low, an area known for producing instrument meteorological conditions, when it iced up. Aloft, an upper-level low helped intensify the weather system's moisture content. The ATR was holding near the Lucit intersection, where PIREPs from two Boeing 727s indicated that rain, heavy rain, and sleet were occurring. A surface warm front was to the south of Lucit, and an occluded front was to the north. One PIREP stated that icing conditions were between 15,000 and 5,000 feet. The ATR was holding at 10,000 feet and began a descent to 8,000 feet in the hold, when it rolled over and made its final dive.*

an altimeter setting of 29.68 in. Hg. In the "remarks" section of the report, there was a note that pressure was falling rapidly and that the ceiling was ragged. Again, another weather warning that would wake up any rookie meteorologist: pressure low and plunging, strong wind out of the northeast (where all that lake moisture is), and temperatures that promise ice just a few thousand feet above the surface.

What about other pilots in the area that day? PIREPs from an Airbus A320 reported icing from 14,000 feet all the way down to 2,000 feet. On final into O'Hare, the A320 pilot said he picked up ½ to ¾ inches of "jagged to bumpy [looking]" ice after 30 minutes in icing conditions, and that the ice stayed with the airplane right down to 2,000 feet. A 727 pilot reported ice between 5,000 and 15,000 feet. Ten minutes after the accident, another 727 pilot flying 10 nautical miles east of the accident site and at 9,000 feet reported "... well, we're in and out of some pretty heavy rain with some sleet in it...started about 14,000 feet and it's continuing still..." Later, this 727 crew would say that the conditions were more like "rain and snow mixed," and not ice pellets or freezing rain.

The NTSB went into great meteorological detail about the icing situation near Lucit intersection. Bottom line: Accurate analysis and prediction of the nature, severity, and precise location of icing conditions has a long way to go. The flight release prepared by American Airlines Weather Services gave the crew of Flight 4148 good information, however. For Lucit intersection at 10,000 feet, for example, the winds were anticipated to be out of 230 degrees at 11 knots, and temperature was forecast to be –6° Celsius. This temperature analysis was backed up by post-accident Doppler radar plots and satellite cloud top temperature extrapolations.

Unfortunately, the accident report doesn't go into much detail about any inflight weather updates the crew might have received. Apparently, the crew didn't learn about the PIREPs, didn't listen to the HIWAS, and didn't call Flight Watch for late-breaking information. Instead, the crew went with the dispatcher information—and their gut feelings—alone. Which was all perfectly legal. But this accident serves as a stern reminder that all pilots, especially the vast majority of us who fly in the lower altitudes, should frequently check with Flight Watch for any new information on hazardous weather.

To reinforce this warning, consider that on January 9, 1997 Comair Flight 3272, an Embraer EMB-120 being vectored for an approach into the Detroit Metropolitan Wayne County Airport, crashed under much the same conditions as American Eagle 4148. The weather was conducive to large droplet icing, the crew was flying on autopilot, and the airplane began showing uncommanded roll motions that look alarmingly like the control anomalies seen in the Roselawn crash. As the Embraer's roll angle passed 45 degrees, the autopilot automatically disconnected and the airplane rolled 140 degrees left wing down. Pitch oscillations of between 20 and 80 degrees nose down occurred up to the time of impact. All 29 persons aboard died.

Roselawn Fallout—Regulations

There was a scramble to find out what went wrong with Flight 4148. First the FAA created an "Inflight Icing Plan," designed in part to explore large droplet icing and rules for avoiding it. The Plan never would have happened if Flight 4148 hadn't crashed—which explains why the FAA is so often called the author of "tombstone" regulations. A reactive agency of generally impaired imagination and foresight, the FAA responds best only when a major crash shakes it from its peculiar type of bureaucratic torpor.

If you looked at both ATR accident reports, you'd rant. Yes, there were two reports—one from our NTSB, and one from France's Bureau Enquêtes-Accidents (BEA, the French equivalent of our NTSB).

You see, the NTSB report listed France's Direction de L'Aviation Civile (DGAC, the French equivalent of our FAA) among the probable causes of the Roselawn accident. The NTSB alleged that the DGAC had information about previous incidents involving roll control problems with ATR. It also blamed the DGAC for not exercising adequate oversight of ATR, and blamed ATR itself for not leveling with the FAA, saying it "failed to disclose adequate information concerning previously known effects of freezing precipitation…when the ATR-72 was operated in [icing] conditions." Turns out, between 1986 and 1996 there were 13 roll-control incidents involving the ATR in ice. Five of them happened in conditions consistent with freezing rain and/or freezing rain. (To return to the Comair accident mentioned earlier, another similarity with the ATR crash must be inserted at this point: six previous incidents where EMB-120s on autopilot experienced significant control problems were uncovered during that accident's preliminary investigative phase.)

The BEA, offended by the NTSB's tone, fired back with some strong points of its own. No airplane is meant to safely fly in severe icing, the BEA said, and it was right. Moreover, the DGAC did too inform the FAA of "all relevant airworthiness or safety of operation information developed from previous ATR icing incidents, including those in freezing rain..." The crew flew for a long time in icing conditions beyond the airplane's capabilities. Large-droplet characteristics and effects weren't known until NASA flew icing tanker tests that duplicated the aileron hinge-moment reversal problem. The Indianapolis ground controller released Flight 4184 knowing that it would have to hold before landing at O'Hare. American Eagle pilots were warned about the dangers of operating in freezing precipitation, and had ample opportunity to ask for a clearance to exit. The BEA also found that American Eagle's policy precluded the distribution of AIRMET Zulu Update 3 for icing and freezing level in Flight 4184's flight release.

The BEA found that the probable causes of the accident was the "...loss of control of the aircraft by the flight crew, caused by the accretion of a ridge of ice aft of the de-icing boots, and upstream of the ailerons, due to a prolonged operation...in a freezing drizzle environment well beyond the airplane's certification envelope, close to V_{FE}, and utilizing a 15-degree flap holding configuration not provided for by the aircraft operating manuals, which led to a sudden roll upset following an unexpected aileron hinge-moment reversal when the crew retracted the flaps during the descent."[1]

Poor situational awareness and cockpit procedures, insufficient awareness of freezing drizzle hazards, and ignorance of the ice-induced hinge-moment reversal phenomenon were listed by the BEA as contributing factors.

The operational upshot of all this? For one thing, the FAA needs to follow the NTSB recommendation to revise the icing certification envelopes to reflect what we now know about large-droplet icing environments. That means scrapping the

[1] *Aircraft Accident Report: In-flight Icing Encounter and Loss of Control, Simmons Airlines, d.b.a. American Eagle Flight 4184, Avions de Transport Regional (ATR) Model 72-212, N401AM, Roselawn, Indiana, October 31, 1994.* Vol. II: "Response of Bureau Euquetes— Accidents to Safety Board's Draft Report."

50-year old requirements, coming up with new envelopes, new aircraft equipment to better protect us against SLD icing, and new flight test procedures for all aircraft hoping to earn known-icing approval.

As for the ATR-72 and -42, redesigned, larger boots were installed on the entire fleet. Where the old boots went to five and seven percent of the wing chord, the new ones went to 12.5-percent chord—or almost double the distance back from the leading edge. Also, flap usage in icing conditions is now prohibited, as is use of the autopilot. The flap setting let the ice run back farther than it would have with flaps zero, it was determined, and the autopilot denied the crew any tactile proof of a deterioration in handling.

Visual cues that tip off the presence of SLD were also developed: ice forming in ridges on cockpit side windows, aft of deice boots, and well aft of propeller spinner tips are all signs that you've entered SLD conditions. So are the appearance of ice fingers or feathers, and visible rain and splashing or splattering rain on the windshield at outside air temperatures near zero degrees Celsius.

The primary, overriding caution, however, transcends the scope of the ATR crash, and predates it: No airplane can take on this or any other kind of severe icing. If it's encountered, ask...no, *demand* a clearance that will allow a quick escape. That goes for icing conditions not just in the Great Lakes, but anywhere in the world.

Roselawn Fallout—Weather Research

One NTSB recommendation in the ATR accident report was directed at the National Oceanic and Atmospheric Administration. It asked that NOAA "develop methods to produce weather forecasts that both define specific locations of atmospheric icing conditions (including freezing drizzle and freezing rain), and that produce short-range forecasts ("nowcasts") that identify icing conditions for a specific geographic area with a valid time of two hours or less..."

The meteorological research community rose to the task, and now we have icing forecast models. As of this writing, the algorithms are still in the experimental stage, but could be

operational at the FAA's Aviation Weather Center (the origina-
tor of SIGMETs and AIRMETs) by early 1999, according to
some projections. The algorithms, one of which is dubbed the
"stovepipe" algorithm, uses local surface observations and
conventional forecast model input to generate graphics showing areas (including altitudes) likely to have "normal" and
SLD icing. The stovepipe algorithm (so called because of its
vertical sampling methodology) is primarily the brainchild of
the National Center for Atmospheric Research in Boulder,
Colorado, and NCAR meteorologists like Marcia Politovich,
who has made a career studying aviation icing environments.
Another icing forecast model, the Neural Net Icing Model, is an
AWC product.

In any event, we may soon have better, more graphic warning of all types of icing conditions. What Doppler and Terminal
Doppler Weather Radar are to thunderstorms and wind shear,
the new icing models will be to icing avoidance. Just remember
that it took Flight 4184 to bring this all about.

Lake Effect Snows

Large-droplet icing is but one cold-weather aviation hazard
typical of the areas around the Great Lakes. Lake effect snows
are another. These occur via two basic mechanisms. One is the
passage of cold air across the Lakes' comparatively warmer
surfaces. The cold air transforms the rising moisture above the
Lakes into snow, which is then deposited downwind on the
nearby shores and inland territory. This type of lake effect
snow can be envisioned as a type of air mass activity—that is,
not associated with a low or front. It occurs on a regular basis
throughout the winter months, and while snowfall may not
necessarily be heavy, it's certainly enough to be a definite safety
problem for non-instrument-rated pilots trying to navigate
under visual flight rules around the Lakes. Lake effect snow
like this is often highly localized, with isolated snow showers
organized in small clusters or bands. Part of a shoreline may
experience good VFR weather, while just 20 miles away a snow
shower can put an airport down to instrument weather minimums. Luckily, much of this air-mass snow activity often
moves along quickly.

That's not such a bad scenario in daylight hours. But at night, when it's more difficult to visually identify and avoid snow showers, it can be easy to stumble into this kind of instrument weather. Then you'd better be prepared with a strategy. Turn around? Divert to an airport with better weather conditions? Push on? It all depends—on the extent of the showers, your experience, qualifications, comfort level, and airplane equipment. A low-time VFR-only pilot in a small piston single has only one option: escape to good weather, now. A more experienced pilot flying a turbocharged or turbine-powered airplane with known icing certification has more psychological and operational capabilities.

The other type of lake effect snow occurs with the passage of a cold front or low pressure system. Here the job of weather flying becomes more serious. Snow—and its attendant parent cloud system—is much more widespread, and so are the areas experiencing instrument weather conditions. In this typical frontal model, a surface low out of Canada travels to the east or southeast, dragging an aggressive cold front along with it. When the front crosses a Great Lake or two, the clouds and precipitation ahead and within it intensify. The naturally-occurring southerly flow of air that precedes a cold front

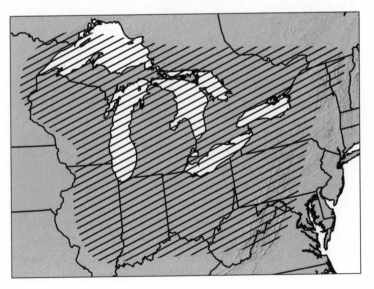

Figure 11-2. Shaded areas indicate the regions susceptible to lake-effect snow. Most lake-effect snow occurs along the eastern coasts of the Great Lakes but, depending on wind direction, heavy snowfalls can take place deep into the Ohio Valley, and as far east as the Appalachians. A second area vulnerable to lake-effect snow is to the east of Lake Champlain, in upstate New York.

begins the job of transporting moisture and instability to the Canadian cold front. Factor in the moisture from the lakes themselves, and it's easy to understand how large-droplet icing and heavy snowfall hang around the Great Lakes.

This all translates into several big weather problems for pilots. Ceilings can lower in either the air-mass or frontal Great Lakes snow setups. Cloud tops can rise to the 10,000- to 20,000-foot level. And in those clouds will lurk the large-droplet, clear and mixed icing we've discussed in the previous section. The pilot who finds himself in this mess has to run a risky gauntlet. It's a lot like any icing situation in any winter front anywhere in the United States—but with the large-droplet problem thrown in for extra risk. Of course, you've turned on your pitot-static heat long before you entered icing conditions. Otherwise, any discussion of escape strategies is moot. Without accurate airspeed or vertical speed information, you're essentially committing suicide.

Climb to on-top conditions? That means running the risk of plating the undersides of the wings with a lot of runback ice, and forcing the airplane's stall speed higher and higher, at a much greater rate than if you remained in level flight, if that's still an option. The longer you climb—and the slower the airspeed/higher angle of attack you use in the climb—the more of this type of ice you pick up. (This is one reason why some manufacturers publish a minimum climb airspeed for use in icing conditions.)

Will you even make it to on-top? Maybe, maybe not. How far do you have to climb? 10,000 feet? 20,000 feet? Then forget about it, if you're flying a non-turbocharged, non-turbine-powered airplane, or any airplane without ice protection. The higher you climb, the more power a normally aspirated engine loses. With a load of ice and an ever-lowering power output, you'd reach stall speed before seeing the tops of the clouds. Moral: unless you know that the cloud tops are easily within reach, don't try a climb. You'll come dead in the water, so to speak, after gaining just 1,000 to 3,000 feet or so of altitude, and your only option then will be to descend—back down through the same icing conditions you endured on the way up.

Descend at the first sign of icing? That strategy can work, but you'll still be faced with the icing problem. Then there could be the added stress of a one-shot, iced-up instrument approach. One-shot, because the airplane may be so iced up that there won't be enough lift or control to perform a successful missed approach. That first approach had better be a good one. A really good one, if it's at night, or if other pilots have the same problem and ATC must sequence a lot of nervous pilots. Time-consuming vectors will probably be the rule, and more ice will build in the process. It's a time to keep your wits, hand-fly the airplane, avoid deploying flaps, and keep airspeeds as high as you can manage.

Turn around? OK, but then you run the risk of lingering for who-knows-how-long in icing conditions. Lake effect snows and clouds can extend deep into Minnesota, Wisconsin, Illinois, Indiana, Ohio, Pennsylvania, and New York—and cover the entirety of Michigan. It may be 100 nautical miles before you fly out of the icy, snowy clag. Can you last that long? It's something to think about when evaluating your pre-flight or inflight weather briefing. If a front is forecast to cross the Great Lakes, make sure you have a realistic alternate plan of action should the weather become unmanageable. That may include the choice to stay on the ground.

Somehow, we tend to think of lake effect snow as only affecting northern Ohio, western Pennsylvania, and western New York state. Wrong. Lake effect snows can hit anywhere downwind of a snow-bearing wind field. With winds out of the east or northeast, Chicago, Milwaukee, Toledo, and other east-facing shores take hits.

It's because upper-air wind flows are so often out of the west that lake effect snows strike New York and Pennsylvania so hard—and can range so far to the east. Sometimes, lake effect snows can extend all the way to the Allegheny, Catskill, and Adirondack ranges. And lake effects aren't restricted to the Great Lakes, either. Lake Champlain, on the New York–Vermont border, generates its share of lake-effect snows. Most of Lake Champlain's snows fall downwind, too—to the east, plaguing the high terrain of northern Vermont and New Hampshire.

There's Summer, Too

The warmer months in the Great Lakes region provide even more examples of ways that large bodies of water exert moderating influences on ambient temperatures, as well as local wind flows. Any nearby lake or ocean affects the weather by keeping high temperatures lower, and low temperatures higher, than they might have been without the water's influence. Also, the differential heating of land and water sets up sea— or lake—breezes (air flowing on-shore), and land breezes (air flowing off-shore).

The Great Lakes bring these same influences to bear on their neighboring states. It's these lake and shore breezes that make the Great Lakes popular with recreational sailors in the summer months, and give the entire area the kind of cooler summer temperatures ideal for vacationers coming from more southerly states. Of course, these localized breezes can also have a profound influence on shore-side airports, and there are a lot of them. Be prepared for the strongest winds from 10 A.M. to 4 P.M. or so, when surface heating is at its maximum. It's the rising, heated air from the surface that draws lake air landward.

All of this assumes that there's enough sun to perform this heating act. Circulations around low pressure systems disrupt lake and shore breezes by bringing their own winds—and cloud cover, precipitation, and thunderstorms.

Deep into summer, the region under the Great Lakes' influence can expect more and more of these disruptions. Yes, cooler temperatures and good flying weather is the rule. (In fact, even in the depths of winter, when IFR conditions are most likely, ceilings and visibilities drop below 1,000 and 3 only about 30 percent of the time).

A typical summer day in Michigan, Wisconsin, and northern Minnesota, Illinois, Indiana, and Ohio might go as follows: in the early morning, temperatures will be in the mid- to high sixties, and there will be a chance of IFR visibilities in fog. As the day progresses, fair weather cumulus, or stratocumulus decks appear, and winds freshen out of the west or southwest. Visibilities reach ten miles or greater. AIRMETs might be published for turbulence or strong surface winds. By the afternoon, those wind flows are firmly established, and surface temperatures climb to the 85°F to 90°F range. If there are to be air mass thunderstorms, they'll happen in the late afternoon.

Come sunset, surface winds die down, clouds dissipate, and the chance of fog is again a factor as the temperature–dewpoint spread narrows. Does this litany sound familiar? It should, since this daily progression of events accompanies nearly every high pressure system east of the Mississippi.

But so much for utopia. This blissful scene is often interrupted in the summer months by a more or less regular passage of lows and fronts, principally cold fronts. On average, two cold fronts pass through the Great Lakes states each week. On these occasions, you can expect the slats to be kicked out from under your hopes of flying in unimpeded VFR weather. Sorry about that. Especially for those of you flying to the Experimental Aircraft Association's annual fly-in at Oshkosh, Wisconsin's Wittman Field.

Why the proliferation of adverse weather? The answer to this question, as with so many others, has to do with the position of the jet stream. Earlier in the year, in the spring and early summer months, the jet stream hovered over the United States somewhere between the 35- and 40-degree north latitudes. This corresponds to the locations of areas such as north Texas, Oklahoma, Kansas, Missouri, and the Ohio River valley—in other words, Tornado Alley (*see* Page 137).

It's no coincidence that the jet stream and Tornado Alley share the same latitudes at the same time of year. The jet stream imparts the kind of upper-air lift and rotation that both creates and intensifies any low pressure disturbances at the surface. A surface low with a strong core of jet stream winds above it is something quite different than a surface low without anything aloft to support its vertical development.

As we move deeper into summer, the jet stream retreats northward. Nothing unusual here, because the jet stream marks the boundary between polar air masses of Canadian origin, and the muggy, tropical air from the Gulf of Mexico. In the spring, the jet moves to about the 45- to 50-degree north latitude position—right where the Great Lakes lie.

Now, Tornado Alley's been transplanted. Accordingly, the frequency of severe thunderstorms increases in the Great Lakes region as summer progresses. Please remember that severe thunderstorms are defined as those that carry one or more of the following: surface winds greater than 50 knots,

¾-inch hail, or tornadoes. They're the worst thunderstorms, and the longest-lasting. No one, not even the most experienced crews with the best-equipped airliners, should attempt to fly in or near severe thunderstorms.

Another feature of Great Lakes weather in July and August is the hot spell. Ordinarily, you wouldn't expect stretches of hot (daytime highs, say, 85°F or better), humid weather to cause much of a stir in the central United States. After all, what do you expect from summer?

But tropical mugginess comes as a shock to northerners who've come to terms with arctic winters and Scandinavian-type summers. On May 9, 1990 Marquette, Michigan received 22 inches of snow, and winds over the upper peninsula of Michigan gusted to 50 MPH. The next day, 80 percent of Waukesha, Wisconsin's 30,000 trees were flattened by the same snowstorm. So when the thermometer hits 90 degrees several days in a row, the local populace always seems to make a big fuss.

Oshkosh Wx

Based on personal experience, the Great Lakes' summertime propensity for severe thunderstorms and scorching heat always seems to reach its apex at time of the Oshkosh fly-in. I suppose like many other pilots, I think Oshkosh week offers the promise of watching an entire range of airplanes and events in a setting that offers respite from summer's most brutal temperatures. Every year I think, "It'll be nice to watch the air show without sweat running into my eyes, or plastering my shirt to my back." But no.

It seems like every Oshkosh fly-in has at least a couple of days of withering heat. Many times, violent cold fronts have passed through Oshkosh, and tornado watches and warnings have also been posted for the Oshkosh area during the week of the fly-in. For all this, thanks once again go in large part to the jet stream's northerly location.

Many times in the summer, high pressure builds over the central United States. In a situation like this, tropical air can easily travel from the Gulf of Mexico as far as the Great Lakes. Once the air is this far north, it becomes the warm sector of a circulation around any nearby lows. That's when surface temperatures soar. The thunderstorms arrive when the next cold front pushes the warm, moist air ahead of it, or localized pockets of moist, rising air create air mass thunderstorms.

It's the really large, stationary high pressure centers that create the hot spells. If a high is big enough, and dense enough (in terms of atmospheric pressure), it can actually prevent any lows or fronts from traveling eastward. It acts as a blockage to the normal progression of weather fronts, and searing heat and oppressive humidity can last for days—until a new trough in the upper air flow pushes it away.

This kind of a blocking high creates some characteristic patterns in the height contours seen on constant pressure charts. You can see how the air from the prevailing westerlies runs into the high, then is forced in a clockwise direction to the north, around the zone of highest pressure. Then the height contours dip southward, following the eastern boundary of the high pressure dome. The height contours look like the Greek letter Omega, so meteorologists call this kind of a blocking high an "Omega block." In effect, it's similar to a stationary Bermuda high, which is a summertime blocking high positioned over the western Atlantic Ocean.

Eventually, the Omega block falls apart, but not for a few days, and not before it's given you a beauty of a sunburn while you explore the sights at Oshkosh. The collapse of an Omega block can also be the signal for violent weather, as the pent-up energy west of the blockage travels through the Great Lakes states.

Pilots flying to Oshkosh will have a special opportunity to follow the weather patterns around the Great Lakes. My advice for those coming from distant locations is follow the weather patterns closely on the days prior to your planned departure—once in the morning, and once at night. This will give you an idea of the weather trend, as well as warn you of any unanticipated worsening of conditions.

On the day of your departure, you'll of course obtain a complete, standard weather briefing, and ask for updated conditions on Flight Watch (122.0 MHz) as you fly. As usual, the best advice is to depart early in the morning. This way you have the best chance of visually avoiding the worst thunderstorms, which peak in the late afternoon.

Those planning on a day-long trip to Oshkosh have a special worry. By leaving early, you may avoid thunderstorms in the first segments of your route, but by the end of the day, afternoon thunderstorms can be a factor at your destination. So always have a way out.

The Oshkosh fly-in is closed for arrivals and departures during the air show, which typically happens every afternoon. This can pose some weather complications, too. Arrive early, and there's the chance of morning ground fog, especially since Oshkosh adjoins Lake Winnebago. Arrive late, and it could be in time for a bout with thunderstorms. The answer is to stay in touch with Flight Watch, and be prepared to alter your plans so as to avoid any adverse weather.

Once at Oshkosh, there's plenty to keep you informed about weather conditions. A flight service station, complete with color radar and other real-time displays, should be at the base of the tower. Manufacturers of weather avoidance equipment will be on hand to show you their latest. I'd pay special attention to lightning detection equipment, which has recently become very competitive in price, and which is one of the best additions you can make to your cockpit.

Best of all, the event's organizers are keen on providing plenty of advance warning if thunderstorms or high winds are on the way. They know just how violent mid-summer thunderstorms can be in the Great Lakes area. There will be a Flight Service Station on the field, with briefers on hand and plenty of weather graphics pertinent to your trip. You say you flew in and forgot to bring tie-downs? Don't worry, Oshkosh rules make you buy a set.

If you're going to Oshkosh, I envy you. Enjoy the sights, keep an eye on the sky and when, after waiting in line for a half hour in the broiling sun, you bite into a Zaug's bratwurst, think of me.

Accidents

On November 15, 1991, at approximately 11:00 P.M., a Mooney M20C collided with a powerline tower during a night instrument approach to the Painesville, Ohio airport. Night instrument meteorological conditions prevailed, and an IFR flight plan was filed for the trip that originated in Keene, New Hampshire. Witnesses said the weather at the accident site was "foggy...with rain showers." The pilot was cleared for an NDB approach, and tracked on radar roughly four miles east of the airport; shortly thereafter, the pilot canceled IFR. A witness saw the airplane flying at a high rate of speed and at low altitude when it hit the tower. The pilot and his single passenger were killed. An area of weak surface low pressure was located over Lake Huron at the time, and its cold front quickly pushed through northern Ohio during the evening of the accident.

The pilot of a Cessna 150 was making a cross country flight from Bryan, Ohio to Waterloo, Iowa on November 11, 1996. He was flying as a flight of two, and both airplanes departed Bryan at about 6:15 P.M. According to the other pilot, night VMC prevailed until the two airplanes ran into IMC in a snow squall. At 6:32 P.M. the pilot of the accident airplane evidently lost control and crashed near Edgerton, Ohio, destroying the airplane and suffering fatal injuries. A strong jet stream was situated over the route of flight. The jet was on an arc from Labrador to Alberta, and beneath it was a surface trough over the southern Great Lakes.

A Piper PA-24-250 Comanche broke up in cruise flight near Akron, Ohio at about 4:30 P.M. on September 29, 1993. The flight began in Austin, Minnesota, with a destination of Harrisburg, Pennsylvania. The first leg of the flight was in VFR conditions, but during a fuel stop in Fostoria, Ohio the pilot learned during a weather briefing that rain showers and marginal VFR weather were forecast along the remaining route of flight. The briefer said that the pilot told him cloud tops along the first leg were at 13,000 feet. The pilot didn't file a flight plan for the trip to Harrisburg. Once the Comanche was en route from Fostoria, ATC radar picked it up at 17,500 feet, making several turns. The pilot's last transmission was, "I am at 16,500 feet and in the soup." A witness on the ground saw the airplane "coming through the cloud layer. I heard a pop sound and then saw the airplane spinning without one wing." The pilot and his two passengers were killed. Unstable air over the Great Lakes and Ohio Valley created locally heavy downpours and IFR conditions all over the northeast quadrant of the United States that day. A surface trough was spread over the eastern Great Lakes, a reflection of the pronounced trough aloft that dipped as far south as the Carolinas.

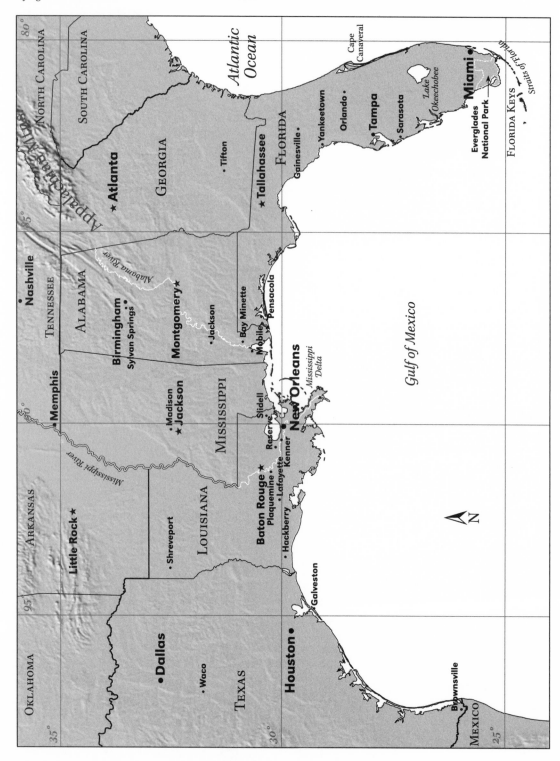

The Gulf Coast
Deep, Damp South

I t's a rare discussion of the United States' weather that goes by without mention of the Gulf of Mexico. That's because the Gulf plays such a powerful role in weather dynamics, and influences almost all the weather from the Rockies to the eastern seaboard. As geographic weathermakers east of the Rockies go, the conditions created by the Gulf of Mexico *far* surpass mountain, lake, or valley effects in terms of ability to create large-scale weather phenomena.

Most of us east of the Rockies notice the Gulf of Mexico's effects any time the wind is persistently out of the southerly quadrants of the compass, or any time a large, stationary high-pressure system is parked off the United States' east coast. This latter situation—called a Bermuda high—is particularly effective in transporting huge loads of the Gulf's warm, moist air. The clockwise flow of air around the high sends Gulf air to the north and east. Many times, especially in the depths of summer, Gulf air can penetrate as far north as Canada.

What happens when air this warm and humid travels north? Sooner or later, it bumps into an air mass that's cooler and drier. It can overrun a cooler air mass (creating a warm front), be pushed away by an invading cold air mass (which produces a cold front), or if there is little movement in the atmosphere, it can just sit there (creating a stationary front). So it's easy to see that Gulf air is a factor in nearly all major frontal systems affecting the eastern United States.

Gulf air figures in winter weather, too. It's the Gulf's moist air that contributes to the east coast's most severe winter weather, and its greatest snowfalls. So any time you encounter a phrase such as "warm Gulf air advecting to the northeast" in a DUATS printout's area forecast, a telephone weather briefing,

Where rain reigns: Take an ocean, enclose it with land, add heat, and what do you get?

187

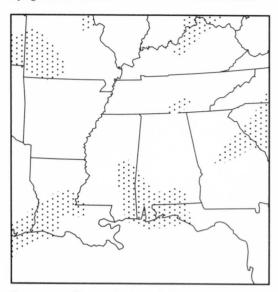

*Percentage of hours in **Spring** when ceiling is below 1,000 feet and visibility is less than 3 miles*

*Percentage of hours in **Summer** when ceiling is below 1,000 feet and visibility is less than 3 miles*

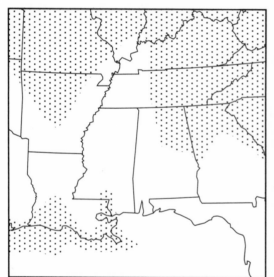

*Percentage of hours in **Autumn** when ceiling is below 1,000 feet and visibility is less than 3 miles*

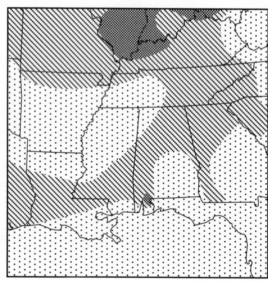

*Percentage of hours in **Winter** when ceiling is below 1,000 feet and visibility is less than 3 miles*

50% or more   **40-49%**   **30-39%**   **20-29%**   **10-19%**   **Less than 9%**

or the synopsis at the end of a surface prognosis chart's 36- and 48-hour forecast panels, use caution. The Gulf is a year-round, permanent moisture machine and when the air above it moves inland, pilots should sit up and take notice. At the very least, visibilities will drop in haze as Gulf air invades. At the worst, in the spring and summer months, severe thunderstorms all over the area east of the Mississippi can result, as the cold air behind a cold front rams into the Gulf's muggy air.

Of course, the Gulf has its greatest effect on its immediate neighbors, and a look at the region encircling it is helpful in understanding not just the extent of the Gulf's impact in that area, but also the nature of the Gulf air mass. We'll call this encircling region the Gulf rim, and include in it the coastal sections of Texas, Louisiana, Mississippi, Alabama, and Florida. The term "Gulf air" is tossed about quite a bit in all kinds of weather reports. But what does this really mean?

First, there are the more obvious characteristics. Naturally, the air over the Gulf of Mexico is warm, thanks to a combination of latitude and prevailing winds, which tend to feed warmer, more tropical air into the Gulf.

The Gulf's ability to act as a great reservoir of heat is reflected in the neighboring states' mean annual number of days with temperatures of 32°F or lower. This number varies directly with distance from the Gulf rim. Areas immediately adjoining the Gulf have ten or less days a year. But travel to Florida's northern border, or the areas along a line running from Tifton, Georgia, to Montgomery, Alabama, to Shreveport, Louisiana, to Waco, Texas, and the days with freezing temperatures rise to a mean of 30 a year. That's a threefold increase in freezing days within just 200 statute miles of the coast.

As for the summers, mean daily surface maximum temperatures hover around the 90-degree mark for the immediate coastal zones. This includes a number of heavily-populated cities—and no small amount of coastal airports. Run an arc from Brownsville, Texas east, through Houston and Galveston, New Orleans, Mobile, Pensacola, and Tampa, and your sectional will show a good helping of both small and large airports.

This same arc takes the prize for humidity levels. From Brownsville to Tampa, count on mean relative humidities in the 80-percent range, all year around. Together with that summertime 90-degree heat, we're talking damp, folks. And remember that we've been talking in terms of mean temperatures and relative humidities. Half of the time, temperatures and relative humidities are either above or below the values we've discussed.

We're also talking high dewpoint temperatures—the temperatures to which air must be cooled in order to reach complete saturation. Relative humidity has a close relationship to dew point, but the two terms are not interchangeable. Both expressions are, however, measures of atmospheric water vapor content. Relative humidity can be thought of as a ratio, or comparison, between the actual amount of moisture in the air and the maximum amount of moisture the air can carry. As such, it's a reflection of the degree of air saturation, and that degree of saturation undergoes diurnal change. Relative humidities are usually lowest in the heat of the day, and highest just before dawn.

Dewpoint temperature is a more stable number. It's a measure of an air mass's inherent moisture-bearing nature, and unless moisture or temperature is added or subtracted from the air mass, the dew point remains more or less constant.

Think of dew point as a primary indicator of the amount of water vapor in the air. A low number indicates dry conditions; higher ones are evidence of more moisture. And all pilots should remember that when temperatures are within five degrees or less of the dewpoint temperature, fog is likely to form.

At what time of day is this convergence of temperature and dew point most likely to occur? In the early morning hours, between about 3:00 and 6:00 A.M. That's when temperatures can fall to the dewpoint level, and that's when pea-soup fogs can surround airports all around the Gulf rim—and well inland.

On the morning of July 16, 1991, Las Vegas recorded a dew point temperature of 26°F, and a temperature of 80°F—not much moisture there. At the same time, Mobile, Alabama reported a dew point of 72°F, and a temperature of 74°F. You guessed it: there was fog, and it reduced visibilities to five miles. In addition, there were multiple layers of clouds at all levels—cumulus, altocumulus, and cirrus.

This is quite typical of Gulf coast weather in the summer months—a direct result of all that southern heat and atmospheric moisture. As the day progresses, temperatures climb, the moisture rises, and air mass thunderstorms crop up.

As a matter of fact, the Gulf coast region experiences the highest number of thunderstorms of any location in the United States. From New Orleans east, thunderstorms occur about 70 days per year. That's more than two months' worth! In the Florida peninsula, that number is even higher—between 80 and 100 thunderstorm days per year. So when flying in the Gulf

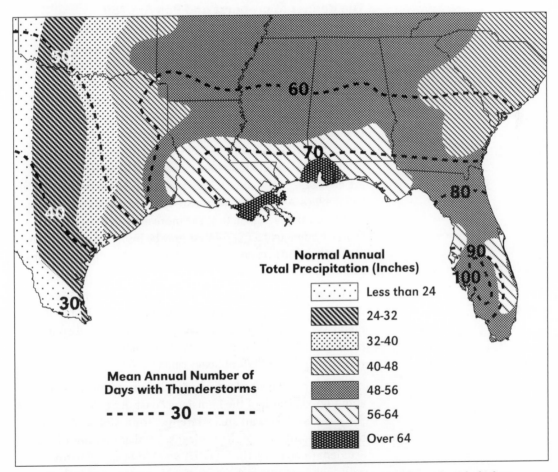

Figure 12-1. Convection, anyone? Southern Louisiana and the Mobile, Alabama region rack up the highest amounts of rainfall along the Gulf coast, while central Florida—with three months-plus' worth of mean annual thunderstorm days—has the nation's highest thunderstorm frequency. Most of these storms are of the afternoon, air-mass type, with plenty of lightning. The area near Tampa has perhaps the highest frequency of lightning strikes of any place in North America (see Page 236, Figure 15-3).

region in the summer be aware of the great likelihood of thunderstorms, especially after midday.

Gulf thunderstorms are frequently of the severe variety (surface winds greater than 50 knots, ¾-inch hail, and/or tornadoes). Winds in excess of 60 knots often occur over a series of days when slow-moving storm systems pass through the area.

The Kenner Microburst and Pan Am 759

Microbursts—highly localized, powerful downdrafts—can occur anywhere in the United States, but here's a Gulf rim variety: A microburst that downed a Pan American Boeing 727 on July 9, 1982 after taking off from the New Orleans International Airport is often touted as a good example of what some meteorologists call a "wet" microburst. Wet, because this type of microburst happens in and around convective weather characterized by air with higher dew points and relative humidities, and lower cloud bases. So-called "dry" microbursts are creatures of the desert, high plains, and the Front Range of the Rockies, where dew points are lower and cloud bases are correspondingly higher. In these more arid regions, the only visible evidence of a microburst may be limited to virga (rain shafts that don't reach the ground) or blowing dirt and debris at the surface.

The microburst that felled Pan American's Flight 759 fits the classic wet microburst scenario. Like the crash of Delta Flight 191 on approach at the Dallas–Forth Worth Airport on August 2, 1985, (*see* Pages 157–160) the microburst's presence was signaled by a shaft of heavy rain.

The day of the accident, a high-pressure center was located about 60 NM south of the Louisiana coast. A SIGMET (SIGMET 38C) was issued for an area stretching from Mobile, Alabama to 60 NM southwest of New Orleans. Valid at the time of the accident (4:09 P.M.), the SIGMET warned of thunderstorms with tops of 50,000 feet, saying the storms showed little movement. The SIGMET was broadcast over the New Orleans International Airport's clearance delivery frequency, as well as the New Orleans tower and departure control frequencies, and Pan Am 759's cockpit voice recorder proved that these warnings were heard by the crew. In any event, the SIGMET did not cover the New Orleans area.

Meanwhile, the National Weather Service's weather radar station at Slidell, Louisiana was painting a different picture. At 3:31 P.M., a special radar observation was made, indicating intense thunderstorms covering three-tenths of an area to the northwest, northeast, east, southeast, and west of the radar site. One cell was located at 223 degrees and 100 NM from the radar antenna. The cells were stationary, according to the observation. The observation was a "special" because the cell tops were within 5,000 feet of the tropopause, which was reported as being 25,000 feet on the radar log.

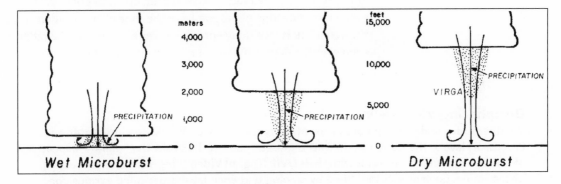

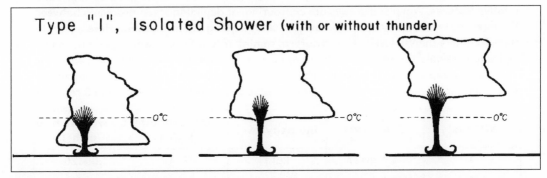

Figure 12-2. Prior to the 1982 JAWS (Joint Airport Weather Studies) experiment conducted by the University of Chicago and NCAR (the National Center for Atmospheric Research), meteorologist T. Theodore Fujita assumed that most microbursts happened in heavy rain and wet climates such as the Gulf coast. After those studies, it was learned that microbursts can occur in dry climates, too. Another misconception was that microbursts are products of large, mesoscale storm complexes. But radar imagery of the microburst-induced crashes of Eastern 66 at JFK and Pan American 759 near the New Orleans International Airport proved that isolated showers — with or without thunder — can also induce microbursts. Fujita calls these "Type I" (for 'isolated') microbursts, and asserts that there is no relationship between the intensity of an individual storm's radar echoes and the wind speeds produced by its microbursts. The bottom illustration shows the locational and seasonal variations in cloud base and freezing levels of isolated showers. (Fujita, The Downburst, *pp. 71 and 76.)*

An hour later, the WSR-57 radar at Slidell was showing radar echoes very near New Orleans International. At 4:35 P.M. another special radar observation was made. It said, "an intense echo cell containing a thunderstorm with intense rain showers was located at 230 degrees at 31 NM from the Slidell, Louisiana, weather radar antenna. The diameter of the cell was eleven nautical miles. The cell was stationary. The maximum top was 49,000 feet."

The departure end of New Orleans International's runway 10—the runway Flight 759 used—is located about 30 nautical miles from the Slidell radar, on a bearing of 237 degrees. Post-accident radarscope photographs of the time of the accident showed a VIP (video image processor, *see* sidebar) Level 2 radar echo over the departure end of runway 10, a VIP Level 2 echo

Deciphering VIP Levels

Weather radar imagery appears in six intensity levels, called VIP (Video Integrator and Processor) levels. The nation's NEXRAD digital Doppler radars take the "digital" aspect of this equipment into account with their DVIP (Digital Video Integrator and Processor) abbreviation. Each level is identified by a color, and each level is assigned various correlative features. When storm cells are contouring, or depicting steep gradients between the intensity levels, it's helpful to know just what's going on inside them. Here's a table that deciphers the VIP levels. The stratiform rainfall rate is for use when continuous precipitation prevails. Convective rates are applicable in thunderstorm situations, when the shape and steepness of VIP contours can predict tornadic activity (hooks and scalloping), squall lines (bow echoes or thin lines), or extreme thunderstorms (level 5 and 6 returns).

VIP level	Color level	Intensity level	Stratiform rate (in/hr)	Convective rate (in/hr)
1	light green	light	0-.10	.05-.20
2	dark green	moderate	.10-.50	.20-1.10
3	light yellow	heavy	.50-1.0	1.10-2.20
4	dark yellow	very heavy	n/a	2.20-4.40
5	light red	intense	n/a	4.40-7.10
6	dark red	extreme	n/a	7.10+

4 NM east of the airport, and VIP Level 3 echoes 4 NM north, 2 NM west, and 6 NM south of the departure end of runway 10.

At 3:10 P.M., a Center Weather Service Unit (CWSU) meteorologist at the Houston Air Route Traffic Control Center called the New Orleans tower to advise of Level 4 and 5 storms south and southwest of New Orleans International. The meteorologist saw the storm echoes on an Air Traffic Control radar—which cannot distinguish levels of storm intensity, only areas of precipitation—but based his Level 4 and 5 determination on the 4:35 P.M. Slidell radar report.

The crew of Flight 759 never received this radar information, because the echoes didn't meet the FAA's southern region criteria for severe weather or convective SIGMETs. Consequently, neither a Center Weather Advisory nor convective SIGMET was required to have been issued.

Low-level wind shear alerts, however, had been issued to the crew. As the airplane taxied from the gate, it was raining, and the NTSB concluded it would have been evident to the crew that the rain was falling from cumulonimbus clouds. However, witnesses agreed there was neither lightning nor thunder. At 4:03 P.M., the tower told the crew of Low-Level Wind Shear Advisory System (LLWAS) alerts in all quadrants, and said that there was a "frontal [sic] passing overhead right now, we're right in the middle of everything."

Between 4:07 and 4:09 P.M., the reported surface winds varied from 060 at 16 knots, to 070 at 17 knots, to 080 at 15 knots.

Between 4:00 and 4:07 P.M., ATC transmitted nine wind shear advisories, but the wind shear that affected Flight 759 wasn't detected until after the airplane began its takeoff. A witness reported that just before the time of impact, a west wind occurred that caused whole trees to move. According to the definitions in the Federal Meteorological Handbook, "whole trees in motion" corresponds to a wind speed of 28 to 33 knots.

As for the weather radar aboard the airplane, the NTSB determined that the precipitation off the departure end of runway 10 was of such intensity that radar returns on the cockpit display screen would have been attenuated to such an extent that effective contouring of precipitation echoes may have been impossible.

Right after hearing the LLWAS advisory at 4:03 P.M., the captain told the first officer, who would be flying the leg in question, to "Let your airspeed build up on takeoff." Then he asked the flight engineer, "Leo, you want to do a no packs takeoff on this thing?"—a strong suggestion that the air conditioning packs be turned off for takeoff in order to develop as much takeoff thrust as possible. "No packs, OK," the flight engineer responded.

At 4:07 P.M., as Flight 759 was waiting for takeoff clearance, the tower advised an incoming Eastern Air Lines flight that "ah...heavy Boeing just landed...said a ten-knot wind shear at about a hundred feet on the final," and the Pan Am crew heard this broadcast. They were then cleared for takeoff.

At 4:07:59 P.M. the first officer called for "takeoff thrust," then just five seconds later said, "need the wipers." An 80-knot speed callout was made 16 seconds later, followed by an increase in the sound of the windshield wiper speed 11 seconds after that.

"Vee R" the captain called out, as rotation speed was reached at 4:08:33 P.M. "Positive climb," he added eight seconds later.

Four seconds after that last callout, however, the captain said "come on back, you're sinking Don...come on back." Eleven seconds later came the sound of the Ground Proximity Warning Indicator (GPWS), "Whoop, whoop, pull up, whoop..." Three seconds later, the first sounds of impact were recorded.

A study conducted by noted meteorologist T. Theodore Fujita found that Pan Am Flight 759 flew from a zone with 17-knot headwinds right after liftoff, to an area of 31-knot tailwinds some 15 seconds later, and at an altitude of just 100 feet AGL. The crew and passengers never stood a chance. The decreasing-headwind type of microburst event that Flight 759 encountered robbed the airplane of lift, physically pushed it down, and took place so close to the ground that recovery was impossible. The airplane climbed to only 163 feet, then crashed into a residential area, killing 152 people, and injuring nine.

The NTSB blamed the microburst's wind shear effects for the accident, a microburst "the effects of which the pilot would have had difficulty recognizing and reacting to in time for the airplane's descent to be arrested before its impact with trees." Contributing to the accident, the NTSB said, was "the limited capability of current ground-based low-level wind shear detection technology to provide definitive guidance for controllers and pilots for use in avoiding low-level wind shear encounters."

Some good came of this catastrophe. The pressure to install Terminal Doppler Weather Radar (TDWR) equipment at most major airports stepped up after the crash of Pan Am 759; it built further after the Delta 191 crash at DFW in 1985. TDWR can see wind shear and contour precipitation echoes where it counts—at altitude, along approach and departure corridors. LLWAS is fine as far as it goes, but wind conditions at the surface can have little relationship to the winds at 100 or 200 feet AGL, as we've seen here.

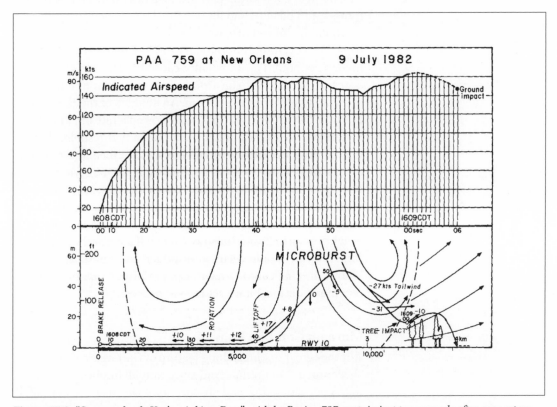

Figure 12-3. *"Come on back. You're sinking, Don," said the Boeing 727 captain just two seconds after gear retraction during the takeoff from the New Orleans International Airport. The airplane flew into a microburst, and one minute, ten seconds after brake release, Pan American Flight 759 crashed in a Kenner, Louisiana neighborhood. This is a depiction of the flight path and indicated airspeed of PAA 759 at New Orleans on July 9, 1982. (Fujita,* The Downburst, *p. 30.)*

At a post-accident hearing, microburst experts from NCAR's Denver-based Joint Airport Weather Study (JAWS) testified about their experiences correlating rainfall rates with microburst intensity. The project co-director stated that "the relationship is zero." Microbursts in the JAWS study were just as likely to "to occur in a little or no-rain situation as in a heavy rain situation." However, he did say that the more severe a thunderstorm becomes, the more likely it will be to produce a gust front.

Since the airplane's loss of altitude coincided with the onset of heavy rain, the effect of heavy rain on airfoil performance was also examined as part of the accident investigation. Rain can, in theory, rob airfoil performance by two mechanisms: a momentum penalty, and lift penalty. The momentum penalty, in which the impact of water droplets causes airspeed loss, is thought to occur only at rainfall rates greater than 500 millimeters per hour. The lift penalty, caused by the rain's imparting a surface roughness to an airfoil, comes into play at rainfall rates of 150 millimeters per hour. An analysis of the rainfall rate at the departure end of runway 10 showed a rate of 144 millimeters per hour—just under the lift penalty threshold. While intriguing, the NTSB was careful to say that the matter of rain effects on airfoils has yet to be verified. It did urge wind tunnel testing to verify or disprove rain-effect theories, inasmuch as current stall warning devices are designed to operate "on the basis of stall conditions for a smooth, or at worst, standard roughness airfoil," and "it is not known if a natural warning (buffet onset) would occur with sudden entry into heavy rain." If any rain-effect studies have been performed pursuant to this recommendation, I have yet to hear of them.[1]

[1] NTSB/AAR-85/01, "Aircraft Accident Report—Pan American World Airways, Inc., Clipper 759, Boeing 727-235, N4737; New Orleans International Airport, Kenner, Louisiana, July 9, 1982."

More on Gulf Rim Rain

Another great distinguishing feature of Gulf weather is the sheer amount of rainfall. And since rainfall implies low ceilings, convection, fog, and obscurations, the measure of rainfall can be construed as a measure of the frequency and intensity of instrument meteorological conditions.

The areas around New Orleans and Pensacola typically receive more than 64 inches of rain per year. As you travel northward, the rainfall rate decreases slightly, but the influence of the Gulf air is plain on a precipitation map. As far north as Little Rock, Memphis, and Nashville, annual rainfall is a very healthy 48 inches per year. These are average figures, and very heavy rainfall can knock the averages for a loop. On August 29, 1962, there was 22 inches of rain in a place called Hackberry, Louisiana. The record for one-day precipitation in Florida goes to Yankeetown, when 38.7 inches of rain fell on September 5, 1950.

The Gulf's rainiest months are in the spring and late summer. New Orleans, for example, racks up about eight inches of rain every July, while Tampa experiences a hefty nine inches. These figures are about double the monthly summer rainfall figures of cities in the northern tier of the United States.

Something else happens in summer. The Gulf of Mexico's surface temperatures begin to reach their highest values after a few weeks of summer warmth. Once the sea temperature reaches about 80 degrees, this heat imparts a lifting action to the surrounding air, and a center of low pressure can form. If it becomes well organized, it can develop winds strong enough—more than 74 MPH—to qualify as a hurricane. After a Gulf hurricane forms, it's difficult for it to not to strike a portion of the surrounding coastal land mass, so beware the late summer and early fall. Hurricanes of Gulf origin typically form in the early part of hurricane season (June and July.)

With all this talk of dripping fogs, torrential rain, microbursts, and hurricanes, it's easy to become convinced that the Gulf coast is a flying nightmare. It's not. With a careful preflight weather briefing, in-flight updates with Flight Watch, and steering clear of cumulus buildups, it's possible to complete many flights in VFR conditions. Even in the winter months, when IFR conditions are most prevalent, the Gulf coast has ceilings and visibilities below 1,000 feet and 3 miles only twenty percent of the time.

Accidents

A Cessna P210 broke up in flight after its gyro instruments reportedly malfunctioned and its pilot flew into convective conditions at about 11:15 A.M. on March 1, 1994 near Bay Minette, Alabama. The pilot received two weather briefings prior to takeoff from New Orleans, Louisiana's Lakefront Airport, and filed an instrument flight plan to the destination—Sarasota, Florida. The pilot and his three passengers arrived at Lakefront at around 9:30 A.M., and numerous thunderstorms were in the vicinity, along with low visibility at the airport. A witness reportedly asked the pilot why he couldn't stay and depart the following day when the weather would be better, and the pilot reportedly responded that "it [the weather] was no problem, and he could handle it." After takeoff, enroute controllers advised pilots in a 10:54 A.M. broadcast that four convective SIGMETs had been issued, and that pilots should tune in HIWAS frequencies, or contact flight service stations or Flight Watch for details. The convective SIGMET relevant to this flight involved warnings of embedded thunderstorms with tops to 35,000 feet, tornadoes, hail to two inches in

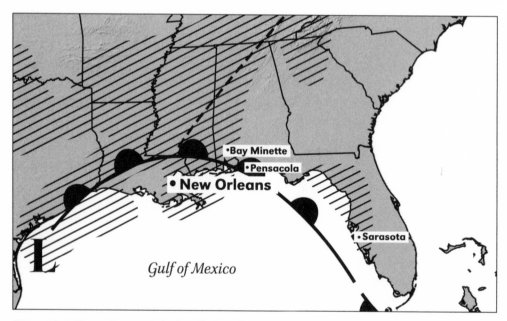

Figure 12-4. The surface analysis chart for March 1, 1994, when a Cessna P210 on a flight from New Orleans to Sarasota crashed in convective weather near Bay Minette, Alabama. The pilot reported that his vacuum instruments malfunctioned before he lost control.

diameter, with the possibility of surface wind gusts to 70 knots. At 10:55 A.M., after reporting reaching FL210, the pilot said it was "a little rough." At 11:00 A.M. he reported problems with the airplane's gyros, and said he was descending. At 11:03 A.M. he said the gyros were "out," and that he was continuing to descend in an attempt to find an altitude suitable for flying in visual conditions. ATC told him that no stations nearby were reporting VFR conditions. The pilot said that he would level at 11,000 feet and attempt to maintain his direction. The 210 was handed off to Pensacola approach control, but the pilot wasn't heard from again. The wreckage was distributed over an area four and one-half miles in length, and all aboard were killed. It was on this day that a low-pressure system formed over the Gulf of Mexico, moved inland with a warm front preceding it over the accident area, and intensified quickly. It moved eastward along the Gulf coast, up the Carolina coasts, and by March 4 was in the Canadian Maritime provinces. It turned out to be a major snow-producing storm for areas extending from western North Carolina to Maine, following a classic northeast snowstorm low-pressure track. But it all began with the thunderstorms of the Gulf coast that felled this airplane.

On July 5, 1994, a Beech H-35 Bonanza had an inflight breakup at about 2:59 P.M. while maneuvering near a thunderstorm near Jackson, Alabama. The pilot and his passenger left Hawkins Field in Madison, Mississippi, bound for Gainesville, Florida. The pilot received a standard weather briefing and obtained VFR flight following service from Jackson approach. After switching over to a Houston Air Route Traffic Control frequency, the pilot reported level at 9,500 feet and asked for radar vectors. He said he was getting into some clouds, thought he was near a thunderstorm, and said he wasn't instrument rated. He was given a heading to turn to, and told that he should be clear of the weather in 2½ miles. The pilot made two Mayday calls, saying he was going down. The pilot and passenger were killed in the ensuing crash. The NTSB preliminary investigation reported that the stabilizers and ruddervators had separated from the airframe in flight. A nearly stationary surface low was over the Alabama–Georgia border that day, and surface dew points were in the low 70s all over the deep south. Daytime surface high temperatures reached 92 and 93 degrees in Alabama and Mississippi. The circulation around the low was drawing huge amounts of moisture as far north as Tennessee. Montgomery, Alabama—80 miles northeast of the accident site—recorded .35 inches of rainfall on the day of the accident.

Continued

A flight instructor and his student died in the crash of their Cessna 152 at approximately 6:30 P.M. on February 28, 1997. The NTSB preliminary accident report indicates only that instrument meteorological conditions prevailed in the vicinity of the accident site, which was over the Mississippi River near Plaquemine, Louisiana. The instructional flight took off from Lafayette, Louisiana at 5:20 P.M., with a destination of Reserve, Louisiana. Just prior to the accident, the airplane was communicating with Baton Rouge approach control, which was providing VFR flight following through the Baton Rouge area. Seven witnesses working on a levee saw the airplane cruising over the river at low altitude, beneath low clouds. One witness said he saw the 152 hit power lines that traversed the river and ran perpendicular to the airplane's flight path. The airplane became hung up in the lines momentarily, then fell into the river. The airplane remained afloat for 10 seconds or so, then sank. Recovery personnel reported that both pilots were still belted in their seats, and that there was no sign of an attempt at egress. Local utility officials said that the height of the power line span was 425 feet AGL. A warm front over the area stretched from south Texas to Georgia, then continued off the New England coast as a stationary front. The accident site was also beneath the southeast quadrant of a pronounced trough aloft. Precipitation had been lingering beneath several fronts that had plagued the area for the previous four days.

A Piper PA-32 Seneca III crashed near Sylvan Springs, Alabama after an icing encounter on December 10, 1994. The airplane was not approved for flight in known icing conditions. The flight, conducted under 14 CFR Part 135, took off from the Birmingham, Alabama airport at 5:36 P.M. Before takeoff, the pilot obtained a weather briefing and filed an IFR flight plan for the trip to Memphis, Tennessee. The FSS specialist advised the pilot of an approaching cold front, and said that "there is [sic] some icing conditions above 12,000 feet." The forecast freezing level in the Memphis area was slightly lower than 9,000 feet, and the temperature at 6,000 feet was 3°C. The forecast ceilings in northern Alabama were 1,000 broken, 5,000 overcast, and the temperature in Memphis was "falling like a rock," according to the specialist's comments in the NTSB preliminary accident report. After takeoff, at 5:50 P.M., the pilot said that she was level at 4,000 feet, and that the cloud bases and tops over Birmingham were 2,000 feet and 3,000 feet, respectively. At about 6:20 P.M., after being handed off to Memphis Center, the pilot advised a controller that "...I'm picking up some, ah, a little bit of rime icing. I'd like to try to get out of it."

A descent to 3,000 feet was approved, but at 6:23 P.M. the pilot said "I'd like to do a 180 and turn back around, probably go back to get out of this." A clearance to return to Birmingham was issued, along with a 3,000-foot altitude assignment. (A pilot talking with Birmingham tower reported that the temperature at 3,000 feet was 1°C.) After a handoff to Birmingham approach, the pilot at 6:36 P.M. said "...I've got a good bit of ice here I'm not able to lose if you could get me in as soon as possible." A descent to 2,500 feet was approved. The controller provided vectors to the Walker County-Bevill Field, which has a VOR/DME approach and which was 11 to 12 miles from the airplane, but two minutes later the pilot said that it looked like "I'm losing a little bit of this...let me keep on, um, coming in for Vulcan [VOR], um, for Birmingham if you can just get me in as soon as possible." Vectors for an approach to Birmingham were issued to the pilot. At 6:42 P.M. the pilot said "I'm still not losing all the ice." At about 6:58 P.M. the airplane hit power lines, a tower, and then crashed to the ground, killing the pilot. Early in the day, a low was over the Jackson, Mississippi area, and a stationary front extended to its northeast—along the accident airplane's intended path of flight. During the day, the low sped to the northeast, where it transformed into a Nor'easter[2] off the Maine coast. Meanwhile, a surface cold front surged south beneath the back side of a trough aloft. It affected the entire deep south. The previous day's surface high and low temperature at Birmingham was 66°F and 59°F, respectively. By the morning after the accident, temperatures had fallen to 26°F.

---

[2] The weather phenomenon called the "Nor'easter" is discussed at length in the chapter on New England, Page 265.

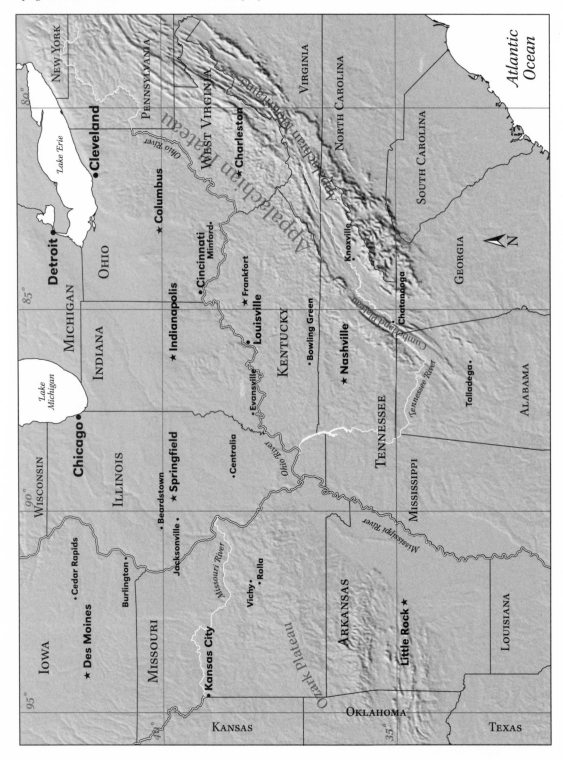

Ohio Valley Pipeline

Southerlies Come North for the Winter

Home of major-league fogs, languid stationary fronts, a second-string Tornado Alley, and southern-style freezing rain

The Ohio Valley is a kind of weather funnel. It's squeezed between the northern air masses of the Great Lakes and the soggy air of the deep south, exposed on its western flank to the massive lows, fronts, and mesoscale storm complexes tracking east from the lee side of the Rockies and the Great Plains. The Ohio, central Mississippi, and Tennessee River Valley states have as big a mish-mash of aviation weather as you'll find in any region of the United States.

And like any other region of the United States, the topography of this region plays a central part in its flying weather. To the west lies the Ozark Plateau, a huge expanse of old (of the Ordovician period, to be precise, or about 450 million years ago—some 300 million years before the first dinosaurs), eroded uplands that cover the entire southern half of Missouri. Over the years, the Ozarks have collected a lot of aluminum, thanks to the tenacity of its fogs and the year-round prevalence of its storms.

The land that surrounds the Ohio Valley serves as great conduits for summertime air mass thunderstorms. Also, some of the worst tornado outbreaks in American history have swept across the lowlands of Illinois, Indiana, and Ohio. The afore-mentioned "Superoutbreak" of tornadoes on April 3-4, 1974 has gone down in history for its sheer number of tornado touch-downs in such a short period of time: 148 documented twisters in 24 hours. The bulk of those tornadoes occurred in Tennessee, Kentucky, Ohio, and Indiana; the map in Figure 13-1 showing the tornado tracks was derived from a map prepared by microburst guru T. Theodore Fujita.

The uplands and mazes of valleys that cover the upslopes of the Appalachian Plateau are what explain, in large part,

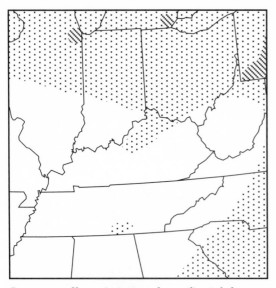

*Percentage of hours in **Spring** when ceiling is below 1,000 feet and visibility is less than 3 miles*

*Percentage of hours in **Summer** when ceiling is below 1,000 feet and visibility is less than 3 miles*

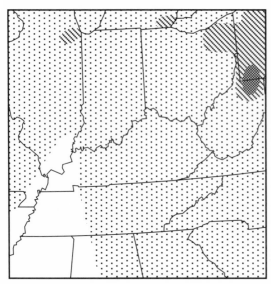

*Percentage of hours in **Autumn** when ceiling is below 1,000 feet and visibility is less than 3 miles*

*Percentage of hours in **Winter** when ceiling is below 1,000 feet and visibility is less than 3 miles*

50% or more   **40-49%**   **30-39%**   **20-29%**   **10-19%**   **Less than 9%**

the large number of days in Kentucky and Tennessee with instrument weather. Low-level southerly winds prevail over these states in all but the winter months. When these winds rise up the Plateau and undergo adiabatic cooling, fog and clouds form in the valleys, and promptly fill them up. Or, at the very least, ridges and mountain are obscured. This can happen any time of year, but it's important for pilots to be on guard in early autumn. That's when nighttime lows start to really plunge along the Plateau. It's a signal that "fog season" has begun, and after having been conditioned by several months of warmer temperatures and less frequent fogs, it's a signal that many pilots can miss. Those who expect to land at night in good VFR conditions may be unpleasantly surprised by unforecast, fast-forming fog and low visibility conditions.

That's a warning that holds especially true for the areas right along the margins of the Ohio and Mississippi Rivers, along a crescent ranging from Burlington, Iowa to Cincinnati, Ohio. This "fog belt" averages anywhere from 10 to 15 days a year with what the National Weather Service calls dense fog—fog with visibilities of ¼ mile or lower. One airport in this fog belt has become famous for its fast-forming rotten visibility: Cincinnati's Lunken Airport. It's best known by its enduring nickname—sunken Lunken—a reference to the airport's meager elevation above the adjacent Ohio River. (*See* "River fog" satellite photograph, Appendix Page 299).

See Appendix Page 292 for a chart showing "average number of days with dense fog" for the U.S., and also the satellite photo of Ohio Valley river fog, Appendix Page 299.

Trapped On Top

I learned long ago how quickly severe thunderstorms can form in the Ohio Valley. In the late 1970s, I was a newly-minted flight instructor eager to build time. Sales of new general aviation airplanes were in their heyday. So, I ferried brand-new Cessnas from the Wichita factory to dealers in Maryland and Virginia. One memorable trip involved a spanking-new Cessna 152. It was August, and IFR in advance of a northeast–southwest cold front would affect the flight from Wichita to southern Illinois. After that, the rest of the route to Leesburg, Virginia promised good VFR—but with a chance of afternoon thunderstorms.

After waiting a day for mechanics to reinstall its propeller, I launched on an IFR flight plan at 7:00 A.M. from Wichita's Mid-Continent Airport. The first leg of the trip would take me

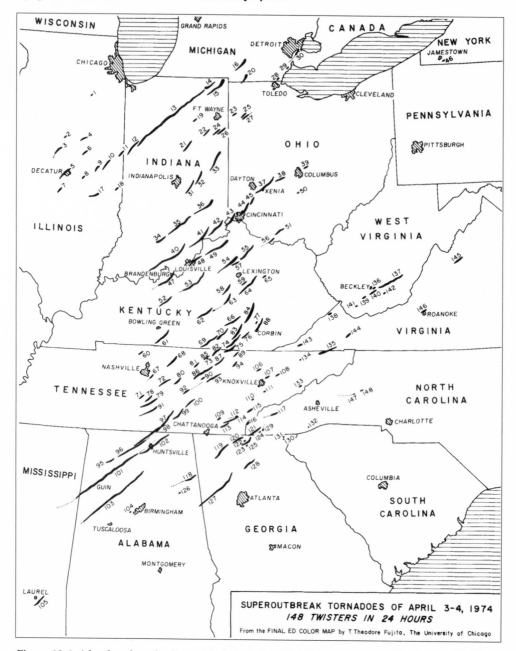

Figure 13-1. *A landmark study of one of the biggest tornado-producing storm complexes — the so-called "Superoutbreak" of April, 1974 — shows that there's a Tornado Alley in the Ohio River Valley, too. The southwest-northeast tracks are typical of most tornado ground paths, and indicative of the southerly wind flows that both precede the passage of a strong cold front and contribute to jet-core-induced instability. (Map by T.T. Fujita, reprinted in* The Thunderstorm in Human Affairs, *ed. Kessler; University of Oklahoma Press, 1988.)*

to the Rolla–Vichy, Missouri airport. At Wichita, ceilings were 500 feet and visibilities were around three miles in haze. The departure procedure was a real instrument flying workout. Why? Because most new Cessna singles left the factory with an avionics "suite" consisting of a single navcom. No transponder, no ADF, certainly no autopilot, and definitely no GPS!

After climbing into the soup, I had to fly a series of 360-degree turns in order for air traffic control to pick up a "skin paint" of the airplane. A skin paint is merely a radar return made up of raw radar signals bouncing off an airplane's aluminum skin. Anyway, the paint was successful, and I was radar identified—even though I filed /X ("slash X-Ray"), the flight plan suffix code for a no-transponder airplane.

Eventually, I climbed the airplane to on-top conditions and settled into a 90-odd knot cruise. The clouds cleared beneath me by the time I reached central Missouri, and the landing at Rolla was uneventful.

The weather briefing for the next leg of the day—to Cincinnati's Lunken Airport—was curious. Forecasts were calling for the standard-issue, summertime, 4,000-scattered-to-broken cloud layers along the route and unlimited visibilities. But the dew points reported at airports all along the Ohio Valley were at the 60-degree mark, sometimes higher. That right there was a warning. With air that soggy, and 90 degree-plus surface temperatures, I knew that the stage was set for thunderstorms—even though the forecasts made an equivocating mention of a "chance" of thunderstorms. I left Rolla nervous. The air was turbulent during climbout; it was smooth when I left Wichita. The air was heating up, and quickly.

By the time I reached the Centralia, Illinois area, moderate turbulence was making my ride in the 152 a really, really aggravating chore. About the same time the gaps between the small puffy, scattered cumulus beneath me began to narrow. Then the clouds began their climb to my 7,000-foot cruising altitude. As soon as I realized this, I asked, and was cleared, to climb to 9,000 feet. On the way to 9,000, it was clear that the clouds would get there before I did.

Another request, and another climb. This time to 11,000 feet. Would the 152 even make it to that lofty altitude in the way-above-standard atmospheric conditions? I doubted it, but I felt I had to try to keep topping these now-menacing clouds.

At 11,000 feet—finally—and somewhere near Bloomington, Indiana, my efforts to stay out of the clouds was becoming desperate. Now the cumulus around me were towering way into the flight levels, and I was having to weave between the slim corridors that separated them. The turbulence increased. I picked up a HIWAS broadcast on my only nav radio and learned that I was right in the middle of a newly-declared Convective SIGMET. It was no surprise. The clouds were becoming darker. And their tops were now blocking the sun.

Lunken's getting closer and I have to face two issues: my fuel status and, of course, how I plan to deal with the weather in what must surely be one of the least-capable cross-country airplanes in general aviation's recent history. I thought about diverting to Louisville, or Evansville. But the weather along those routes was just as bad.

Then more bad news. A call to flight service informed me that I was now flying in a tornado watch box. With Cincinnati so close, I decided to descend and plan for an instrument approach to Lunken.

The trip down through the clouds brought with it a sick feeling of imminence. The turbulence was wild, and even with power at idle, the updrafts conspired against my descent planning. After many nerve-wracking bouts with unusual attitudes in these rain-shot, jarring clouds I was finally vectored for a back course approach to Lunken's runway 3R. Just what I needed now: a back course approach in convective clouds with a single nav receiver and an airplane with a light wing loading.

I broke out at 2,000 feet or so and, in the face of an increasing southerly wind, was vectored around for a landing on runway 21L. The skies overhead were darkening, and the first splatters of rain were hitting my windshield. I had beat a major storm to the airport, but not by much. A lineman, now battered by the gusts flowing out from the oncoming storm, directed me into a hangar. Good thing, because as soon as I pulled the Cessna in, lightning, thunder and, yes, even golf ball-sized hail began pelting Lunken. The field went to minimums, and everyone took cover. The severe thunderstorm lasted the rest of the afternoon and into the night.

I learned a lesson. Well, maybe more than one. Don't try to top building cumulus clouds in an underpowered airplane. If you're flying a light piston-powered airplane, land at the first sign that cumulus clouds are on their way to towering. And never underestimate the Ohio Valley's way of turning ugly on a muggy, late summer day.

East–West Stationary Fronts

Whenever you see a front east of the Mississippi aligned along an east–west axis, it's a sign of IFR weather. Make that long-lasting low IFR (ceiling at or below 500 feet, visibilities lower than one mile) weather. This holds especially true in the Ohio Valley, as well as the territory in and around the Appalachian

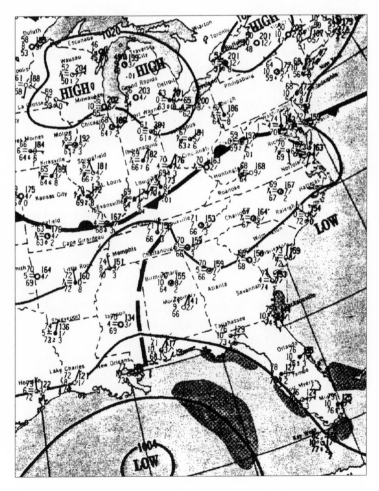

Figure 13-2. An Ohio Valley east-west stationary front on September 17, 1998 — day three of its four-day lifespan. Dense fogs and low ceilings persisted over the area from Missouri to West Virginia until the next day, when high pressure shoved it to the southeast. The front was especially stubborn because it was trapped between a strong high to the north and a strong low over the Gulf of Mexico. The first cool temperatures of the approaching fall played a big part in helping fog to form — one reason why autumn is called "fog season" by meteorologists. (From Daily Weather Maps, *a weekly publication of the NOAA/NWS, September 1998.)*

Plateau. Because these fronts' positions so often roughly coincide with the state demarcation lines between the opposing sides of the Civil War, some meteorologists call them "Confederate" fronts. Appropriate, because the forces at work are advancing from the south, and never quite seem to move too far into Yankee territory.

Here's what typically happens. A Gulf low, born in the waters south of Louisiana or off the Texas coast, migrates inland near the Louisiana/Mississippi border, then heads north under the jet stream's steering winds. At the surface, a southerly flow of warm air sends moisture up the low's east side. That flow of air cuts a swath from east Texas to western Florida, causing a warm front to extend to the southeast of the low. The weather complex usually moves slowly, taking a day or two to move inland.

See Pages 214 to 215 for an example of this typical "Pipeline" weather scenario played out from forecast to actual conditions, in a convective SIGMET, severe weather outlook, and radar summary chart for one April day.

By the time the warm front reaches the latitude of northern Mississippi, it begins to run into higher-pressure air masses centered along, or north of, the Ohio Valley. It also runs into higher terrain, which causes orographic lifting, and the condensation, clouds, fog, and rainfall that this brings about. The movement of the front slows, stalls and becomes stationary. The stage is now set for a days-long siege of instrument weather.

The southerly flow persists, packing more moisture into the frontal zone. By now, that southerly flow has caused the stationary front to assume its classic, east-west orientation. Low clouds, fog, rain, and mountain obscuration will persist until an energetic cold front from the west blows the whole works away, or a large trough aloft sends in colder, drier air.

In the warmer months of the year, this stationary front can cause thunderstorms to pop up, die, and re-energize themselves over the course of a few days. In the colder months, something equally sinister often occurs.

Imagine this warm, southerly air moving north and riding up and over the colder air centered over, say, Ohio and Indiana. Then imagine the pent-up water in the warm air falling into the cold air beneath it. The subsequent rainfall becomes supercooled in the colder air, and presto—freezing rain and clear icing conditions. Often this freezing rain happens in a thin, low-lying slice of the atmosphere. That's because the warm and stationary frontal boundaries aloft that are conducive to freezing rain are so close to the ground. We all know that warm fronts, viewed in cross-section, have shallow frontal boundaries. It's near the boundaries close to the surface front's position that you'll have freezing rain. Farther to the north of this scenario, rain falling out of a warm frontal boundary has farther to fall, and therefore more time to freeze solid before it arrives in lower atmospheric layers. So, it can fall as sleet—or ice pellets, to use the new World Meteorological Organization terminology. Wet snow is also a possibility.

Anyone cruising in the clouds above this kind of warm or stationary frontal setup can run into some serious icing. As always in these situations, flying an airplane certified for flight in known icing conditions makes the most sense—but it's no guarantee of safe passage through really bad ice—or even moderate icing. There's a proper technique for operating deice boots, for example. If a nervous pilot inflates his deice boots the moment he sees ice forming on the wings, he's doing more harm than good. If this is done often enough, ice will continue to form in a bridge that conforms to the shape of the inflated boots' profile—now you've got ice that can't be removed. The best technique (check the pilot's operating handbook for precise information about the ice-protected airplane you may be flying) is to allow a certain amount of ice to build—about ¼ to ⅜ inch thick—before inflating the boots. This helps the boots work the best they can, and helps prevent ice bridging problems.

New theories, however, contradict this decades-old rule of thumb. Evidence has been compiled that rejects the idea that ice can bridge over a leading edge. There's simply no proof, advocates say, that ice bridging has ever been a problem.

Pilots flying airplanes capable of flying in the flight levels may be able to overfly this type of lingering frontal misery. That's because the descending air from high pressure aloft can suppress cloud tops of these fall and winter stationary complexes, create temperature inversions, and keep the real weather down low (if you consider 10,000 to 15,000 feet low).

```
CONVECTIVE SIGMET 17E
VALID UNTIL 1255Z
IL IN KY OH
FROM 60SSE FWA-50E CVG-30W BWG-20NW EVV-60SSE FWA
AREA SVR TSTMS MOVG FROM 2525. TOPS ABV 450.
HAIL TO 2 IN...WIND GUSTS TO 50 KT PSBL.

OUTLOOK VALID 291255-291655
FROM 60NW SYR-AVP-TRI-DYR-IND-60NW SYR
REF WW 174.
CLUSTERS OF STG TSTMS CONT OVR PARTS OF THE OH VLY AND THE LWR
GRTLKS. AMS IS MRGLLY UNSTBL WITH LIFTED INDICES BTWN ZERO AND
MINUS 3. WRMFNT LIFTING NWD ACRS OH/IND AND CDFNT MOVG ACRS WRN
SXNS OF IND/KY WL AID STG TSTM DVLPMT. ACTVTY XPCD TO RQR WST
ISSUANCES THRU MUCH OF THE PD.

FIKE
```

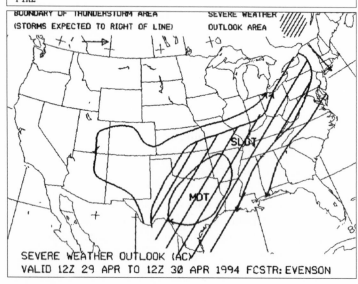

Figure 13-3A. *No matter where you fly in the United States, it's worth taking a look at the Severe Weather Outlook (or AC, to use the NWS abbreviator). It's a forecast product that can be uncannily accurate, and gives a preview of the next 24 hours' severe thunderstorm probability. The textual discussion is mainly for meteorologists, but after learning the abbreviations it's possible for any diligent pilot—or weather briefer—to extract plenty of information. The text mentions that a cold front moving across western sections of Indiana and Kentucky will aid in thunderstorm development and that this activity is expected to require severe thunderstorm warnings through much of the period ...*

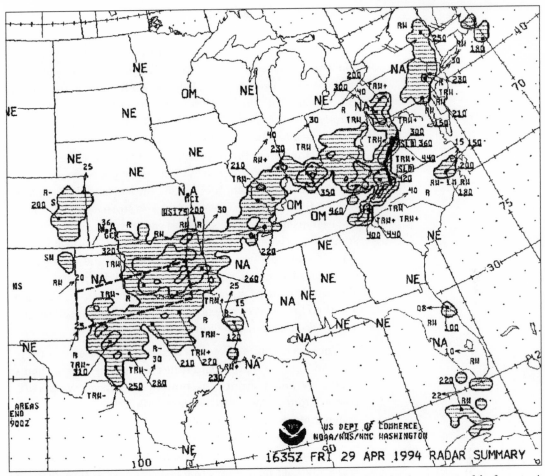

Figure 13-3B. ... *And the radar summary chart issued four hours after the AC proves the accuracy of the forecast. A solid line of thunderstorms with tops to 42,000 feet is over the Virginia/West Virginia border, and a severe thunderstorm watch box is already posted over the north Texas/southern Oklahoma area. And it's only a little past noon.*

215

"Chattanooga Choo-Choos"

In the chapters dealing with the weather on the lee side of the Rocky Mountains, we saw that mountains are major weather-makers. The same holds true for the Appalachian Mountains of the eastern United States. Fall and winter lows approaching the Appalachians via a path from the deep south, and traveling through eastern Kentucky and Tennessee, undergo changes for the worse after they ride northeast along the Cumberland Plateau, then cross the Appalachians. By the time these lows make it to North Carolina or Virginia, heavy snow, rain, or freezing rain can hit the areas along the storm path very hard indeed. Because these types of lows and storms seem to form so often in eastern Tennessee, and can travel so far to the east, some meteorologists call them "Chattanooga Choo-Choos." The "Choo-Choo" gets its initial kick-off from the southeast quadrant of an upper-atmosphere trough aloft's jet stream. That's where the jet stream's core can have its strongest winds, and therefore where vertical and rotational motions in the jet stream do their storm-building work.

Once such a surface low has formed in Tennessee, its trailing cold front can have a hard time crossing the Appalachians. So, the low and its fronts slow down a bit. This allows lots of cold air from the north to be sucked into the storm complex. When it mixes in with the Gulf air in the complex's colder sectors in Kentucky, West Virginia, western North Carolina, and the mountainous parts of Virginia, the result is snow. Sometimes, it's heavy snow that lasts for days as the storm struggles to makes its way up and over the mountains.

Meanwhile, northern Alabama and Georgia experience rain—because these areas are in the warm sector of the Choo-Choo, where it's too warm for snow to form.

If this type of storm complex does make it to the lee side of the Appalachians, then it can re-energize. If it travels as far as the North Carolina coast, it can re-form as a more intense coastal storm. In other words, a Nor'easter. How does this happen? Up high in the atmosphere, the jet core that created the storm in the first place can surge ahead of the sluggish storm's progress at the surface, and move to the northeast. Then the jet core can draw the surface low along and behind its same general track, causing the low to re-intensify as it catches up, and once again subject to the core's lifting forces.

This "dragging" of surface lows is not unique to the winter storms of Appalachia. Surface weather features often trail behind jet cores aloft in many other parts of the United States. The point here is that fall and winter lows in the Cumberland and Appalachian Plateaus must be watched closely. If strong jet cores are perched above them, be on guard. It's a warning that the storm could easily progress to the east or northeast, then cause havoc over the Mid-Atlantic states as a Nor'easter. The pilot who's flying from west to east, hoping to overfly an icy, low-IFR storm complex on his way to the east coast, may find that the storm follows him.

For all the above reasons, it's easy to understand why the Ohio Valley states have so much instrument weather in the fall and winter months. In the higher terrain, climatological records indicate that IFR conditions prevail over 50 percent of the time at those times of the year. For those planning on flying to airports in these states, winter can be most unforgiving.

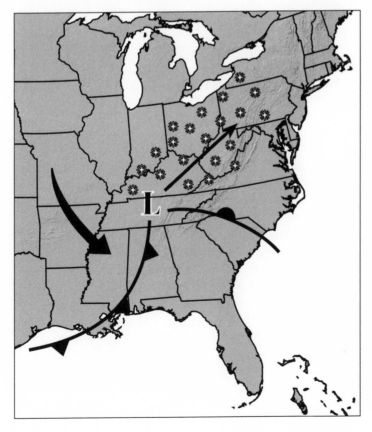

Figure 13-4. Propelled and energized by low pressure aloft, a "Chattanooga Choo-Choo" makes its move from Tennessee to the northeastern United States. Cold temperatures to the north of the system means low ceilings and visibilities in snow and ice. Rain's the rule in Alabama, Georgia, and South Carolina, where the warm sector of the storm is located.

Icing conditions can dog you all the way to decision height or minimum descent altitude. Also, because of the terrain, DHs and MDAs can be higher than standard, and set you up for missed approaches. Finally, decent airports with long, wide runways and good radar service will be few and far between around the higher elevations of the Appalachians. When the weather goes down, your options can be few and far between. At night, the adrenaline level on an IFR crossing of the Appalachians can be sky-high if you'll be landing any time soon. It'll be pitch black, and with ice building quickly the pressure is definitely on. And you say you'll be landing at an airport with an uncomfortably short runway, a nonprecision approach that requires you to circle to land, with a high MDA, surrounded by unfriendly geography?

It can be an uncomfortable—and unsafe—ride for the best of instrument pilots. Let alone those without instrument ratings. It's a good thing that most pilots have sense enough to stand down when stationary fronts or "Choo-Choos" are in town.

Accidents

The pilot of a Beech B-58 Baron and his two passengers died in a crash near Beardstown, Illinois at 7:45 A.M. on June 29, 1993. Instrument weather prevailed at the time, with ceilings reported at 450 feet AGL and visibilities as low as ¼ mile. An IFR flight plan was filed for the trip from Evansville, Indiana to Jacksonville, Illinois. But while on approach to the Jacksonville airport the pilot canceled his flight plan, telling ATC that he was proceeding VFR to Beardstown, Illinois. At Beardstown, witnesses reported IMC with fog and very light drizzle. The pilot apparently lost control of the airplane and crashed one mile southwest of Beardstown's runway 36. The previous day, a low-level trough established itself over the area, causing widespread IMC and rainfall over the entire Ohio Valley. The day of the accident, a stationary front extended on an east–west line from Kansas to southern New Jersey, causing IMC with fog to perpetuate over the Ohio Valley. A weak trough aloft helped sustain the surface front, and prevented it from moving very much. The Ohio Valley remained covered with low ceilings and fog for the next four days.

A newly-rated instrument pilot crashed after takeoff from the Bowling Green, Kentucky airport at about 8:20 A.M. on July 6, 1992. An IFR flight plan was filed for a trip from Bowling Green to Cedar Rapids, Iowa. Weather at the time of the accident was estimated at 500 feet overcast, with visibilities of six miles. Shortly after the pilot and his three passengers took off in a Piper PA-34 Seneca, a call was made to the Bowling Green flight service station. During the call, the pilot reported cloud bases as being 1,300 feet MSL, which would have been about 800 feet AGL. Several witnesses reported hearing the airplane's engines making a "high pitch" sound. A witness sitting in his truck watched the airplane crash not fifteen feet from where the Seneca first hit the ground. This witness said that the pilot appeared to pull the airplane out of a dive. "It was almost completely level but its nose was not," this witness said. The crash happened just one mile east of the departure end of Bowling Green's runway 21. The pilot earned his instrument rating in May 1992, had logged 35 hours of simulated instrument time, and 1.3 hours of actual instrument time when the accident happened. This accident occurred almost immediately after an east–west cold front had passed to the south of the Ohio Valley. In the days before the frontal passage, IMC and precipitation had been affecting the Ohio Valley.

In the crash of a Piper PA-32-260 Cherokee Six at Minford, Ohio on July 24, 1994, morning ground fog appears to have been a major factor. The pilot and his five passengers took off on an IFR flight plan from the Minford airport at 7:30 A.M., bound for an auto race in Talladega, Alabama. However, the preliminary NTSB accident report indicates that the pilot neither requested nor received an IFR clearance prior to departure. The Automated Weather Observation System installation at Minford reported a ceiling of 100 feet, sky obscured, visibility less than ¼ mile at the time of the accident. Witnesses said the visibility was about 200 to 400 feet. The airplane took off from runway 18 and turned right, then witnesses said they heard two loud noises one minute after takeoff, followed by the sound of the engine stopping abruptly. The published instrument departure procedure for the runway in question calls for a climb on a heading of 170 degrees until reaching 1,200 feet, then proceeding on course. The lone survivor of the crash said that the airplane hit two trees before it fell to the ground and caught fire. A large area of high pressure was over the southeastern quadrant of the United States on that day, and low visibilities in fog were prevalent all over the Ohio Valley on the morning of the accident.

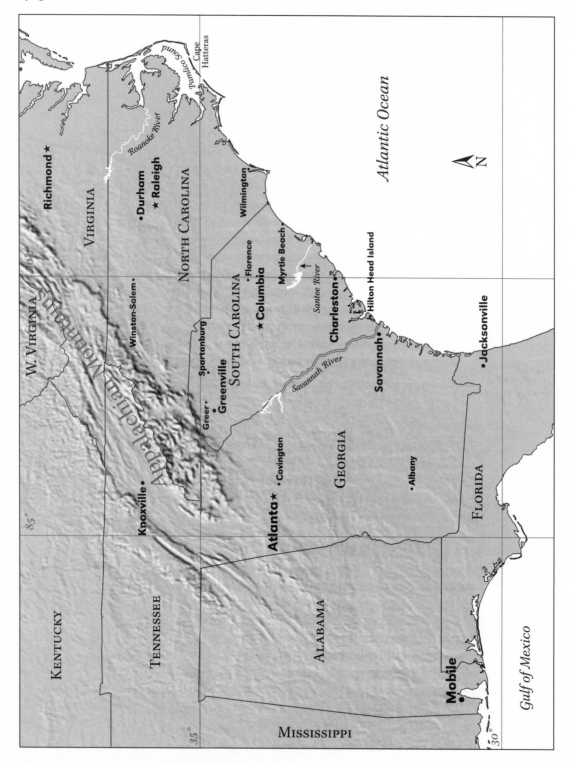

Southeast
The Frontal Graveyard

Betting on the weather has got to be a losing game, but in some cases the odds favor certain phenomena. To illustrate, let me ask you to watch a few days' worth of the Weather Channel, or call up a week's worth of DUAT briefings for the southeast states. I'm going to make a gentleman's wager that you'll come up with at least one front lying across Georgia and the Carolinas. I'll stick my neck out a little farther and say that frontal weather stretches across this area at least one-third of the time, with spring and fall having the greatest chances.

It's easy to understand why fronts hang around the southeast. In a typical synoptic situation, a series of upper-level lows passes through Canada and the northern tier of the United States. These lows help create and intensify fronts at the lower levels of the atmosphere. Fronts—principally cold fronts—trail from these northern lows, and are dragged along behind them as they move from west to east.

Meanwhile, high-pressure air usually dominates the skies over the Gulf of Mexico and the coastal waters off the southeastern states.

So there you have the big picture: cold fronts, oriented in northeast-southwest lines, traveling eastward from the central United States until they run into southern high pressure. High pressure is more of a weather-blocker than a weather-maker, so the fronts tend to slow down and stall by the time they make their way into the southeast.

From there, the situation can take many paths. If the cold front is especially strong and fast-moving, it can bull its way offshore. If it isn't, the high can slow the front until it stops in its tracks, and a stationary front develops. If there isn't much difference between the air masses on either side of the frontal

The southeast states: Where many fronts spend their final days

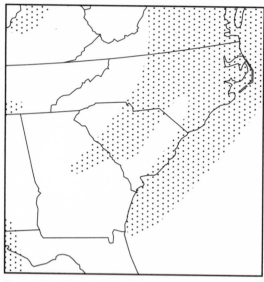

*Percentage of hours in **Spring** when ceiling is below 1,000 feet and visibility is less than 3 miles*

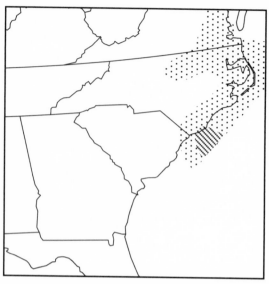

*Percentage of hours in **Summer** when ceiling is below 1,000 feet and visibility is less than 3 miles*

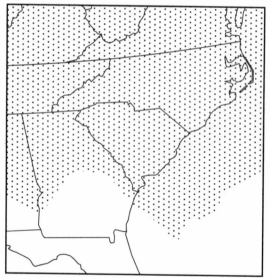

*Percentage of hours in **Autumn** when ceiling is below 1,000 feet and visibility is less than 3 miles*

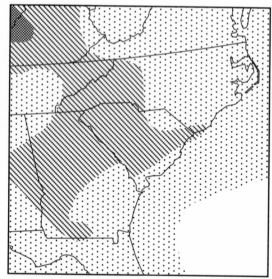

*Percentage of hours in **Winter** when ceiling is below 1,000 feet and visibility is less than 3 miles*

50% or more   **40-49%**   **30-39%**   **20-29%**   **10-19%**   **Less than 9%**

222

boundary, then the front can simply disappear. For all these reasons, many meteorologists call the southeast states the "graveyard" of fronts; it's where they go to end their life cycles.

As pilots, we have to worry about the disappearing-front scenario. There may be clouds at multiple layers, low ceilings, and vast areas of instrument weather—the usual signposts of a deteriorating front in the southeast states. And while large-scale convection may not automatically appear with a dying front, days-long bouts with coastal fogs are commonplace in the southeast. Any onshore wind flows will advect the fog inland, where it can cover entire states.

Other concerns are with situations where strong fronts blow through, or a weakened one become stationary. In either case, SIGMET weather can prevail. Both situations can bring severe thunderstorms. Stationary fronts bring the extra threat of lingering precipitation, low ceilings and visibilities, as the high's moist air feeds the stationary front over a period of days.

Let's look at some examples. On July 1, 1990, a particularly violent cold front spawned a complex of severe thunderstorms. One of them developed right over the Greer/Greenville–Spartanburg airport, then moved on to produce three-quarter to one-inch hail. Witnesses said that after the hail storm stopped, the sun came out. Then, a microburst struck mobile homes and houses three miles southeast of the airport.

For nearly the entire month of January, 1990, stationary frontal conditions plagued the state of Georgia. On January 7, nearly five inches of rain fell on Albany, and rainfall in subsequent days caused major episodes of flash flooding. On January 20, more flooding took place after prolonged rains. On the 25th, a tornado touched down five miles north of Albany.

A cold front entered the southeast on August 10, 1991, then became stationary the next day. On the 12th, a small low formed along the front; by the next day it moved to a position off Cape Hatteras, and another low formed near Mobile, Alabama. Nearly all stations in Georgia and the Carolinas reported IFR and low IFR conditions until August 16, when the front finally collapsed.

But then another weathermaker became a factor. Tropical storm Bob formed north of the Bahamas on August 16th, spreading its moisture all through the southeastern piedmont.

On the 17th, Wilmington, North Carolina reported a 7:00 A.M. visibility of 1/16 mile in fog. Columbia, South Carolina and Savannah, Georgia reported visibilities of one-half mile and two miles in fog, respectively. The 18th brought a repeat performance of IFR weather, and it wasn't until the following day that Bob's departure finally brought VFR weather to the southeast.

***Figure 14-1.** A fronts slows and dies over the southeast states. This surface chart represents a common situation. A cold front that a few days ago ripped through the central United States has slowed down. Why? High pressure over the Atlantic Ocean — the Bermuda High — blocks its movement and causes the front to go stationary. At the same time, the southerly flow off the back side of the Bermuda High packs moisture into the front, creating low ceilings in fog and rain along the coast and as far inland as north Georgia. (**Note:** See Pages 247–248 for an amplified discussion of the Bermuda High. See also the illustration showing the location and effects of the Bermuda High, on Appendix Page 308.)*

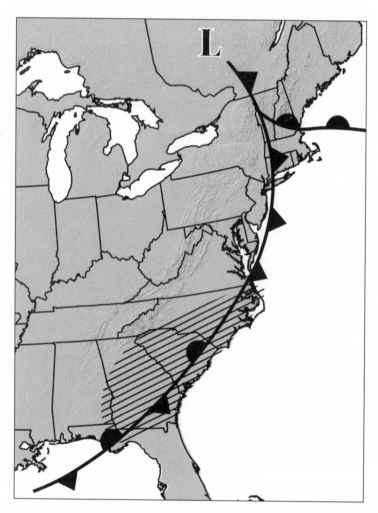

It's important to note that while hurricanes certainly pose some of the most serious weather hazards in the southeast, they occur infrequently—and not without adequate warning. Far more of a problem to pilots are the frequent coastal fogs affecting such airports as Wilmington, Myrtle Beach, Charleston, Hilton Head, and Savannah. At these sites, nocturnal cooling of moist ocean air routinely causes low visibilities in fog, and this situation can occur anytime—not just when fronts or lows are near. In fact, high pressure often brings the most dense coastal fogs in the southeast.

"Graveyard" or not, the southeast's semipermanent front and coastal fogs bear special watching. When winter approaches, there's an additional reason for keeping an eye on the southeast's weather. Georgia and the Carolinas lie right along several very popular north-south routes of flight. A vacationing pilot, bound for Florida and an escape from winter's grasp, should always be prepared to encounter instrument meteorological conditions in the southeast. You may be lucky and be able to make the trip VFR, but don't bet on it.

On a mid-December flight from the Washington, D.C. area to southern Florida, I flew from severe clear conditions into an area of highly localized, deep low pressure in the Savannah area. At my cruising altitude of 7,000 feet, the OAT fell to 0°C, and soon I was picking up ice—at the doorstep to the Florida border! A change of altitude fixed the ice problem, but then it started snowing, and ceilings from Charleston, South Carolina to Melbourne, Florida went below 800 feet. The only good thing about that day was the tailwind—some 50 knots on the tail. That right there was a good indication of the strength of the coastal low aloft that was feeding the goings-on below. Snow aloft persisted right up to the Pahokee VOR, at the south end of Lake Okeechobee, and for the next few days it was unseasonably cold and windy in "balmy" Fort Lauderdale.

So snowbirds, beware. You may have to pay your dues before reaching the promised land. A dying front can ruin your day. If a surface low is off the coast, you can count on it. Now that would be a safe bet.

A Bad Day in November

November 27, 1994 was a very bad day in the southeast United States. The pilot of a Cessna 182 tried two ILS approaches into the Greenville, South Carolina, Downtown Airport. This pilot was on an IFR flight from Gainesville, Florida to Asheville, North Carolina. Both ILS's wound up as missed approaches. After the last missed approach, the pilot was issued vectors for the ILS runway 3 approach at nearby Greenville–Spartanburg Airport in Greer, South Carolina. Not that the weather there was much better: sky partially obscured, measured 300 feet overcast, visibility one-half mile in drizzle and light fog, temperature 41°F, dew point 40°F. Fog, it was noted, covered five-tenths of the sky. The Skylane crashed during the approach, and the pilot escaped with minor injuries—he even walked to a guard shack at a nearby carpet mill to report that he was all right.

However, just a half-hour before this accident, two fatal accidents occurred (which are detailed in the accident section below). The coincidence of these accidents of November 27 underscores a weather problem endemic to the southeast in the fall months. As lows move in from the west, oceanic air masses are drawn inland over Georgia in the Carolinas. This happens any time of year, which explains the year-round chance of coastal fogs. But in the fall months, as surface temperatures drop and the jet stream descends to lower latitudes, the cooling problem intensifies in the southeast. Any ocean air advected inland can easily fall to the dew point, creating statewide dense fogs and low visibilities. That's exactly what happened on November 27.

On that day, a surface low that spent the 26th over northeastern Kansas tracked quickly to the northeast and the upper peninsula of Michigan, shoved along by a cutoff low aloft encircled by wind velocities as high as 110 knots at 18,000 feet. Ahead of the low's surface cold front, a warm front—extending to the surface low's east—took on stationary frontal characteristics over coastal Georgia.

At the same time, another critical ingredient to this low-IFR setup was going to work over New England. There, a strong high-pressure system sent its cold air southward. This air rode on weak northerly winds, and at low altitude. As the cold front pushed in from the west, the high's cold air caused the

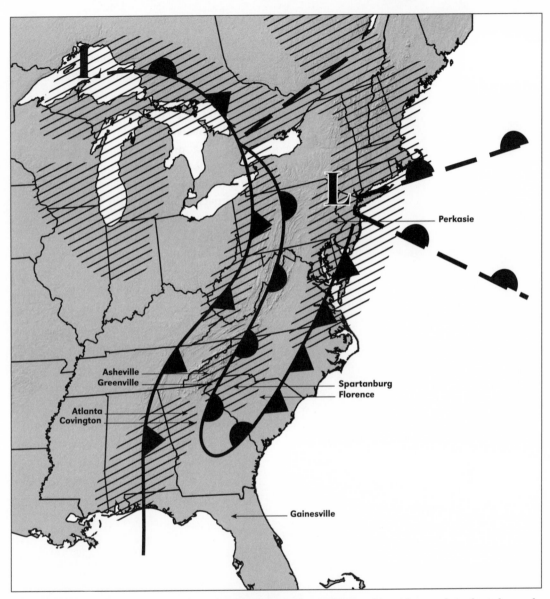

Figure 14-2. *November 27, 1994 was a very bad flying day in the southeast—this surface analysis chart shows why. Cold air, dammed up in the Piedmont east of the Appalachians, shows up as a huge, looping front from the north. No more than 2,000 feet or so deep, this shallow layer of cold air caused temperatures to drop to the dew point and form widespread dense fog. To kick off this situation, strong high pressure over the northeast United States is required. This slows the advance of any cold fronts from the west, and causes distinctive southward bulges in any warm fronts. If you see a chart like this, don't expect the weather in the southeast to improve any time soon. Especially if it's "fog season"—in the fall months when surface temperatures begin their first serious drops. (Note: consult this illustration for further accident accounts of this same November day, given on Page 229.)*

southeast's warm and stationary front to bow southward. Cool air was damming up against the Appalachians—from the Allegheny plateau in the north to the coastal piedmont in the south. It was just cold enough to cause fog to blanket the entire southeast.

It wasn't a deep fog, mind you. This type of cold-air damming phenomenon usually involves a thin layer of fog, maybe just 1,000 or 2,000 feet thick, at most. The point is that it's widespread and a very common fog-producer in the southeast. So any time a forecaster mentions cold-air damming, look out for some varsity IFR approaches, and be ready for missed approaches. Low IFR of the type described here will be the rule. Also, don't expect to find any VFR conditions close by. You may have to fly as far as Florida or the Mississippi Valley to get to better weather. In situations like those that prevailed on November 27, 1994, the entire east coast will be under the low-IFR gun.

Accidents

Another November 27, 1994, accident: A Glasair pilot on an IFR flight plan was cleared for an instrument approach to the Florence, South Carolina airport. Weather for the 10:00 A.M. arrival was 300 overcast, with visibility 2½ miles in fog. While being vectored for the ILS to runway 9, the pilot reported he had lost his gyro instruments. Shortly thereafter, the Glasair crashed, killing the pilot and his one passenger. (*See* Figure 14-2.)

Also on November 27, 1994, the pilot of a Beech B-55 Baron was on a long IFR cross-country flight from Perkasie, Pennsylvania (north of Philadelphia) to Covington, Georgia. He attempted a VOR/DME approach to Covington's runway 9, missed the approach due to the low weather, then diverted to his named alternate—Atlanta's Fulton County–Brown Field, some 38 miles to the west of Covington. Covington is an uncontrolled airport, with no weather reporting, so we don't know how low the weather was at the time. By the time the Baron arrived at Fulton County–Brown—about 6:00 P.M.—the weather records simply state that the airport was IFR. However, earlier in the day, Atlanta's Hartsfield International Airport weather went as low as 150 feet overcast, with 1½ mile visibility in fog. The Baron pilot reported that he had just 15 minutes' worth of fuel left, and proceeded to shoot three consecutive instrument approaches into Fulton County. Each one ended in a missed approach. After the third approach, the Baron ran out of fuel and crashed one mile northeast of the airport, killing the pilot. (*See* Figure 14-2.)

The 6:41 A.M. weather at the Greenville, North Carolina airport was 200 overcast with zero visibility in fog on May 15, 1992. The instrument-rated pilot of a PA-32 Cherokee Six and his five passengers took off from runway 25 on an IFR flight plan, bound for Savannah, Georgia. The pilot received his instrument rating just two days earlier. The airplane crashed one-half mile southwest of the departure end of runway 25, killing all aboard. The conditions that morning in Greenville were duplicated all over the southeast throughout the day. Temperatures were right on top of dew points from D.C. to Jacksonville, from Cape Hatteras to Knoxville. The cause? An east-west stationary front running from Kansas to the Virginia–North Carolina border. A high over New England fed cool ocean air inland and to the south, while an onshore flow from a weak Bermuda high sent muggy air to the west, deep into Georgia and the Carolinas. The entire stagnant mess caused low IFR conditions for three full days.

SOUTH CAROLINA

ALABAMA

GEORGIA

Atlantic Ocean

Savannah•

Pensacola•
Tallahassee ★

FLORIDA

•Jacksonville

Gulf Islands
National Seashore

Gulf of Mexico

Gainesville•

Lake George

•Ocala
•Dunnellon

Inverness•

•Orlando

Melbourne•

Cape
Canaveral

Clearwater•

•Tampa

Lake
Okeechobee

Fort Myers•

•Boynton
Beach

Fort Lauderdale•

Miami •

Everglades
National
Park

Coral Gables•

N

FLORIDA KEYS

85°

80°

30°

25°

Florida
The Sometime-Sunshine State

P alm trees swaying in a gentle breeze, perpetual sunshine, as many beaches as airports, and a few puffy fair-weather cumulus clouds. That's the popular image of Florida, and the one that's most responsible for attracting so many pilots to the sunshine state. There's probably not a single pilot in the eastern half of the United States that hasn't thought about a flying vacation to Florida, and many certainly follow through on their plans. And many stay. With 45,201 pilots living there as of 1995, Florida is the United States' secondmost pilot-dense state. (California comes in first, with 75,801 registered pilots, according to recent statistics.)

Many times, that perfect-flying-weather dream is a Florida reality. But pilots new to the state ought to know this unique region's flip side. Like other states in the nation, Florida has its thunderstorms, fogs, and fronts, but these phenomena behave a little bit differently down there.

A quick look at Florida's geography sets the stage for Florida's flying weather. First, it's surrounded by large bodies of warm water. Its next big geographic feature is its latitude. Within a range from 24 to 31 degrees north latitude, Florida is definitely subtropical. Being at this latitude also subjects Florida to the influence of the subtropical jet stream (STJ), which can help create and/or intensify large thunderstorm cells. The STJ lives at these latitudes because these mark the dividing lines between tropical and temperate air masses, and any time there are temperature contrasts of these order in the upper atmosphere, jet streams occur.

So there you have it—a soggy atmosphere, fed by sea breezes and prevailing easterly winds, and well-heated by a sun high in the sky most days of most months of the year. It's no wonder that Florida experiences so many thunderstorms. It's a convective nirvana.

Coming to terms with Snowbird Mecca, and a pesky stationary front.

231

Percentage of hours in **Spring** *when ceiling is below 1,000 feet and visibility is less than 3 miles*

Percentage of hours in **Summer** *when ceiling is below 1,000 feet and visibility is less than 3 miles*

Percentage of hours in **Autumn** *when ceiling is below 1,000 feet and visibility is less than 3 miles*

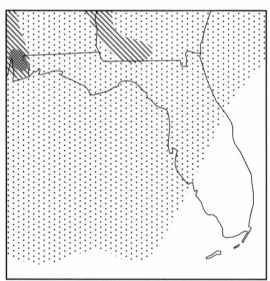

Percentage of hours in **Winter** *when ceiling is below 1,000 feet and visibility is less than 3 miles*

▦ **50% or more**   ◩ **40-49%**   ▨ **30-39%**   ◩ **20-29%**   ⬚ **10-19%**   ☐ **Less than 9%**

A Typical Pattern

Here's what happens almost every day between March and October, somewhere in Florida:

As the sun sets on yet another day dominated by high pressure, surface temperatures drop and by about 4:00 A.M. a temperature inversion forms around 1,000 feet AGL. Fog sets in as nighttime temperatures reach their lowest levels, dropping to the dew point, which will be around 60°F or 70°F.

When the sun rises, so do surface temperatures. The inversion begins to disappear. The temperature–dewpoint spread busts past the 5-degree warning mark we've all been taught to respect, and the fog burns off. This only happens if the sun is able to shine through the fog and heat the surface. Because fog burns off from the bottom up, a layer of overcast skies will prevent the fog from burning off quickly, if at all, so skies must be relatively clear above the low-lying fog for good VFR conditions to develop.

Surface temperatures keep on rising through the day, reaching a peak at 5:00 P.M. or so. Now the atmosphere is absolutely unstable, meaning that any rising parcels of heated air—from a parking lot, kicked up by a sea breeze, or just a choice orange grove—encounter progressively colder temperatures aloft, causing it to rise even faster. With those soggy dew points, the air is saturated with moisture, and the cycle of lifting, condensation, and more lifting continues until a towering cumulus cloud forms.

Within a few minutes the towering cumulus builds to a full-fledged thunderstorm of the air mass variety. The skies open up, all that subtropical moisture comes down in buckets of rain, and cloud-to-ground lightning strikes zap away. By 9:00 P.M. the fireworks are usually over, canceled due to lack of surface heating.

Sometimes, these kinds of air mass thunderstorms cluster together in groups resembling the Mesoscale Convective Complexes seen in midwestern summers. But unlike the midwestern complexes, Florida's large storm complexes are often built with the help of the STJ's lifting forces aloft. The STJ lives around 30 degrees North latitude, and is oriented on an east–west line. Like midwestern MCCs, once a Floridian storm complex forms it's likely to persist through the night, and

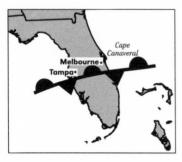

Figure 15-1. *An east–west stationary front running from Tampa to Melbourne is a common synoptic feature of Florida weather. It's especially common in the fall and spring months, when cooler air masses from the north butt up against tropical air to the south. While the front itself sets up across mid-Florida, the clouds and convection it causes can cover the entire state.*

Sea-breeze storms, plus the cloud cover that accompanies a Florida east-west stationary front, are shown in satellite images on Appendix Page 298.

maybe even to the next day. Easterly waves—miniature troughs aloft of the type that trigger hurricanes—are another contributing factor in many Floridian, and Caribbean, thunderstorm setups.

Fronts can also make flying miserable in Florida. Cold fronts from the north frequently make it all the way to central Florida before running out of steam, pushing thunderstorms and widespread rain ahead of them. Then they can stall out, and it will take a day or so before they lose their punch and break up altogether.

Another prominent feature of lousy Florida flying weather is the stationary front you so often see parked on a line from Tampa to Melbourne. This coast-to-coast front can linger for days, and give central Florida 90 to 100 thunderstorm days per year. This front marks the boundary between the more continental air to the north and the tropical air to the south, and so it's not surprising that it, too, hovers somewhere south of 30 North—usually 27 or 28 degrees North latitude, which would put it on a line roughly from Tampa to Melbourne. Forecasters at the Kennedy Space Center on Cape Canaveral despise this front because it can cancel Space Shuttle launches and landings.

Sea breezes, of course, are also big-time considerations, if for no other reason than that so many of Florida's airports are locate along the coasts. Differential heating of land and sea are at work here. During the day, land heats up quickly, causing rising air and lower pressure. Air flows from high pressure to low, so an onshore breeze starts to pick up around 10:00 A.M. When the sun goes down, it's the sea that's warmer than the land, and the process is reversed. Oceans are slow to heat, and once warmed up, slow to give up that heat. So they make excellent heat sinks and have the ability to actually store heat. Couple this with the warm waters of the Gulf Stream just off Florida's Atlantic coast, and the heat contrasts between land and sea can become impressive at night.

For this reason, thunderstorms often form offshore. This frequently leaves overland airways free of convection. On the other hand, it seems that when thunderstorms are forming over Florida, the Gulf and Atlantic are clear of storms. It's something to check into when facing a decision to deviate around storm cells.

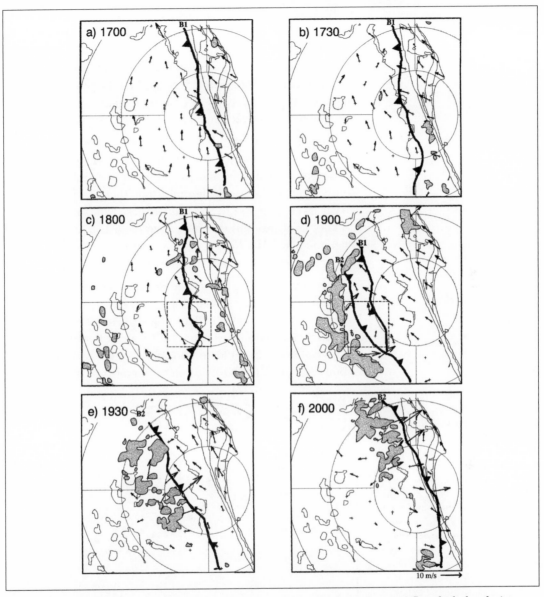

Figure 15-2. *A 1991 NCAR study of thunderstorms initiated by low-level, convergent airflows looked at the interaction of easterly sea breezes with gust fronts coming from the west. Dubbed the CaPE (Convection and Precipitation/Electrification) Project, it produced this illustration which shows the progression of the sea breeze front, wind flows (arrows), and precipitation (shaded areas) for July 15. The location is Cape Canaveral, and the times are UTC. At 1700Z, the sea breeze begins to move inland, and is depicted as a cold front. By 1800Z (2:00 P.M. local time), the first radar returns become organized, and by 1900Z a gust front from the west closes on a sea breeze from the east. At 2000Z a large group of precipitation echoes begins to move toward the Cape. The storms associated with this coastal pattern typically last one to two hours, and are common along Florida's east coast. (*Thunderstorm Initiation, Organization, and Lifetime Associated with Florida Boundary Layer Convergence Lines, *Wilson and Megenhardt;* Monthly Weather Review, *July 1997, AMS.)*

Research has found that offshore breezes have greater potential for causing turbulence and strong vertical currents than onshore breezes. This is especially true if those offshore breezes pass over streams or lagoons before they head seaward. Such is the case at the Kennedy Space Flight Center. As you might guess by now, the Cape Canaveral area is a prime spot for research on convection and sea breezes.

The Bermuda High, a huge semipermanent dome of high pressure situated more or less all the time off the Florida coast, is another Florida wind-maker. It's the winds spiraling off the southern edge of a strong Bermuda high that give Florida's coasts its easterly winds. Sometimes these winds reach the 30-knot level, prompting some meteorologists to call this phenomenon a "dry Nor'easter"—as opposed to the wet variety found in coastal storms farther north.

Frequent lightning is another Florida characteristic worth mentioning. The area just east of Tampa has the highest frequency of cloud-to-ground lightning strikes in the entire United States. Based on airline studies, most lightning strikes to aircraft occur in cloud, in rain, and at altitudes between 8,000 and 15,000 feet. Outside air temperatures near 0°C seem

Figure 15-3. With an annual average of 130 thunderstorms per year, central Florida can be a trouble spot nearly every afternoon in the summer months. Then, you can count on a thunderstorm somewhere in the region every day. Another way to measure thunderstorm frequency comes via the nation's lightning detection network (the dots at right represent reporting points in this network). This illustration shows the mean annual number of cloud-to-ground lightning strokes, in flashes per square kilometer. (Information used to create this chart came from a lightning flash map printed in Storm Data, *June 1996, NOAA/NWS.)*

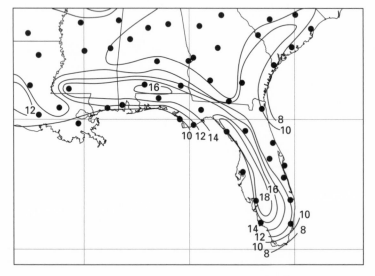

to appear on many lightning strike reports. There's still a lot to be learned about lightning, but one thing we know for sure is that you don't have to be in a cumulonimbus cloud to get hit. Airplanes have, quite literally, been hit by bolts from the blue as they circumnavigated storms by great distances. Which raises the question, 'do airplanes attract lightning?' Answer: maybe. Apollo 13 was hit by lightning as it rose from its launch pad on its ill-fated flight, and research airplanes deliberately flying into thunderstorms have managed to get hit numerous times. But were they hit because they were simply in an area ripe with electrical charges, or did they act as initiating elements?

The Hurricane Season

Let's see, what other Florida weather event are we missing? Oh, yes. Hurricanes. That's a big topic, and one best left treated by tropical meteorologists. Let's just say that Florida—and the entire east coast, for that matter—is susceptible to hurricanes between June and November, and that if they're forecast to come your way, they are good reasons to get in your airplane and head the other way. This is easy to do; since the advent of the Geostationary Operational Environmental Satellite (GOES), ample warning of approaching hurricanes and their likely strike zones has become more and more accurate. Satellite observations, plus the specially-designed hurricane forecast computer models run by the National Hurricane Center in Coral Gables, Florida, have made hurricanes a lot more predictable than they used to be.

I once flew to Antigua in the days before high-rise hotels studded the beaches. It was April, and for the landing at St. John's Airport the winds were out of their customary easterly direction. As per custom, I had no hotel reservations, and criss-crossed the island's central jungle at night, searching for a seaside room. At one hotel, Calaloo Beach, a terrific breeze was blowing; I asked the owner if, in his experience, this meant a hurricane was on the way. He said not to worry, and recited a ditty I still remember: "June, too soon. July, might try. August, don't trust. September, remember. October, all over." Hurricane forecasting has come a long, long way since then.

Customary Conditions, Customary Strategy

The best advice for safe flying in Florida is to depart early enough to beat any building cumulus, and to climb to altitudes high enough to avoid any convection-induced turbulence. That, and following the customary rules to obtain a complete weather briefing and avoid storms by wide margins, will almost guarantee that your Florida flights will be happy ones.

Perhaps the best thing about inflight weather avoidance in Florida is that the state's air mass thunderstorm cells are often so easily avoided visually. If you take off early (say, 7:00 A.M.) and climb to 7,000 feet or more, you will be able to easily spot any building cumulus. Most of the time, you'll find that you can steer clear of them while still flying in the general direction of your destination. Of course, having an instrument rating and filing an instrument flight plan can definitely help here, in case the clouds build all around you and you find yourself with no avenues of escape. Then it's time for a diversion and a landing at a suitable alternate airport, of which there will be many.

VFR But Hairy

Flying in Florida often means that you have to deal with widespread areas covered by cumulus clouds. As long as they remain of the fair-weather variety, there's no problem. If the tops are low enough, and the clouds spaced far enough apart, a good strategy is to simply fly VFR on top. It'll be turbulent beneath cloud base altitude, but smooth above.

With the heat of the day, however, those fair-weather cumulus can take on an attitude, and pose challenges. One thing I've noticed over the years is that if there are towering cumulus or thunderstorms over Florida, the areas offshore are frequently clear of clouds. It works the other way around, too. If there are storms over the ocean, the skies over land are comparatively clear of clouds. When these situations prevail, the choices are clear.

On one trip to Vero Beach, I wove among growing cumulus from Savannah, Georgia to Melbourne, Florida in a Beech A36 Bonanza. It was time to descend for the landing at Vero, but a small storm cell had parked itself about five miles to the northwest of the airport. It contoured well on my airplane's radar, and the Stormscope showed a cluster of dots that confirmed the storm's location. I could even see the storm as I was vectored for the VOR/DME approach to runway 29L. I was in VFR conditions, and smug.

I'd been counting on a well-known assumption about flying around Florida storms: that you can safely circumnavigate them, even if it meant that you skirted them by a close margin. Under this assumption, you could keep a towering cumulus pillar just off your wing tip, and still remain free of turbulence and other nasty storm effects. One well-known radar seminar jokingly refers to this informal rule, saying that you should avoid Florida storms by 1,000 feet, and all other thunderstorms in the United States by an additional 1,000 feet for every mile you're distant from Miami. The first part of the joke is partly true. The second part recognizes the massivity and strong mixing of cold and warm air that takes place in the truly huge storm complexes in the central United States.

Well, the Florida assumption may work aloft—most of the time, anyway, and only when applied to smaller air mass thunderstorms—but don't count on it when you descend to lower altitudes. As I descended down the final approach course to Vero, several strokes of lightning shot down on either side of the approach path. Then there was moderate turbulence. Still, I could see the airport, there was no rain, no apparent strong surface winds, and I was cleared to land. In the distance, the storm revealed itself as a dark smudge over the nearby orange groves.

The first concerns cropped up on short final. I'd obviously flown into a gust front or wind shift line, one pouring out from the nearby storm's low-level outflow. From my perch at 200 feet AGL, the ground seemed to be whizzing past. My ground speed was way too fast for a safe landing.

After declaring a missed approach, ATC cleared me to hold at Eckos intersection, which was well offshore. There, skies were blue and turbulence-free. After holding for a half-hour or so, the storm had subsided and I asked for another shot at the approach. This time everything went well.

It was a good thing I did a go-around and missed approach. Linemen who watched me go by on the first try said *that* approach was timed perfectly. Perfectly, that is, with the passage of a squally gust front with winds as high as 40 knots.

It all goes to show that any thunderstorm, anywhere, deserves a wide berth. With perfect hindsight, I should have held offshore before attempting an approach, and waited for the storm to dissipate or move well away from Vero before descending. That was a day for flying offshore, and waiting out any convective activity. It's a simple rule, but it's tempting to break it when your fuel supply is a factor. And you think that staying visual is a cure-all for flying around thunderstorms.

Accidents

A student pilot flying a Cessna 152 on a solo cross-country training flight took off from Clearwater, Florida, bound for Dunnellon, Florida at 11:18 A.M. on December 2, 1992. IMC prevailed, but a VFR flight plan was filed. The weather was 200 feet overcast, visibility 3½ miles. After taking off, the pilot received radar service until 11:36 A.M., but was tracked on radar until 11:48 A.M., when the flight went out of radar range. The airplane wasn't seen or heard from after that time. The wreckage was found by another airplane at 3:00 P.M. three miles southeast of the Ocala airport. The pilot was killed. On this day, a cold front from the north was advancing toward central Florida, and a weakening stationary front was lying on an east-west line at Florida's southern tip. Jet stream winds were circulating around a trough aloft at 500 millibars.

On February 22, 1994 a private, non-instrument-rated pilot took off at 6:00 P.M. from Savannah, Georgia in a Piper PA-28-161 Warrior. The destination was Tampa, Florida. Night IMC existed along the route, but the pilot filed a VFR flight plan. The pilot asked for flight following 10 miles northeast of Jacksonville, where he was at 8,500 feet. At 7:55 P.M. he asked to descend to 4,500 feet, which ATC approved, telling the pilot to maintain VFR. Radar followed the airplane in a descent to 2,200 feet until contact was lost at 8:03 P.M. A witness fishing on a river near Inverness, Florida saw the airplane descend from the clouds and make a hard right turn at a bank angle of about 45 degrees. The airplane then disappeared below a treeline with its engine running. An increase in engine RPM was heard, followed by the sound of a collision. The pilot was killed in the crash. The ceiling was estimated at 500 feet overcast, and there was little ambient light and no natural horizon other than the treeline, according to the witness. Central Florida was under the influence of a weak cold front across the center of the state, accompanied by strong winds aloft circulating around the southeastern portions of a trough aloft.

A homebuilt Loganair I crashed in night IMC on September 21, 1991 at 5:45 A.M. near Gainesville, killing its pilot and a passenger. The previous day, the pilot declared an emergency, stating that he had lost his gyro instruments. He was given radar service and landed uneventfully at Gainesville. After he landed, the pilot told a lineman about the gyro problem, saying that he would take care of it when he got home. On the day of the accident, the pilot received a weather briefing, identifying himself as the pilot of a Cessna 170, and using that airplane's tail number. VFR was not recommended, but the pilot filed a VFR flight plan to Boynton Beach, Florida. After takeoff, the pilot called ATC, but contact was soon lost. At about the same time, witnesses saw the Loganair making 360-degree turns at 100 feet AGL. It then reportedly pitched up erratically, then descended and hit a tree and then the ground. The engine continued to run until impact. Ceiling was estimated at 600 feet overcast, with a visibility of two miles and light winds. An east–west stationary front lay across central Florida, causing widespread IMC.

The pilot and his five passengers aboard a Piper PA-46 Malibu, north of Ocala, Florida, survived a wild ride after an apparent stall and loss of control resulted in an uncontrolled, high-speed descent from FL180 to 3,000 feet AGL on March 16, 1991. The pilot said he was flying level at FL180 when he saw cumulus buildups five miles ahead. He asked for a climb to FL200 to top them, and clearance was granted. The pilot said he programmed the airplane's autopilot for a 500-FPM climb, but as soon as the autopilot was engaged the airplane pitched up violently. He disconnected the autopilot when he noticed that the airspeed reached zero and the airplane stalled. At that point, the pilot said he noticed the pitch trim wheel trimmed to the full nose-up stop. The airplane entered a spin or spiral, even though the pilot attempted to push forward on the controls. Passing through 15,000 feet, the pilot said "I don't know what's happening...we seem to be diving...we're not getting any airspeed." A TWA pilot broke in on the frequency and said, "Tell that guy to turn on his pitot heat if he hasn't." Another pilot also asked if the Malibu's pitot heat was on. The pilot turned on the pitot heat, then broke out of the clouds into VFR conditions at 3,000 feet. The pilot was given vectors to the Ocala airport and made an uneventful landing. However, numerous rivets in the airframe were loosened, the elevator trim tab was bent, and the airplane lost its right main wheel well door. Thunderstorm activity covered the entire northern half of the state that day, under the influence of STJ activity. This incident was among the Malibu accidents that prompted a certification review of the PA-46 in 1991. Among the recommendations that issued from the review: Install a Pitot Heat On annunciator light.

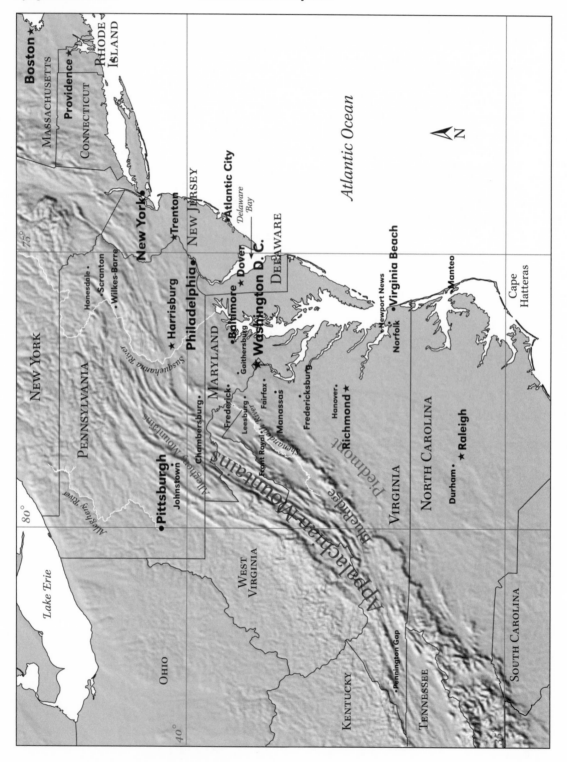

Mid-Atlantic and Pennsylvania
Coastal and Mountain Weather Convergence

Warning signs for the eastern Piedmont and the Keystone State's high country: the Bermuda High, winter snowstorms, beaucoup boomers, plus coastal and mountain effects

All weather is air combat. We've seen that in the previous chapters. Cold air off the North Pacific ocean currents slams into the Cascade, Coastal, and Sierra Nevada ranges in the west. Cold Canadian air drops south, where it rams into the Gulf of Mexico's hot, humid air. Air masses of high and low dew points duke it out over west Texas. A low from the Dakotas tears across Minnesota and Wisconsin, yanking in the refrigerated air over the Great Lakes. Almost daily bombardments of air-mass thunderstorms assault the Florida peninsula in the warmer months. In the Mid-Atlantic states, yet another kind of meteorological warfare takes place.

The list of combatants in this part of the country feature the air masses influenced by the Atlantic Ocean, the area's unique geography, and the upper-level troughs whose axes are so often parked over the eastern half of the United States.

The Atlantic

Whenever you listening to a weather briefing, or trying to parse out a DUAT statement, pay close attention to the movement of the air over the United States' Atlantic coast. If you're planning a flight in the Mid-Atlantic, or over the Appalachian Piedmont country of North Carolina, Virginia, and Maryland, the flow of Atlantic air will play a big part in the weather you might face.

The Gulf Stream—a swath of warm water that flows from Florida to the Canadian maritime provinces—is a conveyor belt, of sorts. The Gulf Stream (and other, similar oceanic circulations) has been compared in effect to the workings of the jet stream. If the jet stream affects weather from the top down, then the Gulf Stream affects weather from the bottom up.

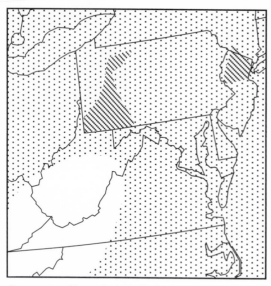

*Percentage of hours in **Spring** when ceiling is below 1,000 feet and visibility is less than 3 miles*

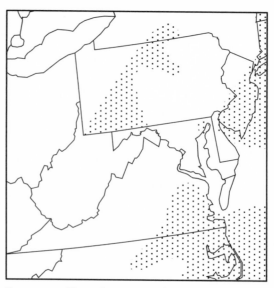

*Percentage of hours in **Summer** when ceiling is below 1,000 feet and visibility is less than 3 miles*

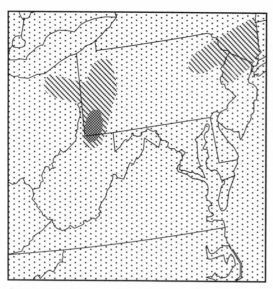

*Percentage of hours in **Autumn** when ceiling is below 1,000 feet and visibility is less than 3 miles*

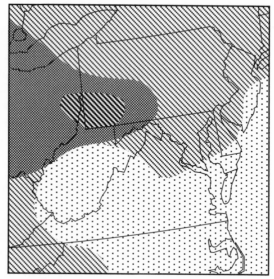

*Percentage of hours in **Winter** when ceiling is below 1,000 feet and visibility is less than 3 miles*

50% or more   **40-49%**   **30-39%**   **20-29%**   **10-19%**   **Less than 9%**

Meteorologists know that the warm Gulf Stream waters just off the North Carolina coast can help intensify any lows or fronts that might be arriving from the west. It does this by adding heat and moisture to the system, causing rising air and condensation.

Cape Hatteras should be on every pilot's briefing checklist. Some experts believe that the concave shape of the North Carolina coast is somehow responsible for the stormy atmospheric circulations so typical of the waters off North Carolina's Outer Banks. These experts point to the concavity of other easterly projections into oceans (Cape Cod, Newfoundland, Greenland,

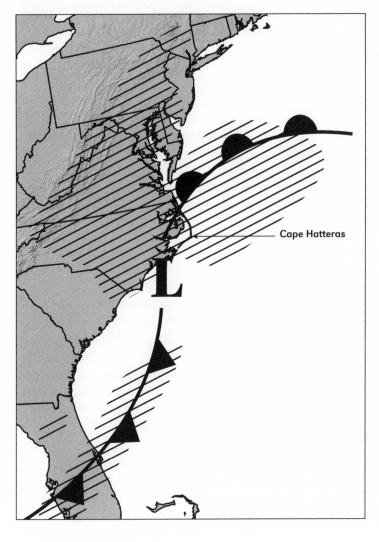

Figure 16-1. Low pressure likes Cape Hatteras. Whether they come from the Appalachians or the Gulf of Mexico, or pop up over the Outer Banks all by themselves, lows and their fronts are a frequent feature of Mid-Atlantic weather. In the winter months, these lows can intensify here, then move up the east coast bringing instrument meteorological conditions in rain, snow, or freezing rain with them.

245

Russia's Kamchatka Peninsula) as other sites known to be conducive to cyclogenesis. It's interesting to note that all these locations are home to warm ocean currents, and semipermanent low pressure. As with so many meteorological theories, however, the exact mechanism at work in these sites is a matter of speculation. Perhaps the release of moist, warm air is energized by an eddy-like process these concavities produce, aggravated by the clashes between air masses of terrestrial and oceanic origin.

Whatever the case, watch Cape Hatteras. If a low is forecast to track that way, expect the weather to deteriorate. If it's already there, study the goings-on over the next 12 to 24 hours to develop a sense of what a Hatteras low can do. At the least, winds out of the easterly quadrants, fog, and MVFR and IFR weather can spread over the eastern halves of North Carolina, Virginia, Maryland, all of Delaware, and perhaps even New Jersey. Worst case: a surface low off Cape Hatteras deepens under the influence of a trough aloft or a strong core of jet stream winds (a.k.a., a "jet streak") and grows to become a Nor'easter—a particularly intense coastal storm. As we'll see later on, Nor'easters often form off Cape Hatteras, then track to the northeast, where they can hit New Jersey and New England with terrific force and a miserable combination of low IFR with high winds.

Mountains and Piedmont

In the chapter dealing with the weather of Utah and Colorado, we looked at how lows often form in the lee of the Rocky Mountains. To briefly recap, some meteorologists think that the spinning actions (vorticity) in the upper atmosphere are enhanced when a low from the west crosses the Rockies. A column of air goes from being compressed over the Rockies to being elongated over the flatter terrain to their east, causing cyclogenesis. This process is called vorticity stretching, which causes the type of counterclockwise circulations that create surface lows.

East of the Appalachians, it seems that vorticity stretching is less of a factor in cyclogenesis than it is in the lee of the Rockies. Perhaps it's because the mountains aren't as high. Most of the lows that strike the Appalachians come fully-formed from the Ohio Valley or deep south, and pass over, and to the east of, the mountains without being significantly transformed. That said, it's important to emphasize that any storm approaching higher terrain will get a boost from orographic lift.

Powerful air mass thunderstorms can form in the complex of ranges that make up the Appalachian chain. According to *Storm Data* (the monthly compilation of unusual weather conditions published by the National Climatic Data Center), strong thunderstorm complexes formed in the southern Appalachians on May 5 and May 24, 1996. The storms of the 24th drifted south, pelting western North Carolina with 1¾-inch hail, downbursts, and 50-knot wind gusts. It was noted that nearly every car dealership in Catawba County had severe hail damage. During the night of the 24th, the storm complexes underwent regeneration along their western flanks, and caused even more hail to fall the following day.

The Piedmont to the east of the Appalachians is a land that starts in the west as hilly uplands interspersed with meandering rivers and lakes, then trails off to flat coastal plains near the Atlantic. The important point here is that any easterly flow will travel upslope as it makes its way inland. And if the flow's from the east, it's an Atlantic-influenced air mass. As the air rises up the terrain, cooling and fog can occur—sometimes covering entire states.

The Piedmont is also prime thunderstorm country. *Storm Data* recorded a whopping 221 mentions of North Carolina hail, lightning, or strong thunderstorm winds for May 1996 alone. On May 11, a 55-knot gust from a thunderstorm over the Raleigh-Durham International Airport ripped off part of the terminal's roof.

More On Thunderstorms

The Bermuda High, a semipermanent air mass centered over the western Atlantic, is a major player in the Mid-Atlantic's many thunderstorms. The mean annual number of thunderstorms in the Mid-Atlantic runs from 70 in southern North Carolina to 40 in Pennsylvania. By "mean," read that half the time the number of storms are above the mean, and half the time the number is below the mean. It's a measure of averaging, and the logic behind this type of storm reporting differs from that used in the *Storm Data* monthly publication. *Storm*

See the Bermuda High illustration in the Appendix on Page 308.

247

Data is a log of total observed storm events; one storm could earn as many as 30 entries in *Storm Data*, depending on its track and severity. Meteorological maps that show mean numbers represent storms or other phenomena (e.g. heat waves, lightning strikes, cold snaps) as individual events, and are used in a climatological context. *Storm Data* is a compendium of the bizarre that records financial and human loss, and is intended for insurance companies, the legal community, federal disaster agencies, meteorological researchers, and weather freaks like you and me. (To obtain a subscription, contact the National Climatic Data Center at 704/271-4800.)

Anyway, that Bermuda High sends a hot, moist, southerly flow over the Mid-Atlantic in the warmer months of the year. Together with heating of the earth's surface, it sends dew points and instability soaring. The air mass thunderstorms that follow can be spectacular. They're even more spectacular if a cold front is shoving them eastward. Often, you can tell if this is about to happen when the wind abruptly picks up from the south. As in the midwest, a strong southerly flow frequently precedes a strong, thunderstorm-laden cold front.

Don't think that the worst storms are in the southern Mid-Atlantic, either. On June 9, 1990, a thunderstorm with 100-MPH winds and 1½ inch hail hit the Leesburg, Virginia airport, destroying two parked airplanes and damaging 10 others after their tiedown ropes broke. On September 6, 1996 a thunderstorm associated with Hurricane Fran snapped trees in the Shenandoah and George Washington National Forests, caused similar damage along the Blue Ridge's Skyline Drive, and ultimately traveled as far east as Fairfax, Virginia, near the Washington–Dulles International Airport. Winds at 2,000 feet were recorded as gusting to 79 MPH.

And let's not forget the 130-knot microburst that struck the Andrews Air Force Base in Maryland on August 1, 1983. What makes this microburst special is that Air Force One, with President Ronald Reagan aboard, landed at Andrews at 2:04 P.M., on a dry runway. Six minutes later, that 130-knot, northwesterly gust on the front side of the microburst hit Andrews. Then the wind speed dropped to two knots (in the eye of the microburst), followed by another peak gust of 84 MPH out of the southeast, as the microburst moved on.

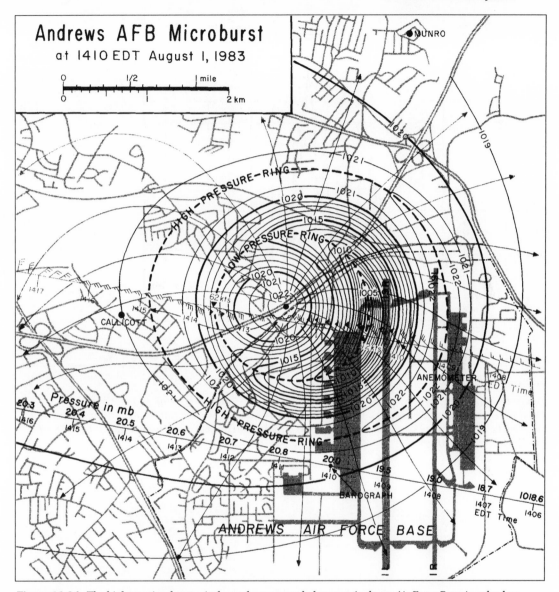

Figure 16-2A. *The highest microburst wind speed ever recorded was at Andrews Air Force Base in suburban Washington, D.C. on August 1, 1983. The scary part was that it hit the airport just six minutes after president Ronald Reagan touched down in Air Force One. Dr. Fujita's illustration shows "wind and pressure fields ... constructed by time-space conversions of wind and barograph traces." On the edge of the microburst's effect at Callicott, tree damage occurred, while not far away at Munro, winds peaked at only 5 to 6 knots.* (Fujita, The Downburst, p. 107)

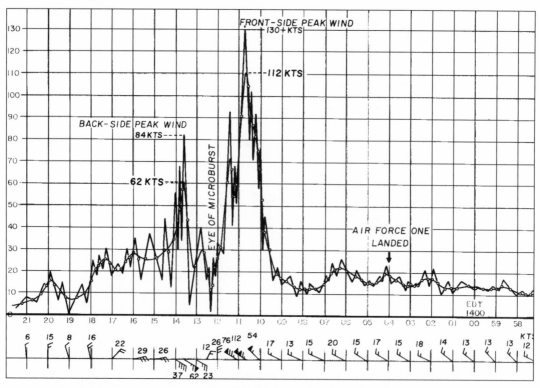

Figure 16-2B. *An anemometer data trace shows the huge spike in wind speed as the Andrews microburst hit. The time sequence runs from right to left, and the wind barbs along the bottom of the trace give another view of the abrupt changes in wind speed and direction. Data revealed that this burst had an "eye" at its center. (Fujita,* The Downburst, *p. 108)*

Troughs and Snowstorms

Any trough aloft is a warning sign of adverse flying weather—especially east of the trough's axis (i.e., an imaginary line extending from the trough's southernmost projection to its most northerly, parent area of low pressure). In the winter months, a trough in the Mid-Atlantic states should make you sit up and take notice. Upper-level lows from the west and south are the major culprits in Mid-Atlantic and Northeastern snowstorms.

Typically, a surface low from the Gulf states, parked under the southeast, trouble-making quadrant of an upper-level trough-with-a-jet streak, will wind up tight once Atlantic moisture is drawn into the storm. The storm tracks to the northeast, along the Atlantic coast. About 200 miles to the north and northwest of the surface low, snow bands form first in the Piedmont, then migrate to the northeast with the storm track. Ultimately, this type of snowstorm hits southern New England before turning out to sea near Newfoundland. According to two of the nation's top winter storm forecasters, Paul J. Kocin and Louis W. Uccellini, it's the troughs with a "negative tilt" (an axis that runs from southeast to northwest) that produce the most intense storms. In their book *Snowstorms Along the Northeastern Coast of the United States: 1955 to 1985,* Kocin and Uccellini found that of the twenty storms they studied, nineteen had negatively-tilted trough axes at the time of the storms' maximum intensity. Any pilot who flies in the Northeast and Mid-Atlantic in the winter months ought to consider buying Kocin and Uccellini's book.[1]

The book also identifies a winter storm type that's unique to the east coast of the United States. The garden-variety of storm—called a Type-A storm, has a single surface low and one central area of low pressure. But it's the Type-B storms that are found so often off the Mid-Atlantic. A Type-B coastal low-pressure setup involves an occluding primary low over the Ohio Valley, and a secondary surface low over the east coast. The secondary low forms along a warm frontal boundary from the primary low. Between the two lows, a wedge of cold air juts down from the north, filling the area between the Atlantic and the Appalachians. Under this concept, the Atlantic air provides the moisture, and the cold air damming up against the mountains chills it enough for snow to fall. And, of course, create widespread severe icing.

[1] Their book is available through the American Meteorological Society, 45 Beacon Street, Boston, Massachusetts 02176.

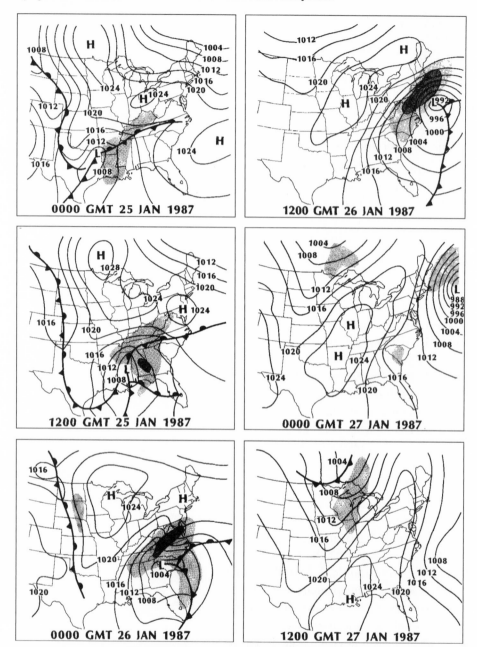

Figure 16-3A. *The surface progression of a northeast snowstorm that meteorologists Kocin and Uccellini call a "Type A" storm. It has a single surface low that began life in Texas, picked up more moisture as it moved along the Gulf coast, then shot up the east coast—all in 36 hours. The low deepened significantly once it reached the Carolina coast. Heaviest snowfalls are in dark shading. (*Snowstorms Along the Northeastern Coast of the United States, 1955 to 1985, *Paul J. Kocin and Louis W. Uccellini; American Meteorological Society, 1990; p. 260)*

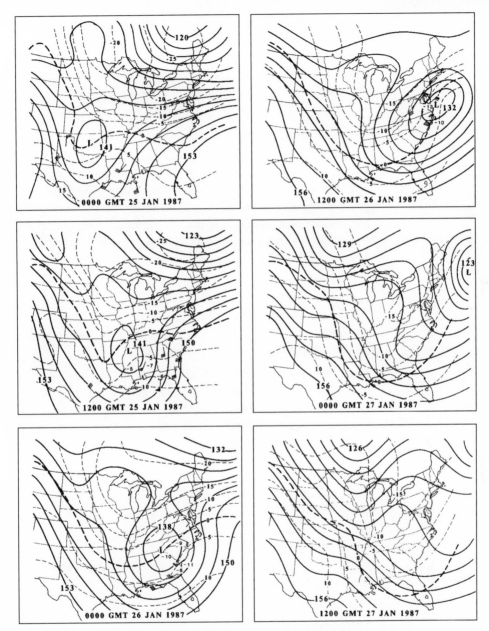

Figure 16-3B. A look at the 850 mb charts for the same period reveals that the surface low pressure center of the January 25-27, 1987 storm always stayed to the east of a cutoff low situated at approximately 5,000 feet MSL. (Kocin and Uccellini, p. 262)

So if there's low-pressure regeneration east of the Appalachians, it's more apt to fit the "Type-B" category than the vorticity-stretching antics in the lee of the Rockies. Then again, who knows? The A and B storm concept types were first advanced in 1946, and some meteorologists doubt its validity.

Cold-Air Damming

For a look at cold-air damming as revealed in a surface analysis chart, *see* Page 227.

There's another phenomenon unique to the weather of the Mid-Atlantic. It happens when conditions are similar to those just discussed. Cold-air damming brings cold air from high-pressure systems in the New England states to as far south as the Carolinas. As it piles up ("dams") against the Appalachians, tenacious, low-lying fogs can settle in for a day or two. It can bring even the scheduled airline operations to a halt.

Cold-air damming in the fall often happens like this: An aging low with an occluded front or trough extending to its northwest, and a cold front lying to the southwest, is west of the Appalachians, or in the Ohio Valley. A warm front extends from it also, in a southeasterly direction.

A big high-pressure system to the north sends the cold air south, and this can be seen on surface analysis charts as isobars drooping southward. To anthropomorphize things a bit, the warm front would like to head north, but the high pressure prevents it. Instead, as the cold front pushes from the west, the warm front buckles southward, and the wedge of dammed air stays in place. The fog caused by the cold, dammed-up air may only top out at 1,000 feet or so, but at the surface, ceilings and visibilities can fall to zero-zero. Rain can also cover the dammed-up zones. If it were winter, then a coastal storm, complete with ice and snow, might have formed along the warm front. But in the early fall or late spring, temperatures are too warm for that.

Thundersnow

I don't know if it was a Type-A or Type-B snowstorm I faced one April day in a Cessna 172RG, but it was an unforgettable experience. I was flying under VFR from Newport News, Virginia to Gaithersburg, Maryland. During the preflight telephone weather briefing, the briefers mentioned a fast-moving line of snow squalls approaching from the west, but said that the weather shouldn't affect the flight. It would arrive after I'd be safely on the ground at Gaithersburg's Montgomery County Airpark. Hah!

Approaching the Brooke VOR near Fredericksburg, Virginia it was evident the storm was moving faster—much faster—than predicted. At my cruising altitude of 4,500 feet, it started to snow. Then the fog snuck in over the ground below—or was it blowing snow? Whatever the cause, visibility started going down.

I tuned in Dulles International Airport's ATIS and heard the bad news: a special observation had the ceiling at 2,000 feet, the visibility at two miles, the barometric pressure falling fast, and strong winds out of the northwest gusting to 30 knots.

A quick call to Washington Center provided me with an IFR clearance to Gaithersburg. The controller handed me off to a Dulles approach controller. It was one of those days where each hand-off was prefaced by yet another update on a crummy situation heading further downhill. Now the ceiling was 1,000 feet, and the visibility was one mile in blowing snow. Next controller, it was 500 and one. The next, 200 and one-half.

It became crystal clear that I wouldn't be able to safely shoot one of Gaithersburg's non-precision approaches. It was also clear that if Dulles' trend held up, the airport would go to Category II—or maybe even III!—weather minimums. And it would happen quickly.

By this time I was near Manassas, about 15 miles south of Dulles. The sky was dark with the weather. Like every other soul in the sky that day, I asked for an ILS approach to one of Dulles' long, wide runways. It would be just what the doctor ordered for the situation I was about to face. The approach frequencies were filled with anxious voices, all of them belonging to pilots fooled by this fast-moving storm.

The heat was on, and the controllers were in a state of high alert. Sooner than I thought, I was vectored for the ILS to runway 1R. I was on instruments, with an ancient Cessna "Nav-Pac II" avionics "suite," no autopilot, in turbulent air, and facing an approach to minimums. What a change from the easy, two-hour VFR trip I was expecting just a few short minutes ago.

When I switched to the tower I was informed that the weather was holding at 200 and one-half, and that the surface winds were occasionally hitting 35 knots. Was ATC lying a little, in hopes of accommodating as many airplanes as he could? It's been known to happen on occasion, but I was hoping this wasn't one of them.

The approach was tense, but the needles stayed in the center. Approaches like these have a way of focusing the mind, and extracting your best performance. Sure enough, I broke out at minimums, with a huge crab angle. There, stretched before me, was a wonderful, well-lit, huge stretch of asphalt. I was more than ready to land.

But it was not to be. An airliner had been breathing down my neck ever since passing the final approach fix. Now the tower felt that we were getting too close. I was told to break off the approach, turn right 90 degrees, climb, and come back around for another try. I should have refused the clearance. After all, the airliner had ice protection, two pilots, and a whole lot more going for them in the avionics department.

On the second approach I noticed that wet snow was now adhering to the Cessna's leading edges. The needles weren't as perfectly centered on this trip down the ILS, but I saw the approach lights before me, and eventually made my way to the threshold. It occurred to me that perhaps the ceiling was slightly lower than 200 feet, and that the visibility was maybe under one-half mile, and that it could be possible that the sky was obscured quite effectively by fog and blowing snow.

Flying the approach was one thing. Taxiing to the ramp was quite another. Four inches of slick, slushy snow covered the airport now. With all that wind, taxiing was a slow, skid-stop-creep forward process. It was a long way to the ramp, and visibility was becoming a real problem. I couldn't see more than 100 feet ahead of me, let alone the tower or other airport landmarks.

Then, over the frequency, the tower said that the airport was closed. I just made it in. I was one of the last to land. Later, after leaving the terminal building, and while stuck in a traffic jam in the ever-worsening conditions, a bolt of lightning hit the ground nearby. Thundersnow, they call it.

Pennsylvania

The land north of the Mason–Dixon line deserves special mention. Pennsylvania's flying lore is rich with hair-raising tales of killer ice, and its many ridges are filled with decades' worth of airplane crashes. In large part, this lore came about because some of the first airlines, flying radial twins, so often flew below 10,000 feet. In other words, they couldn't top the clouds—which were loaded with ice, a lot of it, of the large-droplet kind discussed in the Great Lakes section of this book.

Pennsylvania is prime ice country for two reasons. First, the moist flow off the Great Lakes saturates almost the entire state, causing a semipermanent cloud deck that usually tops out at 7,000 to 8,000 feet in the winter, and about 10,000 feet or higher in the summer months. Those altitudes are for quiet days; when a northeast-southwest cold front (the alignment typical of a Mid-Atlantic cold front) passes through, cloud tops will naturally be higher, and a reading of the area forecasts will reflect this. Area forecasts are one of the few places where aviation meteorologists make cloud top predictions, so they're particularly important to check.

Then there's the lifting forces caused by Pennsylvania's many parallel ridges. Again, even on a docile day cloud streets will form along these ridge lines. Below the clouds, the ride will be turbulent. Above them, it should be smooth. Anywhere along the Appalachians, when a strong westerly air flow crosses mountains, hills, and ridges, the up- and downdrafts of mountain wave activity is common.

Western Pennsylvania, with its broad upland plateau, is a unique piece of climatological real estate. Lake-effect snows are common in the winter, with these snowfalls extending all over the plateau, and beyond. After a vigorous cold frontal passage, these snows can blanket the entire state, and can even surge beyond the Appalachians (the typical eastern boundary of lake-effect phenomena) in Maryland and Virginia.

Even if it doesn't snow in the wake of a frontal passage, the instability created by western Pennsylvania's high terrain often sets up a vast cloud deck over many portions of the state. In them, there'll be icing conditions. Beneath them will be the slate-gray skies, low ceilings, and raw winds so often associated with Pennsylvania in the winter.

For every ridge in Pennsylvania, there's a valley. And almost every valley has a river. That spells fog in the fall, when surface temperatures begin to drop during the ever-shortening days, and any time of year when high pressure creates early morning fog. Look on your sectional charts and you'll find that many airports are located in valleys, which means that places like Pittsburgh, Johnstown, Harrisburg, and Philadelphia can be socked in with IFR in fog any time the above conditions prevail. Meanwhile, the airports on higher ground, such as Wilkes–Barre/Scranton, while not free of clouds, can have higher ceilings and visibilities. Thank the stronger winds of higher elevations for this phenomenon, and the fact that cold air drains down from ridge to valley floor during the cooler parts of the day.

Pennsylvania's weather "bottom line": Instrument weather prevails over the entire state almost fifty percent of the time in the winter. The average is higher than that in the southwestern corner of the state, where the climate is similar to another home of IFR—the northern half of West Virginia's Morgantown-to-Weirton corner, where low clouds and fog tenaciously cling to Appalachian ridges and valleys. The rest of the year is no picnic, either. There's less IMC, but as native pilots know, Pennsylvania's more often a cloudy place than a clear one.

High Enough?

The Minimum Enroute Altitudes (MEAs) across Pennsylvania's mountains generally run between 4,000 and 6,000 feet. A good tactic for crossing these mountains is to climb high enough to hopefully clear any cloud tops, and then make your flight in on-top conditions. This way, you avoid icing in the winter months, and can see well enough to visually circumnavigate thunderstorms in the warmer months of the year. Come to think of it, this strategy works well in practically all areas of the nation.

Of course, your ability to climb "high enough" depends on the airplane you're flying, and the weather you're facing. In a jet, getting on top is usually no trouble. Some modern turbofan-powered airplanes can cruise as high as FL510, where what little weather there may be—the tallest thunderstorms—can be easily avoided. Turboprops are fine for mountain flying, too.

Their maximum operating altitudes are usually no more than 35,000 feet, but this is still high enough to avoid some of the worst weather. Besides, jets and turboprops typically have ice protection equipment as well as radar to help their pilots deal with adverse weather.

It's in non-turbocharged piston-powered airplanes that strategy becomes most important. In order to safely cross the Appalachians or any other mountain chain, you want to fly as high as practical. The chapters dealing with the Rockies should have convinced you of that earlier in the book.

Non-turbocharged piston singles and twins usually have service ceilings in the 14,000- to 17,000-foot range. That may seem high for flatland flying, but over mountains it's a different story. A flight may start out on top, but over the Appalachians those tops can rise and thicken. Have oxygen? Have an airplane that's approved for flight in known-icing conditions? Have plenty of fuel? If so, fine, keep on trucking.

But without these luxuries you run some pretty grave risks in the winter months over Pennsylvania and the rest of the northern Appalachians. Should you run into icing conditions, you may be forced into a descent, culminating in an instrument approach to a remote, valley-fringed airport in foggy and/or snowy conditions. During that descent, you'll be on pins and needles, hoping against hope you don't pick up any more ice. Then come the worries that go with shooting an approach, knowing that a missed approach may not be successful in an ice-impaired airplane.

The rule here should be to make sure clouds are few below your cruising altitude, and temperatures are above freezing. Bottom line: You don't want to pick up ice as you descend.

The strategy works. One late fall afternoon I was flying an A36 Bonanza westward across Pennsylvania. I was at 8,000 feet, and in clouds. The freezing level was at 6,000 feet—the minimum enroute altitude. The first part of the flight—from Frederick, Maryland to Muncie, Indiana—was incident-free. But after I passed the Martinsburg VOR, ice began to form. A slow descent to 6,000 feet resolved the situation, and ice soon began to shed. I stayed at 6,000 feet until reaching the area near Portsmouth, Ohio, where the clouds parted and all was well.

If the freezing level was any lower than 6,000 feet, I would've postponed the trip until conditions were better. That's the only way to fly a nonturbocharged, non-ice-protected piston single or twin around the Appalachians in the colder months. It's those who break this informal rule who risk running into icing problems.

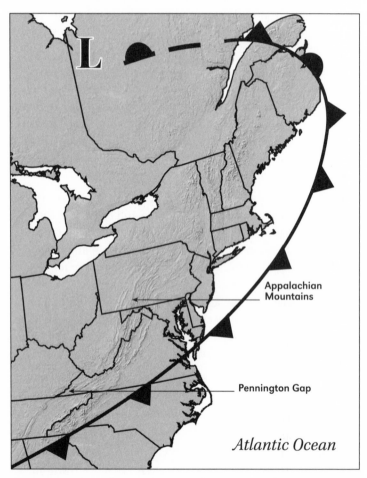

Figure 16-4. *The surface analysis chart for July 24, 1991, when the pilot of a Beech Bonanza crashed after taking off in low IFR conditions in fog. Low-level moisture, supplied by thunderstorms the day before, teamed up with a frontal passage to create low ceilings. A brief discussion of this accident follows on the next page.*

Accidents

The pilot of a V-35 Beech Bonanza and his three passengers were killed on July 24, 1991 after taking off on an IFR flight plan from Pennington Gap, Virginia in the extreme southwest corner of that state. The airplane hit a mountain 2½ miles northwest of the airport at about 9:15 A.M. According to witnesses, the airplane took off into a 200-foot overcast and a visibility of two miles. The published IFR departure procedure calls for climbing visually over the airport to 2,800 feet, then continuing the climb to 5,000 feet while flying direct to the Long Hollow NDB holding pattern before proceeding on course. Departure minimums for this procedure are a 2,800-foot ceiling and a one-mile visibility. A high over the Gulf states sent muggy air north to the Appalachians, the Ohio Valley, and the Mid-Atlantic the previous day, causing afternoon thunderstorms and rainfall. The day of the accident, instrument conditions formed in the valleys around the accident site after a cold frontal passage, with the fog and clouds no doubt intensified by the moisture from the saturated ground from the day before, plus the warm (70°F) early morning temperatures.

On August 8, 1992, at about 11:00 A.M., a Rutan Long-Eze crashed into trees in the Shenandoah National Park near Front Royal, Virginia. Instrument weather prevailed at the time of the crash. The pilot and his single passenger were flying from Hanover, Virginia to Chambersburg, Pennsylvania. A flight plan was not filed, and the airplane apparently never established radio contact with anyone. Park rangers said there were low clouds and fog near the accident site. There was a post-crash fire, and both occupants were killed. Low pressure over Michigan that day trailed a warm front to the southeast. The frontal complex's warm sector drew humid air up the Appalachians, where fog formed, and a band of rain advanced from the Ohio Valley eastward, through West Virginia, Virginia, and Maryland.

Continued

A Piper PA-32-260 Cherokee Six with five persons aboard also crashed into trees and terrain in the Shenandoah National Park, 11 miles southeast of Front Royal, Virginia at around 1:42 P.M. on August 16, 1994. Instrument weather was present, but there was no flight plan for the flight from Manteo, North Carolina to Delaware, Ohio. At a refueling stop in Fredericksburg, Virginia, the pilot reportedly received a weather briefing for the remainder of the flight. A witness at the 2,300-foot level of the 2,900-foot-high mountain said that the airplane was flying low over the mountains, that it was foggy, and that clouds obscured the mountains. She also said she heard what was later determined to have been the sound of the collision. The airplane hit at the 2,700-foot elevation, and the forward section of the fuselage caught fire. All aboard died in the crash. On his last medical certificate application, the pilot listed 220 total hours of flight time. On this day, the synoptic features included an tropical depression coming on shore in the western panhandle of Florida, sending rain northward to the Mid-Atlantic Appalachians, and setting up an east–west stationary front through central North Carolina. On the morning of the crash, IFR ceilings and visibilities—many of them low IFR ceilings and visibilities—were all over the Appalachians and Mid-Atlantic piedmont. The following day, the tropical depression weakened, and transformed into a surface low over southern West Virginia, with a stationary front extending to the east and moderate rainfall covering an area from West Virginia to eastern Pennsylvania.

The pilot of a Piper PA-32-300 Lance ran into strong headwinds over Pennsylvania while on a flight from Bridgeport, Connecticut to Columbus, Ohio on October 16, 1995. VMC prevailed, but the pilot was on an IFR flight plan. Because of the headwinds, the pilot asked for a descent from 8,000 feet—where he was on top of a cloud layer—to 6,000 feet. The request was granted. During the descent into the clouds the airplane's windshield was covered with ice, and the pilot reported there was ice on his pitot tube and wings, saying that he could not maintain altitude. The pilot asked for, and received, vectors to the nearest airport, which was at Honesdale, Pennsylvania. The airplane descended clear of clouds at 4,500 feet, but the pilot still couldn't maintain altitude. At 4:15 P.M., he landed downwind on Honesdale's runway 17, and the right wing hit runway lights during the final turn to the runway. Neither the pilot or his passenger were injured. Conditions at Honesdale at the time were: 6,000 scattered, 8,000 broken, visibility 20, with wind 250 degrees at 14 gusting to 24 knots. High pressure, strong westerly winds, lake-effect moisture, and terrain-induced low-level instability helped create cloud decks all over Pennsylvania that day.

The 4,000-hour pilot and a passenger aboard a Beech F33 Bonanza crashed into mountains near Doylesburg, Pennsylvania around 7:30 P.M. on October 8, 1996. Night instrument conditions prevailed along the route of flight, which began in Pittsburgh, Pennsylvania and was to have ended with a landing at Harrisburg. No flight plan was filed, although the pilot did receive a preflight weather briefing. During the briefing, the flight service specialist advised the pilot of a SIGMET for occasional moderate to severe turbulence below 12,000 feet. The pilot said "we're certainly not going to get up in anything. We'll be staying low." Asking if there was anything precluding VFR flight, the briefer advised that VFR flight was not recommended because of the many low clouds across the ridges, and said that there would be low ceilings obscuring mountainous terrain along the route of flight. Residents near the crash site said it was rainy and foggy the night of the accident. The airplane hit a mountain at the 2,000-foot elevation. The weather of October 8 involved a coastal low off the North Carolina–South Carolina shore. The low began as tropical storm Josephine in the Gulf of Mexico the previous day; during the night, the storm weakened as it crossed the southeast states. To the north of the low, rain and IFR ceilings stretched from the Carolinas to eastern Pennsylvania. There was heavy rainfall in North Carolina and Virginia. The easterly flow off the Atlantic sent moist, unstable clouds all the way into the Pennsylvania interior, as well.

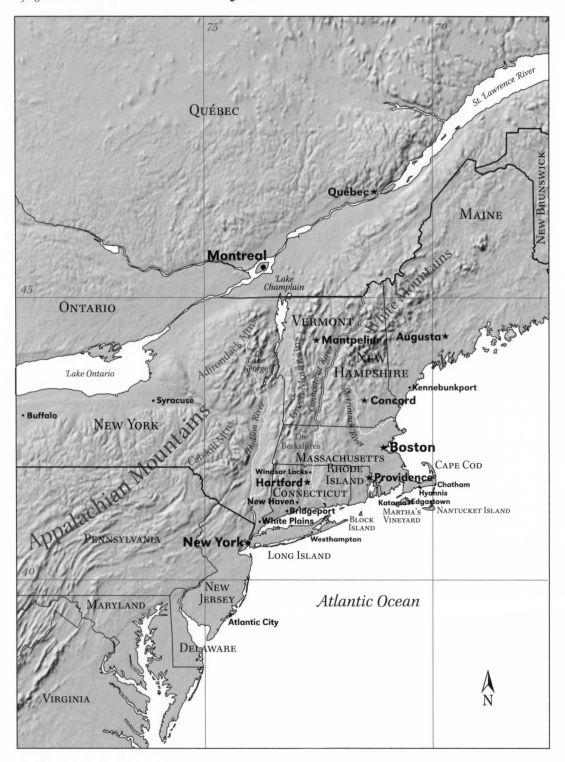

75°   70°

QUÉBEC

St. Lawrence River

Québec ★

MAINE

NEW BRUNSWICK

Montreal

Lake Champlain

45°

ONTARIO

Lake Ontario

Adirondack Mtns.

Lake George

VERMONT

★ **Montpelier**

White Mountains

★ **Augusta**

NEW HAMPSHIRE

Green Mountains

Connecticut River

Merrimack River

• **Kennebunkport**

• **Syracuse**

• **Buffalo**

NEW YORK

Catskill Mtns.

★ **Concord**

Hudson River

The Berkshires

★ **Boston**

MASSACHUSETTS

CAPE COD

Appalachian Mountains

Windsor Locks •

RHODE ISLAND

★ **Providence**

• **Chatham**

Hartford ★

★

• **Hyannis**

CONNECTICUT

Katama • Edgartown

New Haven •

MARTHA'S VINEYARD

NANTUCKET ISLAND

• **Bridgeport**

PENNSYLVANIA

• **White Plains**

BLOCK ISLAND

New York ★

Westhampton

LONG ISLAND

40°

NEW JERSEY

Atlantic Ocean

MARYLAND

• **Atlantic City**

DELAWARE

VIRGINIA

N

New England
Nor'Easters and More

Where the weather changes three times a week—guaranteed.

In the Northeastern states, "normal" weather simply doesn't exist. "If you don't like the weather, just wait for ten minutes and it's bound to change." This hackneyed old saw is tossed about in all parts of the United States, but there are few locations where this saying carries more validity than in New England.

I lived in New England off and on over the years, and like most Americans I had picture-postcard expectations of the weather. Summers would consist of mild, dry days, and refreshingly cool nights. In the fall months, severe clear would prevail, giving me unlimited views of New England's beautiful autumn colors. Winters would be equally picturesque, with just ornamental amounts of snow.

But I'm a pilot, not a tourist, and the awful truth about New England weather soon became evident. Here, it seems to rain all the time. It's always turbulent at lower altitudes over the Green Mountains of Vermont, the White Mountains of New Hampshire, and the Berkshires of Massachusetts. All up and down the Connecticut, Merrimack, Hudson, and any other river valley, lake, pond, kettle hole, low stretch of ground or even back yard, morning ground fog is more the rule than the exception. Cape Cod, Nantucket, Martha's Vineyard, Block Island, and just about every other place offshore is also prime fog country. We're talking dense fog, the kind that routinely cuts surface visibilities to one-quarter-mile or lower.

Winters can be extremely hazardous, with the special brand of wet snow, freezing rain, and "Nor'easters" that frequent this area on a regular basis. The freezing rains seem to plague southern New England—from Massachusetts south—with regularity. In addition, there is a semipermanent, lake-effect

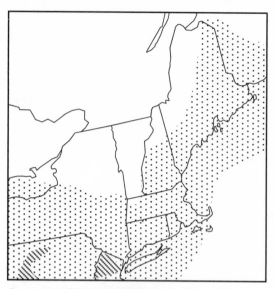

Percentage of hours in **Spring** *when ceiling is below 1,000 feet and visibility is less than 3 miles*

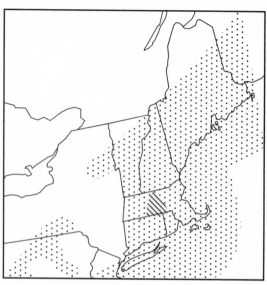

Percentage of hours in **Summer** *when ceiling is below 1,000 feet and visibility is less than 3 miles*

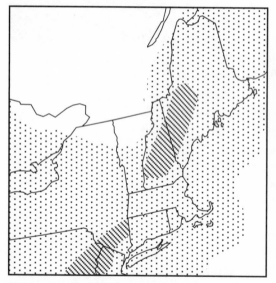

Percentage of hours in **Autumn** *when ceiling is below 1,000 feet and visibility is less than 3 miles*

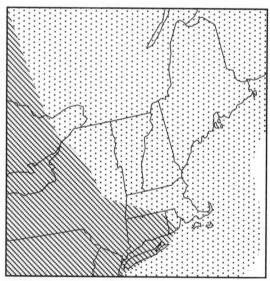

Percentage of hours in **Winter** *when ceiling is below 1,000 feet and visibility is less than 3 miles*

50% or more　**40-49%**　**30-39%**　**20-29%**　**10-19%**　**Less than 9%**

snowfall east of New York's massive Lake Champlain and
Lake George.

In the spring, IFR (ceiling 1,000 feet or less, visibility at or
below 3 miles) prevails one-third of the time throughout most
of New England. This frequency drops to about fifteen percent
of the time in the summer (except for central Massachusetts,
where the one-third figure still holds), then rises again in the
fall, when the airports near New Hampshire's White Mountains
and central Maine have IFR weather almost fifty percent of
the time.

Take away the icing hazards—and the occasional
Nor'easter—and winter might provide New England's best
flying weather. Then, IFR weather holds sway for somewhat less
than ten percent of the time. Except for western Connecticut,
that is, where statistics show instrument ceilings and visibilities
occur about thirty percent of the time in the winter months.

Please bear in mind that these figures are generalizations.
Climatologists, who pride themselves on associating weather
trends with seasonal and monthly patterns, find New England
weather especially puzzling because of its unpredictability. For
example, Connecticut's "normal" precipitation total for August
is four inches; this is based on averages accumulated over a
thirty-year period. However, in 1990 Connecticut had over
eight inches of rain in August. This kind of departure from
"normal" weather is, in itself, a permanent feature of New
England weather. No one month or season is ever the same
from year to year. For that matter, daily weather hardly ever
stays the same—hence the ten-minute rule mentioned earlier.
Actually, ten-minute weather variations do stretch the truth a
mite. However, it's a documented fact that measurable precipitation occurs—on average—once every three days, somewhere
in New England.

What is it about New England that makes its weather so
fickle? First of all, many different geographic features are
packed closely together. As is the case in California, vast
stretches of ocean shoreline are not far from mountainous
terrain. But unlike California, New England is at a much
higher latitude. The cold, polar winds and high pressure air
masses of Canada blow out of their customary northwesterly
direction all year round, save for a few weeks in late summer
when a strong Bermuda high may shunt them northward,

toward Newfoundland, Greenland, and eventually the cold waters of the North Atlantic.

But most of the time, these Arctic blasts make straight for New England, preceded by cold fronts and unimpeded by the flattest, oldest, most glaciated terrain in North America. Unimpeded, that is, until these Canadian fronts run into New England's major geographic features: the northern reaches of the Appalachian Mountains, and the ocean surrounding its southern and eastern flanks.

The first effects on flying weather occur as a result of this air's traveling over New England's high terrain. Turbulence and orographically-induced rain- and snowshowers are common, as well as thunderstorms and upslope fogs that produce mountain obscurations. As Canadian air moves farther east and south, conditions are perfect for the intensification of frontal weather, and we'll learn why very shortly. It's not at all uncommon to find fronts stretched across most of southern New England many, many times during any given season.

It's the movements of this semipermanent front that can give forecasters fits. As continental and maritime air masses are propelled north and south—or stagnate into occluded or stationary conditions—weather conditions can rapidly fluctuate over very short distances.

Sometimes, Nor'easters are byproducts of this frontal battleground. Lows frequently develop along a front off the New England shore, then quickly deepen. Along with their maturity come strong winds and heavy precipitation. Because of the counterclockwise flow of air around a low, onshore winds out of the northeast ("Nor'east") can bring copious amounts of rain or snow, depending on the season.

Most of the time, however, Nor'easters come from the south. This may sound odd, but it's the truth nonetheless. In low-pressure systems forming off the North Carolina coast are where most Nor'easters originate. The area off Cape Hatteras is a place that might as well be named "the birthplace of Nor'easters." So anyone planning to fly in New England would be wise to pay attention to the conditions off North Carolina's Outer Banks. If an organized low forms there, it will probably make a beeline for Long Island, bringing fronts, IMC, and high winds with it. If it doesn't head for Long Island, then chances are it will track more to the east, for example, Cape Cod. It all depends on the steering currents of the jet stream that helped create the Nor'easter in the first place, and the location of the warmest zones of Gulf Stream water, which help close the feedback loop that bring about Nor'easters (which we'll talk about later in this chapter).

As long as we're on the subject of lows, it seems only fair to mention that New England attracts its share of hurricanes. Recent seasons have been kind, but in the past several very destructive hurricanes have visited New England between June and October.

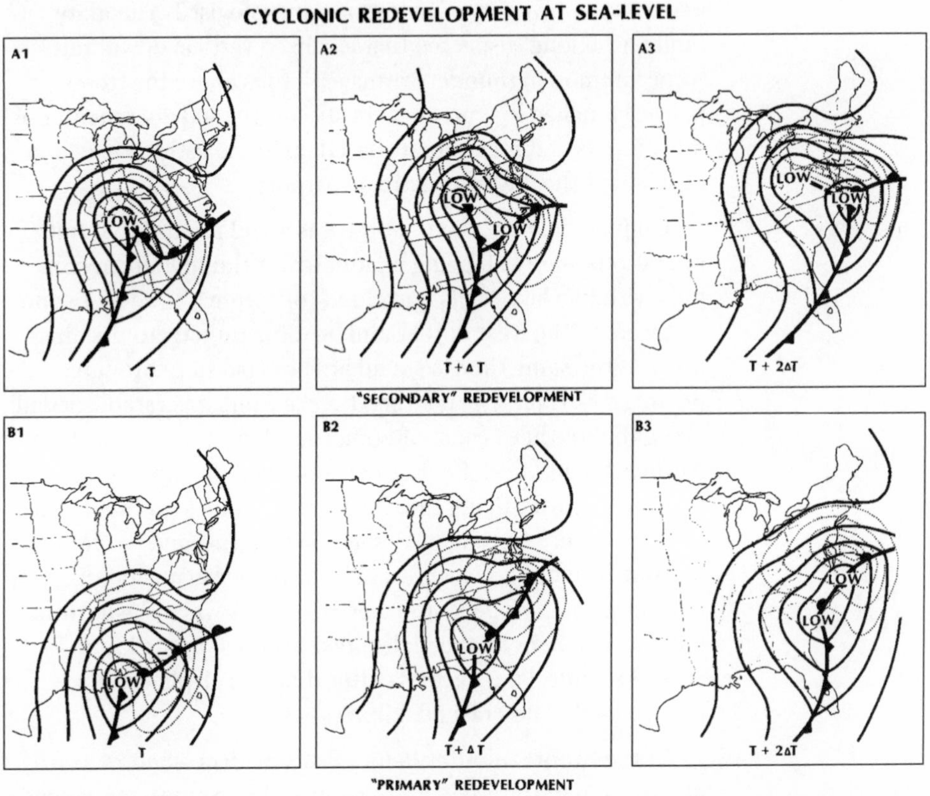

CYCLONIC REDEVELOPMENT AT SEA-LEVEL

Figure 17-1. Northeast snowstorms can redevelop from parent lows by one of two methods. In secondary redevelopment (top row, left to right) we have an Ohio Valley low that yields a second low over Cape Hatteras. The Hatteras low then dominates, while the originating low dies out—a phenomenon called "center jumping." With primary redevelopment (bottom row, left to right), any additional lows form in close conjunction with the parent low, which in this case forms on the Gulf coast and generates a second surface low south of New England. Notice how, in both cases, Cape Hatteras is a prime location for storm intensification. (Kocin and Uccellini, p. 25)

Several weather progressions seem to be commonplace in New England. In the summer months, air mass thunderstorms love to breed in—or aim for—the Berkshires, then move east in lines that run north and south. Anyone planning to fly in the summer months should always check the stations in this vicinity or Albany, New York for any early signs of convective activity.

The JFK Downburst and Eastern 66

Though we think of the midwest as prime convective territory, don't ever forget that New England has its share of violent thunderstorms. University of Chicago meteorologist T. Theodore Fujita, who long suspected that localized vertical downdrafts were common in thunderstorms with tops above the tropopause, launched his career as the discoverer and documenter of downbursts and microbursts based on his investigation of a 1975 accident at the JFK International Airport.

On June 24, 1975, the weather was awful around JFK, but operations were still being conducted. A thunderstorm complex with two large cells and cloud tops from 35,000 to 49,000 feet were to the west of JFK, and heading directly to the airport. At the same time, a squall line was passing through northern New Jersey, and a sea-breeze front was established all along the southern coast of Long Island. At 4:05 P.M. Eastern Airlines Flight 66—a Boeing 727—crashed on approach to runway 22L after flying into heavy rain and a downburst. The airplane entered a rainshower at 700 feet AGL, and the rain became heavy at 500 feet AGL. The airplane began sinking below the glide slope at 400 feet AGL, that's when the bottom fell out. The 727's airspeed dropped from 138 to 122 knots in seven seconds. Four seconds after that, the airplane hit approach lights and crashed, killing 113.

In the twenty minutes before Eastern 66 crashed, eleven airplanes made approaches to runway 22L. Some experienced wind shear, some didn't. A Flying Tigers DC-8 encountered strong, sustained downflow from 700 to 200 feet AGL, and the pilot reported having to apply an abnormally high amount of power for an unusually long period of time. From 200 feet to touchdown, the DC-8 was in a moderate downflow, but had a strong right crosswind. Just above the ground, wind velocities were 50 to 55 knots. Once the aircraft was on the runway, however, there was practically no wind.

Next in line was Eastern 902, an L-1011. It flew into a heavy rain shaft, and its airspeed dropped from 144 to 121 knots. Power was applied to pull up, and a missed approach was initiated. The L-1011 kept on sinking to 60 feet AGL before the pilot was able to arrest the descent using "considerable" power and raising the nose to an "abnormally high" pitch attitude, according to Fujita's interviews. After the missed approach, Eastern 902 landed at the Newark, New Jersey airport.

Then came a Finnair DC-8. Fujita's notes say the pilot reported, "Rain was heaviest between six and three miles final. The **INS** wind at 1,500 feet was 230 degrees at 30 knots. At about two miles final, the aircraft lost 25 knots IAS. The subsequent approach and landing were normal."

A Beech Baron was next in line. It "encountered light turbulence and moderate to heavy rain from just outside the outer marker down halfway to the middle marker. The approach continued normally until about 200 to 300 feet, where a heavy sink rate was experienced."[1] The airspeed dropped about 20 knots, the pilot applied power to recover from the sink, and the remainder of the approach was normal.

Then came Eastern 66. Why did that airplane crash, while the others were spared the worst wind shear? Fujita theorized that there were three downburst cells near the approach end of runway 22L, each of them affecting an area less than three miles in diameter. In between them were areas of calm winds. Fujita went on to examine dozens of other downburst- and microburst-related accidents, all of them landmark studies that revolutionized aviation meteorology and quickly brought about pilot training programs designed to avoid and escape severe downbursts and microbursts. (A downburst is defined as a vertical current with downward velocities exceeding 720 feet per minute, and affecting a surface area greater than 2½ miles in diameter, and that lasts anywhere from five to thirty minutes. A microburst is a downburst with a diameter of less than 2½ miles.)

What causes downbursts and microbursts? Fujita believes that when a well-developed cumulonimbus cloud penetrates the tropopause, the cold, dense air of the cloud top collapses and sinks, sending intense columns of air down through either the parent storm cell or the areas on the periphery of the storm complex. Although the downburst or microburst can occur

INS. Inertial Navigation System, a navigation aid that computes an aircraft's position by formulas using the measured acceleration and flight vectors of an airborne gyro-stabilized platform.

[1] Quoted from Fujita, *The Downburst*, page 37.

271

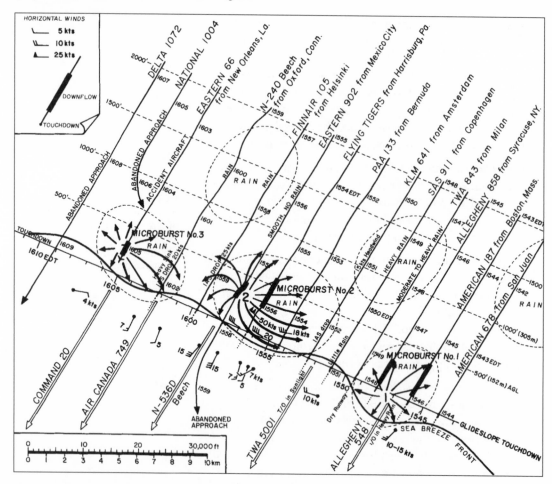

Figure 17-2A. *Many airplanes landed safely on JFK's runway 22L on the afternoon of June 24, 1975 as shown on Dr. Fujita's flight path vs. flight time graph. Between 3:44 P.M. and 4:10 P.M., 14 airplanes landed on that runway in highly localized, variable-intensity microburst conditions. Only two airplanes experienced difficulties. Eastern Flight 902, a Lockheed L-1011, flew into Microburst No. 2 and its captain performed a missed approach. Seven minutes later, Eastern 66 hit Microburst No. 3 and crashed short of the runway. (Fujita,* The Downburst, *p. 38)*

without the presence of rain, rain shafts can and do mark downbursts and microbursts in wetter climates. (The so-called "dry" microbursts are common to the high-cloud-base thunderstorms of the western United States, where drier air masses can prevent rain from reaching the ground, causing virga—itself another warning sign of downburst activity. *See* the Colorado and the Rockies chapter, Page 79.)

So it wasn't a tornado-spewing, mammoth mesoscale convective complex from the Midwest that gave birth to the downburst and microburst theories we now know so well. It was a storm in New England.

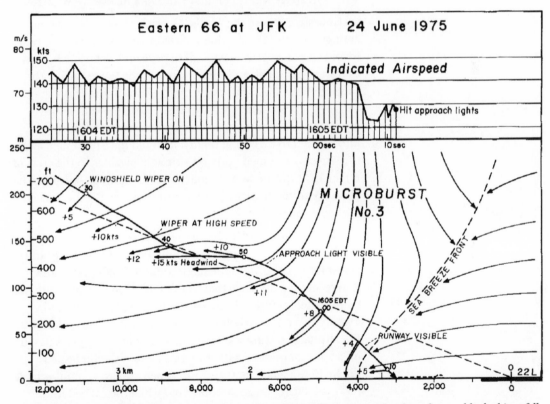

Figure 17-2B. Airspeed and flight path data from Eastern 66's flight data recorder shows how suddenly things fell apart. Fujita believed that interaction with a sea breeze front may have given Microburst No. 3 especially strong downdrafts. That, and the fact that the airplane flew right into the center of the strongest winds. A Flying Tigers DC-8, on the other hand, flew near the eastern edge of a preceding microburst (see Figure 17-2A), and evaded the worst winds. (Fujita, The Downburst, p. 39)

Pressure Drop

Need more proof that New England can be a convective nightmare? Then consider the fate of American Airlines Flight 1572, an MD-80 that crashed on Windsor Locks, Connecticut's Bradley International Airport after hitting trees on Metacomet Hill, a stretch of high terrain along the VOR runway 15 approach path to Bradley.

That crashed happened at 12:55 A.M. on November 12, 1995—a day that featured a very deep surface low over Quebec with an occluded front extending across eastern New York state. There were strong southerly winds ahead of the front, strong westerly winds behind it, and rain all over New England.

How strong were the winds? Gusting to 43 knots. Strong enough to cause the windows of the Bradley tower cab to bow in and leak rain. Strong enough to pose and electrical hazard to tower personnel, and therefore close the tower during the time of Flight 1572's approach. At the time of the crash the tower supervisor was the only person in the tower. He was monitoring repairs, as well as providing wind and runway information to incoming flights. It would have been nice had the supervisor issued updated altimeter settings to the crew of Flight 1572, but he wasn't required to. Technically speaking, he wasn't required to provide information to any flights—because the tower was officially closed.

The crew was well aware of the forecast conditions for Bradley that night—strong winds, moderate turbulence, and possible low-level wind shear. En route to Bradley, the crew also received a message that Bradley's barometric pressure was falling rapidly (PRESFR, to use meteorological shorthand). Twenty-five minutes before the crash, the crew was told that the altimeter setting was 29.42 in. Hg. That setting was based on a 29-minute-old weather report. Boston Center issued Flight 1572 a 29.40 in. Hg altimeter setting three minutes later, but that setting was 22 minutes old when the MD-80 hit the trees. The NTSB accident report concluded that, since the crew knew the pressure was falling rapidly, it should have requested an updated altimeter setting from the Bradley approach controller upon initial radio contact. (The controller is supposed to provide this information as a routine matter, but didn't on this particular occasion.)

The correct altimeter setting was 29.38 in. Hg, and the NTSB figured that if the crew had set this in their altimeters the airplane would have been 40 feet higher than it was when it hit the trees. They would have cleared the trees on Metacomet Hill—not by much, but they would have cleared them.

Complicating all this is American Airlines' practice of using two altimeter settings for instrument approaches—one, set to QNH (station pressure), and another, set to QFE (an adjusted setting designed to show the airplane's height above the airport surface). Below 10,000 feet, American crews are told to switch their primary altimeter settings from QNH to QFE. But the QFE the crew used (29.23) was incorrect, because it was based on old information. The correct QFE at the time of the accident was "about 29.15 in. Hg," according to the NTSB.

This meant that the airplane's QFE altimeter was about 76 feet too high (based on the 29-minute-old setting), and resulted in the airplane being 76 feet lower than indicated.

When they were receiving vectors for the approach, controllers stated that the surface winds were "170 at 29, gusts 39." The captain turned on the radar briefly, saw no convective activity, and turned the radar off. The descent and approach were flown using the autopilot. The captain selected the VOR/LOC mode for the autopilot, but when the autopilot attempted to apply a 30-degree wind correction angle to the airplane's heading to stay on the approach course, the autopilot couldn't hack it. The airplane drifted left of course. At this point, the pilot selected the HDG SEL (heading select) mode, so that he could use the heading indicator's heading bug to compensate for crosswind effects.

A descent to 2,000 feet, to cross the final approach fix inbound, was then made using the autopilot's vertical speed mode for pitch control. During the descent, moderate turbulence and heavy rain were encountered. After passing the final approach fix, the captain asked the first officer to select a 1,000-FPM descent rate to the MDA (minimum descent altitude)—again, using the autopilot's vertical speed mode.

The tower supervisor provided the crew with wind shear alerts, and the first officer then noticed that he had ground contact. The airplane was at the base of the clouds. The first officer looked back at his altimeter, and then noticed that the airplane had sunk below the MDA, saying to the captain, "you're going below your…" (the captain stated that the first officer called out "100 below"), at which point the captain punched the autopilot's altitude hold button.

The cockpit voice recorder (CVR) then sounded the "sink rate" warning, and four seconds later the airplane hit the first trees. Severe turbulence then rocked the airplane, the captain called for a go-around, "firewalled the throttles," and the on-board wind shear and ground proximity warning system sounded. After "a second or two," according to the captain, the turbulence stopped. But now there was a new problem. "Left motor's failed," the captain said to the first officer.

The airspeed began to decrease, and the airplane began descending. The right engine wasn't developing full thrust. The rain stopped, however, and the first officer saw the runway ahead.

"Tell 'em we're going down," the captain told the first officer. The first officer made the radio call. Then he thought twice, saying "you're going to make it" to the captain. He then asked if the captain wanted the landing gear down. He did, and the gear were lowered.

The next move was a call for the flaps to be lowered to the 40-degree position—to achieve a ballooning effect to gain some altitude and hopefully reach the runway. The airplane clipped the top of a tree near the end of the runway, then crashed into an ILS antenna array, landed on the edge of another runway's stopway, continued down runway 15, and came to a stop. The drama was over. Of the 78 persons aboard, only one sustained injuries—and they were minor.

Both engines had tree branches and sticks in their inlets, and the left engine had damage to its low-pressure compressor and other turbine components. The right engine also had damage to its compressor stages.

The NTSB ruled that the probable cause of the accident was the crew's dropping below MDA. Contributing factors were: (1) the failure of the Bradley controller to furnish the flight crew with a current altimeter setting; and (2) the flight crew's failure to ask for a more current setting.

Hitting the Beach

Anyone visiting New England will feel the urge to fly to Cape Cod, Martha's Vineyard, or Block Island. If you do, be ready for a fog encounter—hopefully timed so that it occurs when you're safely on the ground, or at your rented cottage. Almost every time I've made a summer trip out there, sea fogs have been factors. And each time that it has, sea breeze influences have been at the heart of some of the densest and fastest-forming fogs I've ever observed.

Let the temperature off the Atlantic shoreline drop just a few degrees, and the air nearly always reaches its dew point, creating fog. Once fog forms offshore, it tends to move landward as a result of sea breeze effects. Coastal land masses that have been heating up all day release their heat into the atmosphere as the sun sets. Colder air from the ocean then breezes in to replace it, causing routine dense fog as temperatures drop to dew point. Though the chances of a fog encounter are greatest near coastal areas, sea breezes can bring oceanic fogs as far inland as New England's mountains, where its movement is blocked. Some experts have attempted to associate the densest coastal fogs with the times of high tide.

Sea fogs work the other way around. Mainly a winter problem, these fogs happen when cold air moves over the comparatively warmer sea surface—warmer because of the warmth of the Gulf Stream currents that snake their way up from Floridian latitudes, past North Carolina's Outer Banks, and on up toward Newfoundland's Grand Banks, Iceland, and ultimately, Ireland. The cold air lowers the air temperature just above the sea surface to its dew point, and a shallow, widespread fog forms.

Maritime fogs often catch vacationing pilots unaware. Early in the day, conditions all across New England may be VFR. But by late afternoon, places like Nantucket and Martha's Vineyard can be socked in with low IFR ceilings and visibilities. One time, I flew to the Katama Shores airport on Martha's Vineyard, a great little grass strip within walking distance of the beach. Things were sunny and clear until about 4:00 P.M., when a fog bank appeared about one-half mile off shore. Within an hour the fog rolled in, the ceiling went to 300 feet AGL, and the visibility plunged to one-eighth of a mile. I spent the night in Edgartown, and flew out the next morning—after the fog burned off. Now, after learning that Nantucket and Martha's Vineyard experience—on average—dense fog one out of every four days, I know better than to count on a late afternoon or early morning departure under VFR.

Truth to tell, the area around Cape Cod, Nantucket, Martha's Vineyard, and Block Island average nearly 100 fog days per year. But that's what you should expect from the North Atlantic at these latitudes. Anyone planning to visit these areas should have an instrument rating, and the recency of experience to back it up. The FAA recognizes the uniqueness of this region, and provides a toll-free PATWAS telephone number that reports solely on Cape and island weather.

Fogs over the Cape and the coastal islands are seldom very deep. Most times, you can break out on top at 1,000 to 3,000 feet. After flying inland for 30 miles or so, it's very typical for the undercast to vanish completely, leaving the remainder of a north- or westbound flight in visual meteorological conditions. That's fine for instrument departures. But if you're facing a fog-shrouded approach into a New England airport dominated by an oceanic fog, expect a descent on instruments all the way to decision height—and be spring-loaded for a missed approach.

Northeast Snowstorms

Lows love southern Canada, and depending on their location and direction of travel, New England can suffer as a result. If a Canadian low tracks to the central United States, New England will usually be in the warm sector of a frontal complex. That means southerly winds, and oceanic fogs inland. If a low passes to the north, through Quebec, then it's the showery precipitation, convection and turbulence of a strong cold frontal passage—especially if the cold front is aligned north–south.

What about winter, you say? Once again, the Atlantic plays a big factor. Oceans and other large bodies of water exert a moderating influence on temperatures. They are slow to heat up, and slow to lose any heat they may have accumulated—whether over the course of a day, weeks and months. This means that in the summer months, ocean temperatures are cooler than those over land; in winter, the reverse is true.

With warmer waters offshore and a stationary or occluded front inland, the environment is ideal for drenching wet, warm air masses to feed northward to the frontal boundary. In the winter, this kind of warm frontal behavior causes freezing rain, severe icing conditions and, of course, low IFR ceilings and visibilities. Precipitation falling from warmer air aloft turns into freezing rain as it drops through the lower layers of a cold frontal boundary. Often, this freezing rain can be highly localized in New England's many valleys—precisely where so many airports are situated. Here the problem is cold air sinking, draining downslope, and filling in the valleys—when rain falling from an inversion or warm front passes through these pockets of colder air, it can produce clear icing due to freezing rain.

Farther away from the coast, adverse winter weather is usually influenced more heavily by Canadian air masses. While warm front icing can be a serious threat whenever low-pressure centers move toward northern New England, so-called "back door" cold fronts must also be reckoned with on occasion. "Back door" cold fronts descend from the north and move southward, over New England, and can travel as far south as the Carolinas if the high pressure behind it is strong enough. Since cold fronts typically travel from west to east, and are aligned northeast-southwest, these fronts are meteorological oddballs —hence the "back door" moniker. When these fronts come in the back door, they often bring strong turbulence and snow squalls in the winter months, and convection in the warmer times of the year.

Freezing rain, pea-soup fogs, routine precipitation, and constant frontal warfare between Canadian and North Atlantic air masses—that's why New England's weather is so changeable. It's a place where an instrument rating can really get a workout on short notice, and where good weather interpretation skills, a knowledge of local conditions, and good judgment are necessary items on any preflight checklist.

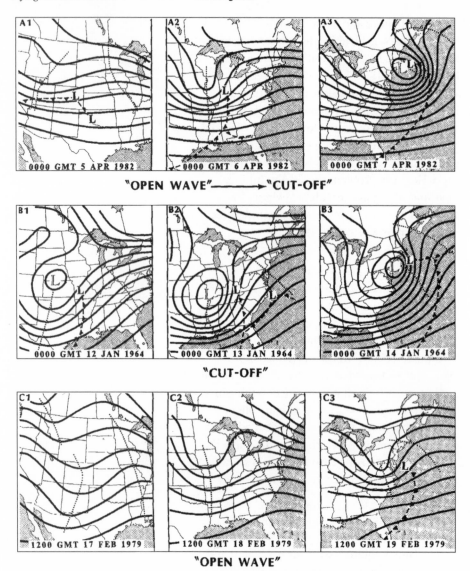

"OPEN WAVE"——————▶"CUT-OFF"

"CUT-OFF"

"OPEN WAVE"

Figure 17-3. *To scope out the chances of a snowstorm in the Mid-Atlantic or Northeast, look to the 500-millibar charts for the patterns shown above. The top sequence shows the progression of height contours from an open wave shape to a cut-off low. Middle charts show how a cutoff low can move from west to east. Bottom charts indicate an open wave pattern persisting through the eastern United States. Locations of surface lows and fronts are plotted to the east of these troughs aloft. (Kocin and Uccellini, p. 47)*

Nor'Easters—Not as Quaint as They Sound

Hurricanes often visit New England, causing plenty of damage and even temporarily closing airports; but back in 1991, the most destructive Atlantic storm of the year wasn't a hurricane at all. It was a northeaster—it was the storm popularized by the 1997 book, *The Perfect Storm* by Sebastian Junger.

What's a northeaster or, in native jargon, "nor'easter"? In very broad terms, it has come to mean any substantial force of wind out of a northeasterly direction. Because northeasters are usually considered indigenous to Atlantic coastal areas, heavy precipitation usually accompanies the wind. Depending on the temperature, this precipitation can come in the form of rain, snow, freezing rain, or a combination of all three.

But in the classic, stricter sense, a northeaster is defined as a well-developed low pressure system that meteorologists call an extratropical cyclone. That is, a storm that originates or migrates well away from equatorial regions. While northeasters can occur at any time of year, they tend to form in the winter months and off the North Atlantic coast, anywhere from Cape Hatteras, North Carolina, to Maine.

Most often, a northeaster begins when an offshore surface low deepens, then backs into coastal areas. A trough aloft is usually present, which helps deepen the low, intensify the storm's counterclockwise circulation, and steer it westward. Typically, a zone of high pressure, or a front, is present over the eastern United States. When the northeaster's low pressure collides with such a high or front, a very steep pressure gradient forms. That's when isobars become heavily packed over coastal regions, and winds out of the northeast (hence the name) start really kicking up. It's not unusual for these winds to reach hurricane strength—meaning greater than 74 miles per hour, or 64 knots.

That's when the damage begins. The wind alone is bad news, but the wind also creates high waves—up to 25 feet high. When these waves crash against the shore, homes are destroyed, bridges collapse, and widespread flooding takes place. Northeasters spell real trouble for areas like Cape Cod, Massachusetts, and North Carolina's Outer Banks. Barrier islands and narrow strips of coastal land can be overrun by wave action, causing breaches in the land structure and severe erosion of sand dunes. Under the constant pounding and heavy backwash of the waves, beach sand is carried offshore. Eventually,

Figure 17-4. This is how meteorologists depicted the "Perfect Storm" of 1991. In this case, the low moved from east to west, backing into a ridge of high pressure that intensified this northeaster's already-strong winds. The chart may look benign enough, but what isn't shown are the many tightly-packed isobars surrounding the surface low.

281

wave surges can attack dunes. What's left are steep, unstable cliffs of sand, if anything at all.

Here's another problem: Unlike hurricanes, northeasters can linger for days. So day after day, more and more damage occurs to low-lying coastal regions. And don't forget that each day brings high tides. Throw a high tide, 25-foot waves, and hurricane-strength winds together for three days or so, and you've got a permanently altered shoreline. According to one expert on coastal research, the first high tide takes the beach away, the second starts hitting the dunes, and the third moves into coastal buildings.

This, and more, is exactly what happened on October 30 through November 1, 1991. On Wednesday, October 30, a deep low formed about 300 nautical miles east of Cape Cod. There was a cold front over the Mississippi Valley. Ahead of it was a ridge of high pressure over the eastern United States. The setup was perfect (hence the title of Junger's book), with the low backing into the ridge. On the west side of the low, winds ranged from 45 to 75 knots—from the surface all the way up to the flight levels. Beaches from Maine to Virginia started going away.[2]

Early Wednesday evening, the 106th Air Rescue Group of the New York Air National Guard responded to a call for help. A Japanese sailor bound for Bermuda in a 30-foot yacht radioed a Mayday, saying his ship was in danger of capsizing. He was 210 NM south of Nantucket island, in the heart of the northeaster. An HH-60 helicopter with five crewmen was dispatched from Long Island's Suffolk County Airport. The crew located the yacht, but 40-foot waves, darkness, and high winds prevented them from lifting the sailor off his ship. Life rafts, survival equipment, and an ELT were dropped. (Later, the sailor was picked up by a merchant vessel.) But now the helicopter was running low on fuel. Its crew attempted to refuel from a C-130 some 60 NM south of Westhampton, Long Island, but the storm's turbulence made it impossible. The helicopter was ditched at about 9:45 P.M., all five crewmen jumping from the HH-60 before it crashed into the sea. Four were rescued six hours later. The fifth crewman, Sergeant Arden (Rick) Smith, was last believed spotted on Thursday afternoon, some 80 NM south of where the ditching took place. In spite of a search involving thirteen aircraft and three ships, he was never found. Some of his survival gear was found off the Maryland coast.

[2] It was at this point that the fishing boat in Junger's book presumably began to sink.

On Thursday, the northeaster reached peak force. With tides already running 4 to 5 feet higher than normal, waves ate away 30 feet of beach from areas between Long Island and Maine. The first floor of President Bush's home at Kennebunkport, Maine, was destroyed, as were thousands of beach-front homes. Damage estimates went into the hundreds of millions of dollars, and portions of Maine, Massachusetts, and New Jersey applied for disaster relief. There were four deaths.

Then history repeated itself on Saturday, November 9, and Sunday, November 10. This time, a surface low formed off the southeast coast, then tracked to the north, fed all the time by a deep closed low over South Carolina. By Sunday morning, the low was directly over Cape Hatteras, generating 50-MPH (43-knot) winds out of the northeast and 14-foot waves.

The already-fragile Outer Banks took a severe pounding. Waves broke through sand dunes in four places on Pea Island. In Kitty Hawk, the ocean almost crossed the island's only highway. In many, many other places, dunes that had been partially re-built after the previous northeaster were wiped out once again.

What does all this mean to pilots? First of all, northeasters serve as a reminder that adverse weather can come from the east as well as the west. Most of us are accustomed to thinking of fronts and storms as traveling from west to east, but it's not always so. Second, always keep an eye on the areas east of Cape Hatteras and Cape Cod. These projections into the Atlantic are frequent breeding grounds for storms of varying intensity. Finally, treat any mention of northeasters with respect. Hurricanes may get all the press, but year in, year out, it's the north-easters that create the most damage and occur more often. One look at a sectional or world aeronautical chart tells you that there is an abundance of airports along the Atlantic coast, from large terminals like Logan and JFK to small, beachfront airports like the ones at North Carolina's Ocracoke Island, Cape Hatteras's Mitchell Field, or Katama Shores Airport at Martha's Vineyard. None of them are far from the ocean, and none have very high elevations.

If you plan to fly in northeaster country, pay careful attention to your weather briefing. If winds are out of the northeast and increasing, the barometer is falling, and a trough aloft is nearby, it would be wise to consider postponing the trip. You'll see why on television the next day.

Accidents

Action Air Charters Flight 990, a Piper PA-31-350 Navajo Chieftain with eight passengers, crashed at Bridgeport, Connecticut's Sikorsky Memorial Airport on April 27, 1994 at 10:56 P.M., killing all but one aboard. Because of a persistent stationary front that extended from upstate New York, southward to Delaware, and back to the northeast off Cape Cod, low ceilings had caused the flight to delay its morning departure from Hartford, Connecticut's Brainerd field. Conditions were only slightly better for the flight's last leg of the day—from Atlantic City, New Jersey to Bridgeport. The pilot filed an IFR flight plan for the Part 135 charter flight, but never activated it. Upon reaching the Bridgeport area, the pilot learned that the weather was deteriorating quickly. At 10:25 P.M. a Learjet called the Bridgeport tower, saying that visibility was about ½ mile and that a VFR landing would not be possible. The Learjet evidently landed VFR anyway. At 10:30 P.M. the Bridgeport tower closed. A weather observer who left work at the airport at about 10:00 P.M. said that the "horizontal visibility was zero." At 10:37 P.M. a Sabreliner 65 declared a missed approach during a VOR approach to Bridgeport's runway 29, and diverted to White Plains, New York. At 10:42 P.M. a Twin Commander on final for runway 24 at Bridgeport lost sight of the airport, performed a missed approach and flew to New Haven to land. The Navajo pilot apparently called the Learjet pilot on the ground, asking "how was the ground fog?" "Not bad until you get on the ground," the Learjet copilot replied. A tower controller backed up that observation, saying that at about 10:30 P.M.—the time the tower closed— that the fog was thicker near the ground, had tops of 150 feet AGL, and that there were

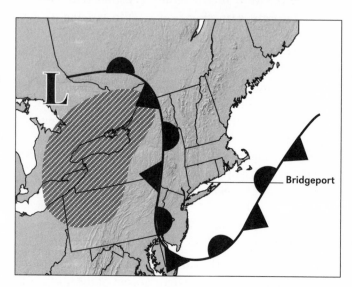

Figure 17-5. On April 27, 1994, an Action Air Charters Piper Navajo crashed at Bridgeport, Connecticut in dense fog associated with a stationary front's influence over southern New England. Above is a brief discussion of the accident.

VFR conditions on top of the fog layer. The Navajo encountered 20-knot tailwinds during its approach to runway 6, and as a consequence landed 3,471 feet from the threshold of the runway. Touchdown speed was calculated as being between 93 and 107 knots (70 knots is a normal touchdown speed for this Navajo). The airplane began leaving skid marks 4,200 feet down the runway, then crashed into a blast fence at an estimated 69 knots. The occupants survived the impact, but a post-crash fire erupted, and burn injuries were responsible for the deaths. In addition, the NTSB found there were improper seat belt installations in the airplane, and some passengers didn't have their seat belts on at the time of the crash. The NTSB said the probable causes of the accident were the pilot's failure to use the available ILS glide slope, and his failure to go around. The fatalities were caused by the presence of a nonfrangible blast fence and the absence of a clear safety area at the end of the runway.

At 8:15 P.M. on November 18, 1994, a Mooney M20J crashed during a missed approach from the Chatham, Massachusetts airport. Weather for the NDB approach was 300 feet overcast with a two-mile visibility in fog. After an approach controller told the pilot to switch to Chatham's advisory frequency, he noticed the airplane deviate from the final approach course and descend. When the controller's altitude alert sounded, he re-established contact with the pilot, who said he had run into some "rough weather," and said that he didn't think he could see the airport. The controller advised the pilot to climb to 2,000 feet, then tried to give him vectors to the Hyannis, Massachusetts airport. But there were no more transmissions from the pilot, who died in the crash near Brewster, Massachusetts. Hurricane Gordon, which was off Cape Hatteras earlier in the day, had set up an east–west stationary front off the New Jersey coast, and as a consequence rain and IFR ceilings and visibilities were affecting the entire northeast. The following day, Gordon weakened to tropical storm status and drifted to the south, where it eventually dissipated to tropical depression status off central Florida.

On the same day—November 18, 1994—an Island Airlines Cessna 402 crashed at 10:00 P.M. on an instrument approach to the Hyannis airport, killing the pilot. The airplane hit wires at 300 feet AGL two miles north of the airport, where conditions were: sky obscured, 100 feet overcast, visibility 1¼ in fog, with winds out of 140 degrees at 12 knots gusting to 22 knots.

Appendix

Percent frequency of low instrument meteorological conditions, commonly known as "Low IFR"—ceilings less than 500 feet and/or visibilities below one statute mile

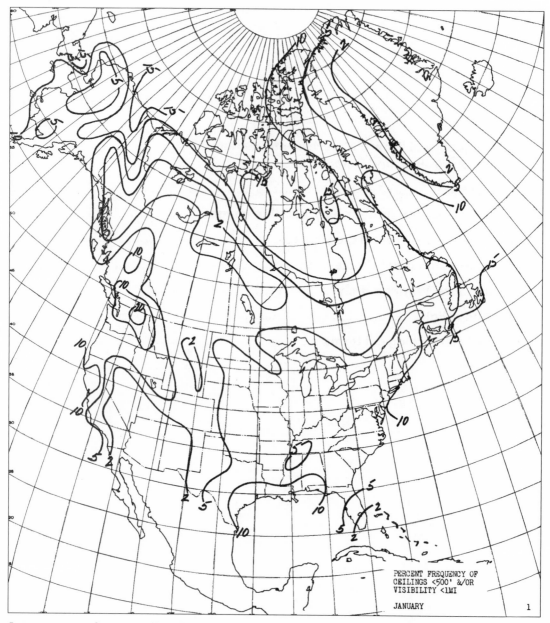

January percent frequency of low IFR. The Pacific northwest, northern California, Gulf coast, and Cape Cod take the prize.

April percent frequency of low IFR. *The Pacific northwest, northern California, and Gulf coast come out of the gloom, but the southern coast of New England still has its 10 percent share of low conditions — along with the upper peninsula of Michigan.*

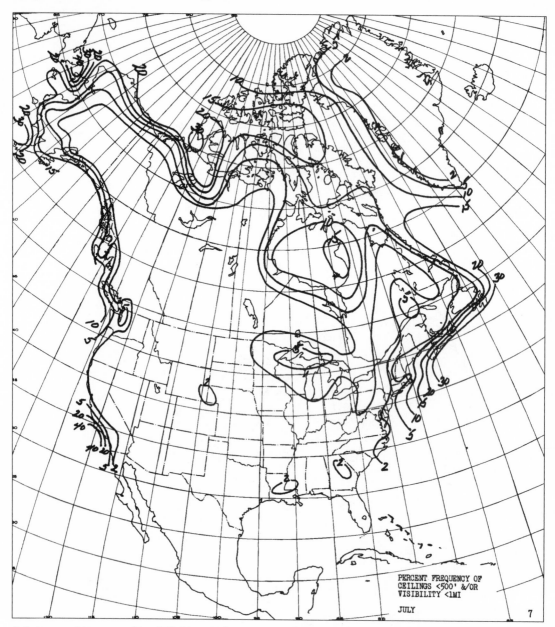

PERCENT FREQUENCY OF
CEILINGS <500' &/OR
VISIBILITY <1MI

JULY

7

July percent frequency of low IFR. *Marine effects impact all coastal regions, save those in Florida and the Gulf coast.*

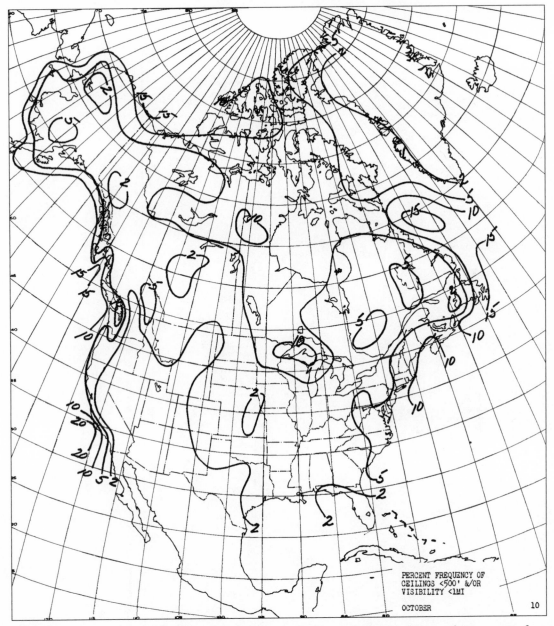

October percent frequency of low IFR. *Advection fogs return to the southeast United States after a summer of abatement, and low conditions in southern California abate.*

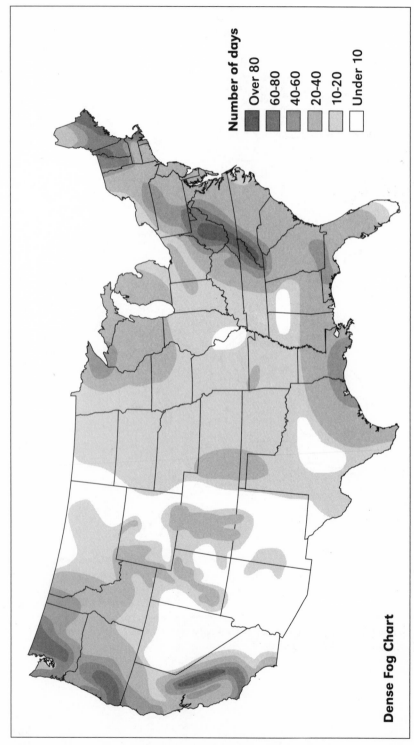

Dense Fog Chart

This chart shows the average number of days per year when dense fog (visibility ≤ ¼ mile) is present.

Number of days

Over 80
60-80
40-60
20-40
10-20
Under 10

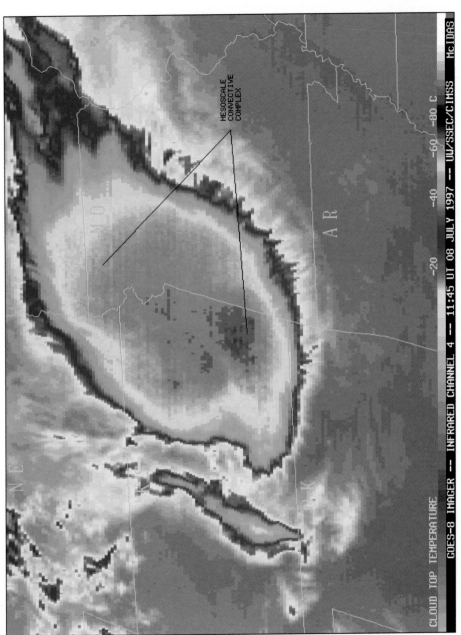

Mesoscale Convective Complex (satellite). This GOES-8 infrared image shows just how large a Mesoscale Convective Complex (MCC) can be. This complex, which occurred on July 8, 1997, is unusual in that it has a cyclonic circulation, rather like that of a hurricane. The west-central portion of the storm complex shows an eye-like center of circulation, and the southwest edge of the complex has a hooklike appendage that indicates rotation. The "eye" formed in what meteorologists call the "rear stratiform precipitation region" of the MCC, where stratus clouds and continuous precipitation prevail. The outflow boundary at the southeast portion of the MCC later created thunderstorms in Arkansas. (Courtesy of CIMSS)

Circular lenticular clouds, near Nederland, Colorado.
*Stable air flowing over mountain ranges can set up some
rowdy flying conditions. The lenticular clouds in the
photo at top were created in the turbulent eddies downwind of an isolated mountain peak. The clouds and their
rotating bases were formed by the processes indicated in
the diagram at right — and closely resemble the behavior
of water in rapids, as it flows past boulders. Hazardous
small-scale vortices can exist in the clear-air region below
these types of clouds. (*Hazardous Mountain Winds and
Their Visual Indicators, *p. 46)*

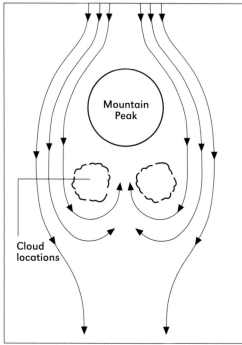

© S. Horne

Desert microburst. *Are we flying too close to a microburst? This shot is a great example of the kinds of microburst-spewing high cloud bases that can happen over the desert southwest. Fortunately, this microburst is marked by a fairly dense rain shaft. Other times, virga (rain that doesn't reach the ground) accompanies desert microbursts. But sometimes the air is so dry that there are no clouds or precipitation to help you locate these intense downdrafts.*

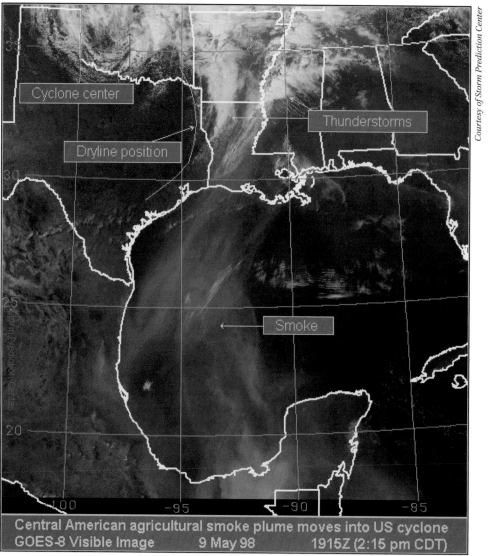

Courtesy of Storm Prediction Center

Cyclone center

Thunderstorms

Dryline position

Smoke

Central American agricultural smoke plume moves into US cyclone
GOES-8 Visible Image   9 May 98   1915Z (2:15 pm CDT)

(above) **Texas dryline.** *Smoke from agricultural burning is drawn northward and into the moist air ahead of a Texas dryline in this May 1998 GOES shot. The dryline is the boundary between the two different air masses. Dry air is over most of Texas, while the muggy air of east Texas, Louisiana, and Arkansas is being primed for thunderstorms later in the day. The smell of smoke from the fires was strong in Norman, OK, and air pollution hazard statements were issued. (top right)* **The Golden Gate bridge** *isn't just a way to get from San Francisco to Sausalito. It's also the spot where a whole lot of fog and marine stratus makes its way inland, smothering airports in instrument weather along the way. (bottom right)* **GOES-7 photo** *shows California's Central Valley filling up with dense fog. Often, this phenomenon begins with fog flowing through low-lying areas around San Francisco and other gaps in the coastal range, and over a period of days, the fog fills up the valley. It's also not uncommon for the southern part of the valley to commence the fogging-in process. Then the fog travels north, covering the whole valley after a few days of progress.*

San Francisco Bay and Central Valley fog

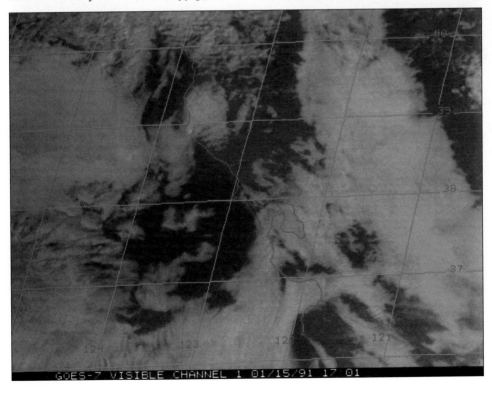

GOES-7 VISIBLE CHANNEL 1 01/15/91 17:01

Florida fronts. *Sea breezes are daily events along coastal Florida. As they move inland, they can form fronts as they collide with inland rising air masses. The satellite shot at right shows how an additional source of rising air — from a forest fire — can make for a huge thunderstorm. Compare its size with the rest of the storm cells around it. The GOES-7 image below has a band of clouds and precipitation running east–west across central Florida — created by one of the typical east-west stationary fronts that affect the area.*

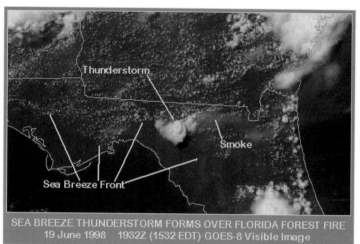

SEA BREEZE THUNDERSTORM FORMS OVER FLORIDA FOREST FIRE
19 June 1998   1932Z (1532 EDT) GOES-8 Visible Image

Courtesy of Storm Prediction Center

GOES-7 1KM VISIBLE   2 DEC 92   17:01 UTC

RIVER FOG - GOES-8 IMAGER VISIBLE - 8:45 AM EDT 20 SEP 1994

LK ONTARIO

LK ERIE

Ohio River Valley fog. *Early fall 1994, and the first cold air of the season drains to river beds and other low-lying areas of the Ohio Valley, Pennsylvania, and New York. The fog formed in the early morning hours, but by daybreak it had yet to burn off from the lowest elevations. This is a concern because so many airports are located in valleys and in the flood plains along rivers. (Courtesy of CIMSS, Univ. of Wisconsin)*

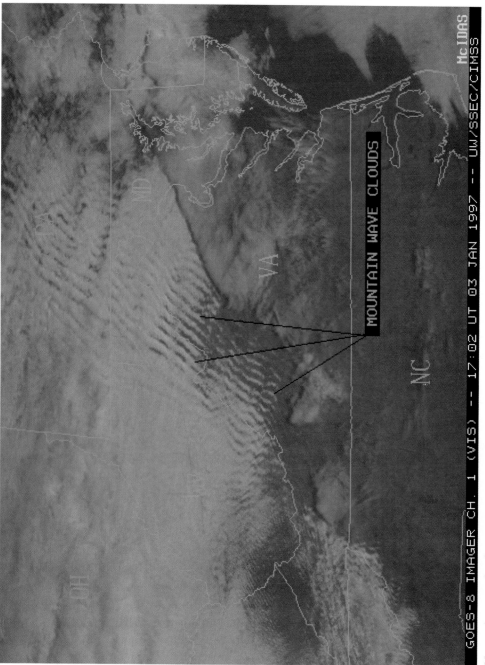

Mountain wave clouds near East Coast. *Everyone thinks of standing waves as being creatures of the Rockies, but this satellite shot proves otherwise. The Appalachians can set up their share of wave effects, including lenticular and rotor clouds, and these mountain wave clouds. (Courtesy of CIMSS, Univ. of Wisconsin)*

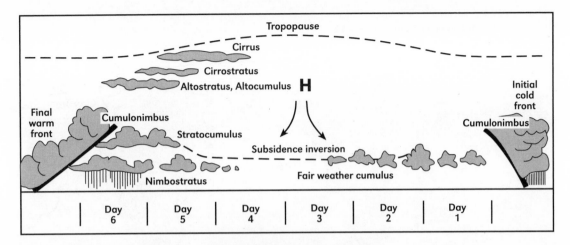

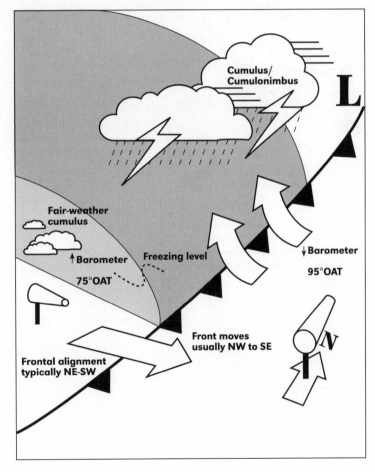

(top) A representation of a typical, day-by-day progression of a large high-pressure system. The sequence runs from right to left, and begins with the arrival of a cold front and its associated cumulus build-ups. After frontal passage, day one dawns with low-level, fair weather cumulus and brisk surface winds out of the west or northwest. The high's subsiding air forms an inversion as the center of the high passes overhead on days two through four. By the fifth day, the "back side" of the high arrives, bringing southerly surface winds and warmer temperatures. The warm front from the next low pressure system arrives on day six, with lowering ceilings and rain showers falling from stratus decks.

(bottom) **Cold fronts** occur when advancing cold air displaces the warmer air mass ahead of it. Expect a bumpy ride, clear ice in clouds above the freezing level, and a good chance of thunderstorm activity in the summer months.

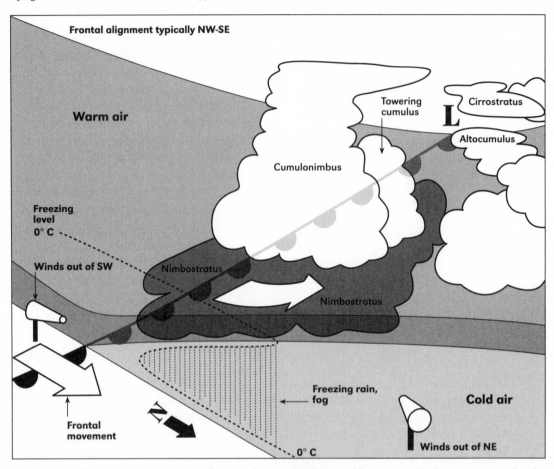

Warm fronts happen when warmer air rides up and over a retreating, colder air mass. In the warmer months of the year, vast cloud cover and embedded thunderstorms are typical results. In winter, rain falling through the colder air near the frontal boundary can set up a freezing rain situation. Warm fronts typically announce their arrival well in advance, with high cirrus or cirrostratus layers preceding the surface front by 300 to 500 miles.

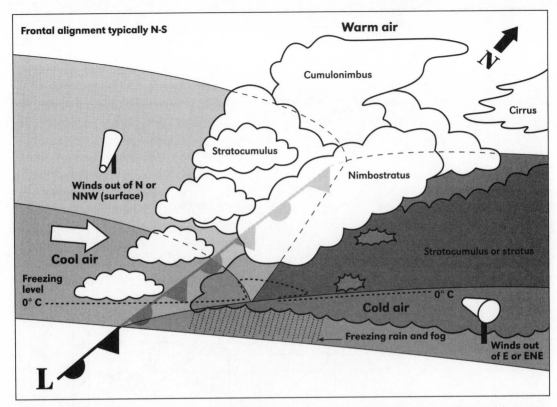

Frontal alignment typically N-S

Warm air

N

Cumulonimbus

Cirrus

Stratocumulus

Nimbostratus

Winds out of N or
NNW (surface)

Stratocumulus or stratus

Cool air

Freezing
level
0° C

0° C

Cold air

Freezing rain and fog

Winds out
of E or ENE

L

*This shows a **warm-front occlusion**, a type of **occluded front** where cool air catches up with the warmer air mass ahead of it. These are common in the western United States, where cool Pacific air runs over the warm sector of a continental low-pressure system. Cold-front occlusions, another type of occluded front, happen when cold air from the north wedges beneath the relatively warmer air in the cold sector of a frontal complex. These are common in the central and eastern United States, where much colder Canadian air masses move south to strike an already-established cold front. Be they of the warm- or cold-front type, occlusions are usually signs that a frontal complex is dying. Slow to move, occlusions can cover large areas with low clouds, fog, and precipitation.*

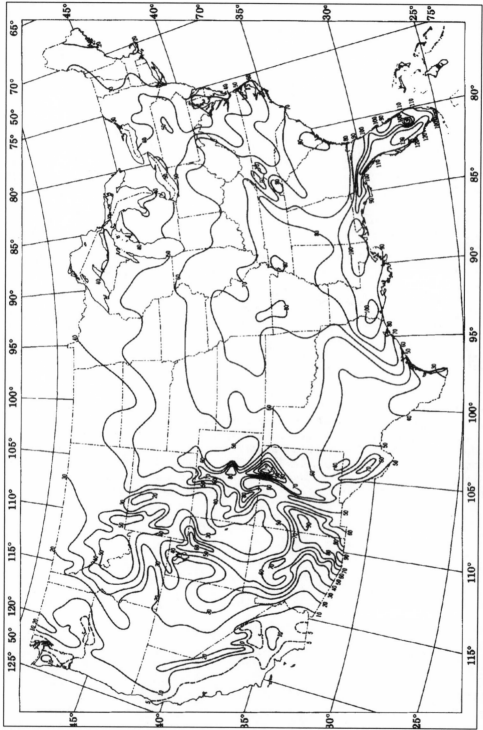

Mean annual number of thunderstorms per year. *This represents the arithmetic middle ground between a range of thunderstorm frequencies, and as such should be considered as rough approximations. For example, central Florida's mean annual number of 130 thunderstorms indicates that approximately half the time the number of storms is higher than that. And that the other half of the time the number of storms is lower than 130 per year. Data is based on 30 years' worth of observations, from 1955-1985. (Storm Data, NOAA.)*

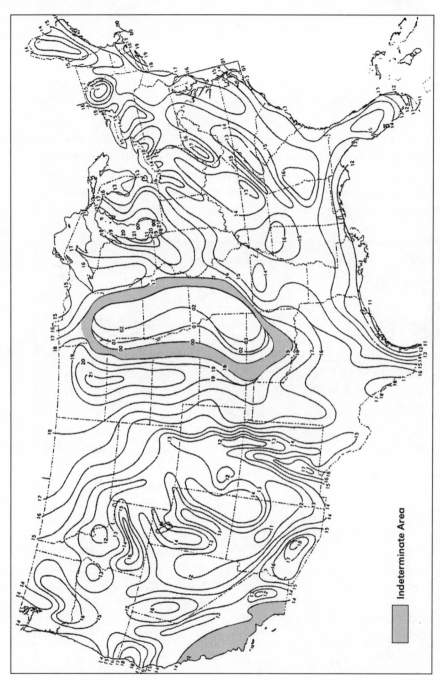

Average local hour of thunderstorm onset, using the 24-hour clock. It's obvious that late afternoon is the usual time for thunderstorm formation over most of the United States. The interesting exception is the band from southern Minnesota to northern Oklahoma, where Mesoscale Convective Complexes typically form in the hours after midnight. (courtesy of NOAA)

Indeterminate Area

Height Contours: What Are They?

Most pilots are familiar with isobars—those lines of equal pressure that show up on surface analysis charts. Isobars and the patterns they make show us what's happening with atmospheric pressure at the surface. *Height contours* do the same thing for pressure patterns aloft.

Height contours are found on constant pressure charts (*see* below). These charts show pressure patterns at selected levels of the atmosphere, as identified by a pressure level expressed in millibars of mercury. Because of standard pressure lapse rate effects, these pressure levels roughly correspond to altitudes above mean sea level. For example, a 500-millibar constant pressure chart shows the pressure distribution at about 18,000 feet

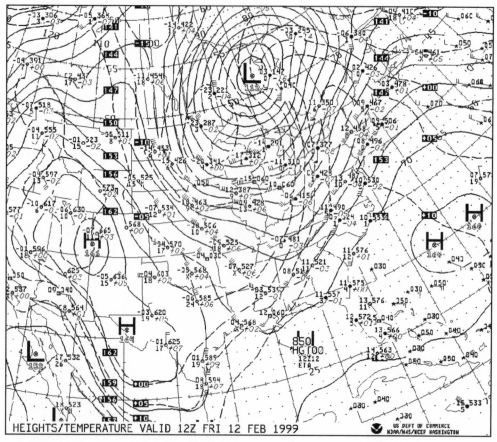

HEIGHTS/TEMPERATURE VALID 12Z FRI 12 FEB 1999

US DEPT OF COMMERCE
NOAA/NWS/NCEP WASHINGTON

850-millibar chart *shows a cut-off low north of the Great Lakes; trough in Ohio Valley.*

MSL. I say "about" because as pressures rise and fall the 500-millibar pressure surface rises and falls. Would this or any other constant pressure surface touch the ground? Yes—depending on the height of the terrain. But if it's surface pressure you're worried about, you should check the surface analysis charts.

The height contour lines show the height of the 500-millibar pressure levels, and are labeled in meters printed in a three-digit, abbreviated form. A contour encircling a low aloft may be labeled "528," for example. This is an abbreviation for 5,280 meters, or 17,323 feet. Farther away from the low, let's say, 300 nautical miles, a height contour may read "558," or 18,307 feet MSL. Now we can see that the surface of the 500-mb level drops about 1,000 feet in 300 NM. Imagine this pattern in three dimensions, and you can visualize the pressure surface sloping downward, toward the low aloft.

Constant pressure charts are published for 850 mb (5,000 feet); 700 mb (10,000 feet); 300 mb (30,000 feet); 250 mb (34,000 feet); 200 mb (39,000 feet); 150 mb (45,000 feet); and 100 mb (53,000 feet). The altitudes in parentheses are approximate altitudes for each level of constant pressure. To decipher the altitudes of the pressure surfaces in some of the most-often used charts, remember the following: On 850-mb charts (such as the one shown at left), the first digit is a 1, and is omitted; for 700-mb, the first digit is a 3 or 2, and is omitted; for 500-mb, the last digit is a 0, and is omitted; for 300-mb, the last digit is a 0, and is omitted; and for 250- and 200-mb the first digit is a 1 or a 0, the last digit is a 0, and both the first and last digits are omitted.

Sometimes, it's valuable to look at several constant pressure charts to get an idea of the dynamics aloft. If you see a closed low (one completely encircled by a height contour or two, or three) aloft at several successive pressure levels, you've got what's called a deep low, or a stacked low—one that you could envision as a kind of hole in the atmosphere, with steeply-sloping, funnel-like pressure surfaces descending down through the altitudes. That's a sign of a dying, slow-moving system with plenty of precipitation and low clouds at the surface.

By the same token, closely-spaced height contours indicate fast wind speeds aloft, much the same as closely-packed isobars on surface analysis charts show strong surface winds. But at altitude, these strong winds are signs of jet stream activity. And as we've seen, jet streams and their cores, or jet streaks, of the strongest winds can create and/or intensify surface lows and severe weather.

Finally, troughs aloft can be identified by height contour patterns. If the same trough repeats itself vertically, appearing on all the charts from 850- through 200-mb, then you've got one major ingredient that all meteorologists check for when predicting just about every type of severe weather.

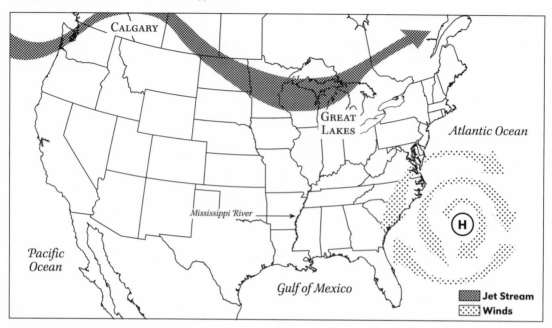

The Bermuda High. *Summertime east of the Rockies, and high density altitudes rule. Why? Usually, a large high-pressure system over the Atlantic Ocean — the Bermuda High — is firmly in place, sending hot, muggy air inland off the clockwise flow coming from its western flank, or back side. The high keeps the jet stream far to the north, lasts for days, and is a main feature of the "dog days" of August.*

Glossary
Meteorological Terms

adiabatic process. The process by which fixed relationships are maintained during changes in temperature, volume, and pressure in a body of air without heat being added or removed from the body.

advection fog. A type of fog caused by the movement of moist air over a cold surface, and the consequent cooling of that air to below its dew point. Sea fog is one type of advection fog that involves moist air in transport over a cold body of water.

ageostrophic flows. Air flows that move across isobars or height contours at an angle toward either high or low pressure.

air mass. In meteorology, an extensive body of air within which the conditions of temperature and moisture in a horizontal plane are essentially uniform.

altitude, density. The altitude in the standard atmosphere at which the air has the same density as the air at the point in question. An aircraft will have the same performance characteristics as it would have in a standard atmosphere at this altitude.

altitude, pressure. The altitude in the standard atmosphere at which the pressure is the same as at the point in question. Since an altimeter operates solely on pressure, this is the uncorrected altitude indicated by an altimeter set at standard sea level pressure of 29.92 inches or 1013 millibars.

anemometer. An instrument for measuring wind speed.

anticyclone. An area of high atmospheric pressure which has a closed circulation that is anticyclonic, i.e., as viewed from above, the circulation is clockwise in the Northern Hemisphere, counterclockwise in the Southern Hemisphere, undefined at the Equator.

ASOS (Automated Surface Observation System). A suite of weather instruments that automatically report certain weather conditions, such as sky cover, temperature, and wind.

atmospheric pressure (also called barometric pressure). The pressure exerted by the atmosphere as a consequence of gravitational attraction exerted upon the "column" of air lying directly above the point in question.

Beaufort scale. A scale of wind speeds.

bush flying syndrome. A defect in judgment caused by overconfidence born of successful past encounters with adverse weather in Alaska.

ceilometer. A cloud height measuring system. It projects light on the cloud, detects the reflection by a photoelectric cell, and determines height by triangulation.

Celsius temperature scale (abbreviated C). A temperature scale with zero degrees as the melting point of pure ice and 100° as the boiling point of pure water at standard sea level atmospheric pressure. *Also* Centigrade.

Chinook. A warm, dry foehn wind blowing down the eastern slopes of the Rocky Mountains over the adjacent plains in the U.S. and Canada.

Chinook effect. The temperature response to downslope winds. Most often used in the context of the Rocky Mountains, Chinook effects can increase surface temperatures by 20 to 40°F in as little as 15 minutes. The temperature increase is the result of subsiding air, which heats up and lowers humidities as it flows down the leeward slopes of a prominent mountain or ridge.

cirrocumulus. A cirriform cloud appearing as a thin sheet of small white puffs resembling flakes or patches of cotton without shadows; sometimes confused with altocumulus.

cirrostratus. A cirriform cloud appearing as a whitish veil, usually fibrous, sometimes smooth; often produces halo phenomena; may totally cover the sky.

cirrus. A cirriform cloud in the form of thin, white feather-like clouds in patches or narrow bands; have a fibrous and/or silky sheen; large ice crystals often trail downward a considerable vertical distance in fibrous, slanted, or irregularly curved wisps called mares' tails.

clear air turbulence (abbreviated CAT). Turbulence encountered in air where no clouds are present; more popularly applied to high level turbulence associated with wind shear.

cold air damming. A situation in the Atlantic piedmont and coastal plain where low-level cold air is shunted southwards, ahead of an approaching cold front. High pressure to the northeast of the advancing cold front is necessary to help provide the mechanism for advecting the cold air to the south. The low-level cold air "dams up" against the Appalachians, hence the term. It is an event common to the fall and winter months.

cold front. Any non-occluded front which moves in such a way that colder air replaces warmer air.

constant pressure chart. A chart of a constant pressure surface; may contain analyses of height, wind, temperature, humidity, and/or other elements.

contour. In meteorology, (1) a line of equal height on a constant pressure chart; analogous to contours on a relief map; (2) in radar meteorology, a line on a radar scope of equal echo intensity.

convection. (1) In general, mass motions within a fluid resulting in transport and mixing of the properties of that fluid. (2) In meteorology, atmospheric motions that are predominantly vertical, resulting in vertical transport and mixing of atmospheric properties; distinguished from advection.

convergence. The condition that exists when the distribution of winds within a given area is such that there is a net horizontal inflow of air into the area. In convergence at lower levels, the removal of the resulting excess is accomplished by an upward movement of air; consequently, areas of low-level convergent winds are regions favorable to the occurrence of clouds and precipitation. *Compare with* divergence.

cumulonimbus. A cumuliform cloud type; it is heavy and dense, with considerable vertical extent in the form of massive towers; often with tops in the shape of an anvil or massive plume; under the base of cumulonimbus, which often is very dark, there frequently exists virga, precipitation and low ragged clouds (scud), either merged with it or not; frequently accompanied by lightning, thunder, and sometimes hail; occasionally produces a tornado or a waterspout; the ultimate manifestation of the growth of a cumulus cloud, occasionally extending well into the stratosphere.

cumulonimbus mamma. A cumulonimbus cloud having hanging protuberances, like pouches, festoons, or udders, on the under side of the cloud; usually indicative of severe turbulence.

cumulus. A cloud in the form of individual detached domes or towers which are usually dense and well defined; develops vertically in the form of rising mounds of which the bulging upper part often resembles a cauliflower; the sunlit parts of these clouds are mostly brilliant white; their bases are relatively dark and nearly horizontal.

cyclogenesis. Any development or strengthening of cyclonic (counterclockwise, in the northern hemisphere) circulation in the atmosphere. It is applied to the development of cyclonic circulation where it previously did not exist (commonly, the initial appearance of a low or trough).

cyclone. (1) An area of low atmospheric pressure which has a closed circulation that is cyclonic, i.e., as viewed from above, the circulation is counterclockwise in the Northern Hemisphere, clockwise in the Southern Hemisphere, undefined at the Equator. Because cyclonic circulation and relatively low atmospheric pressure usually coexist, in common practice the terms cyclone and low are used interchangeably. Also, because cyclones often are accompanied by inclement (sometimes destructive) weather, they are frequently referred to simply as storms. (2) Frequently misused to denote a tornado. (3) In the Indian Ocean, a tropical cyclone of hurricane or typhoon force.

derechoes. Families of strong downbursts, embedded in thunderstorm lines or clusters.

dew point (or dewpoint temperature). The temperature to which a sample of air must be cooled, while the mixing ratio and barometric pressure remain constant, in order to attain saturation with respect to water.

diurnal. Daily, recurrent variations in meteorological variables. Some diurnal variations at the earth's surface include (1) Temperature maximums near or after local noon, and temperature minimums just before sunrise; (2) Relative humidity and fog minimums in late afternoon, and maximums near sunrise; (3) Increase of winds during the day, and decrease of winds at night.

divergence. The condition that exists when the distribution of winds within a given area is such that there is a net horizontal flow of air outward from the region. In divergence at lower levels, the resulting deficit is compensated for by subsidence of air from aloft; consequently the air is heated and the relative humidity lowered making divergence a warming and drying process. Low-level divergent regions are areas unfavorable to the occurrence of clouds and precipitation. The opposite of convergence.

downburst. A strong downdraft which induces an outburst of damaging winds on or near the ground. The sizes of downbursts vary from one-half mile or less to more than ten miles. *See also* micorburst.

dry adiabatic lapse rate. The rate of decrease of temperature with height when unsaturated air is lifted adiabatically (due to expansion as it is lifted to lower pressure). *See* adiabatic process.

echo. In radar, (1) the energy reflected or scattered by a target; (2) the radar scope presentation of the return from a target.

eddy. A local irregularity of wind in a larger scale wind flow. Small scale eddies produce turbulent conditions.

foehn. A warm, dry downslope wind; the warmness and dryness being due to adiabatic compression upon descent; characteristic of mountainous regions. *See* adiabatic process, Chinook, katabatic wind, Santa Ana.

fog. A cloud on the ground; formed when temperature and dew point are within a few degrees of each other.

freezing level. A level in the atmosphere at which the temperature is 0°C (32°F).

freezing rain. Rain that falls in supercooled liquid form, but freezes on impact with an airplane or other object.

front. A surface, interface, or transition zone of discontinuity between two adjacent air masses of different densities; more simply the boundary between two different air masses. *See* frontal zone.

frontal zone. A front or zone with a marked increase of density gradient; used to denote that fronts are not truly a "surface" of discontinuity but rather a "zone" of rapid transition of meteorological elements.

funnel cloud. A tornado cloud or vortex cloud extending downward from the parent cloud but not reaching the ground.

GOES satellite. Geostationary Operational Environmental Satellite. These satellites orbit at altitudes of approximately 22,300 statute miles. At this height, the satellites orbit with the earth's rotation, and therefore give continuous, overlapping coverage of the cloud cover, surface temperatures, and vertical distributions of the atmospheric temperatures and humidities below. There are two such satellites— GOES-East, centered over the Equator at 75 degrees west longitude, and GOES-West, centered at 135 degrees west. GOES-East covers the Atlantic Ocean; GOES-West the Pacific. Both cover large portions of eastern and western North and South America. GOES satellites provide visible, infrared, and water vapor imagery.

gradient. In meteorology, a horizontal decrease in value per unit distance of a parameter in the direction of maximum decrease; most commonly used with pressure, temperature, and moisture.

Gulf stream. A warm, well-defined, swift, and relatively narrow ocean current that originates where the Florida current and the Antilles current begin to curve eastward from the continental slope off Cape Hatteras, North Carolina.

high. An area of high barometric pressure, with its attendant system of winds; an anticyclone. *Also* high-pressure system.

humidity. Water vapor content of the air; may be expressed as specific humidity, relative humidity, or mixing ratio.

ice pellets. Small, transparent or translucent, round or irregularly shaped pellets of ice. They may be (1) hard grains that rebound on striking a hard surface, or (2) pellets of snow encased in ice.

insolation. The total solar radiation received at the Earth's surface; also, the rate of delivery of direct solar radiation per unit of horizontal surface area.

instability. A general term to indicate various states of the atmosphere in which spontaneous convection will occur when prescribed criteria are met; indicative of turbulence.

inversion. An increase in temperature with height—a reversal of the normal decrease with height in the troposphere; may also be applied to other meteorological properties.

INS. Inertial Navigation System, a navigation aid that computes an aircraft's position by formulas using the measured acceleration and flight vectors of an airborne gyro-stabilized platform.

isobar. A line of equal or constant barometric pressure.

katabatic wind. Any wind blowing down an incline. The same as a "gravity wind," a katabatic wind that is warm is called a *foehn*. If it's cold, it's called a "fall wind," or a *bora*.

lapse rate. The rate of decrease of an atmospheric variable with height; commonly refers to decrease of temperature with height.

lee wave. Any stationary wave disturbance caused by a barrier in a fluid flow. In the atmosphere when sufficient moisture is present, this wave will be evidenced by lenticular clouds to the lee of mountain barriers; also called mountain wave or standing wave.

lenticular cloud (or lenticularis). A species of cloud whose elements have the form of more or less isolated, generally smooth lenses or almonds. These clouds appear most often in formations of orographic origin, the result of lee waves, in which case they remain nearly stationary with respect to the terrain (standing cloud), but they also occur in regions without marked orography.

microburst. A localized, extremely high-intensity column of descending air.

millibar (abbreviated mb). An internationally used unit of pressure equal to 1,000 dynes per square centimeter. It is convenient for reporting atmospheric pressure.

monsoon. A seasonal pattern of onshore (summer) and offshore (winter) precipitation movements.

mountain wave. A standing wave or lee wave to the lee of a mountain barrier.

nimbostratus. A principal cloud type, gray colored, often dark, the appearance of which is rendered diffuse by more or less continuously falling rain or snow, which in most cases reaches the ground. It is thick enough throughout to blot out the sun.

obscuration. Denotes sky hidden by surface-based obscuring phenomena and vertical visibility restricted overhead.

occluded front (commonly called occlusion, also called frontal occlusion). A composite of two fronts as a cold front overtakes a warm front or quasi-stationary front.

orographic. Of, pertaining to, or caused by mountains as in orographic clouds, orographic lift, or orographic precipitation.

POES satellite. Polar Orbiting Operational Environmental Satellite. These satellites orbit along north–south tracks at nominal altitudes of approximately 530 statute miles. This is a comparatively low orbiting altitude, but it allows greater resolution of the weather features below, and better remote sensing of atmospheric soundings. POES satellites measure in the visible, infrared, water vapor, and various radiometric spectra, one of which is used to make ozone measurements. POES satellites also contain SARSAT (Search and Rescue Satellite Aided Tracking) equipment, which allows them to locate and relay emergency locater transmitter (ELT) and other emergency broadcasts from pilots and mariners in distress. Two POES satellites make 14 orbits each per day. This provides nearly complete coverage of the earth below.

polar front. The semipermanent, semicontinuous front separating air masses of tropical and polar origins.

quasi-stationary front (commonly called stationary front). A front which is stationary or nearly so; conventionally, a front which is moving at a speed of less than 5 knots is generally considered to be quasi-stationary.

radiation fog. Fog characteristically resulting when radiational cooling of the earth's surface lowers the air temperature near the ground to or below its initial dew point on calm, clear nights.

relative humidity. The ratio of the existing amount of water vapor in the air at a given temperature to the maximum amount that could exist at that temperature; usually expressed in percent.

ridge (also called ridge line). In meteorology, an elongated area of relatively high atmospheric pressure; usually associated with and most clearly identified as an area of maximum anticyclonic curvature of the wind flow (isobars, contours, or streamlines).

roll cloud (sometimes improperly called rotor cloud). A dense and horizontal roll-shaped accessory cloud located on the lower leading edge of a cumulonimbus or less often, a rapidly developing cumulus; indicative of turbulence.

rotor cloud (sometimes improperly called roll cloud). A turbulent cloud formation found in the lee of some large mountain barriers, the air in the cloud rotates around an axis parallel to the range; indicative of possible violent turbulence.

rotors. Intense, localized parcels of air with strong rotating motions.

Santa Ana. A hot, dry, foehn wind, generally from the northeast or east, occurring west of the Sierra Nevada Mountains especially in the pass and river valley near Santa Ana, California.

sea breeze. A coastal breeze blowing from sea to land, caused by the temperature difference when the land surface is warmer than the sea surface.

sea level pressure. The atmospheric pressure at mean sea level, either directly measured by stations at sea level or empirically determined from the station pressure and temperature by stations not at sea level; used as a common reference for analyses of surface pressure patterns.

squall. A sudden increase in wind speed by at least 15 knots to a peak of 20 knots or more and lasting for at least one minute. Essential difference between a gust and a squall is the duration of the peak speed.

squall line. A narrow band of extremely active thunderstorms, which often precede the passage of a fast-moving or otherwise violent frontal zone. Squall lines often produce heavy precipitation, hail, strong winds and wind shear, and tornadoes.

stability. A state of the atmosphere in which the vertical distribution of temperature is such that a parcel will resist displacement from its initial level. (*See also* instability.)

standard atmosphere. A hypothetical atmosphere based on climatological averages comprised of numerous physical constants of which the most important are:
   (1) A surface temperature of 59°F (15°C) and a surface pressure of 29.92 inches of mercury (1013.2 millibars) at sea level;
   (2) A lapse rate in the troposphere of 6.5°C per kilometer (approximately 2°C per 1,000 feet);

(3) A tropopause of 11 kilometers (approximately 36,000 feet) with a temperature of –56.5°C; and

(4) An isothermal lapse rate in the stratosphere to an altitude of 24 kilometers (approximately 80,000 feet).

standing wave. A wave that remains stationary in a moving fluid. In aviation operations it is used most commonly to refer to a lee wave or mountain wave.

stratocumulus. A low cloud, predominantly stratiform in gray and/or whitish patches or layers, may or may not merge; elements are tessellated, rounded, or roll-shaped with relatively flat tops.

stratosphere. The atmospheric layer above the tropopause, average altitude of base and top, 7 and 22 miles respectively; characterized by a slight average increase of temperature from base to top and is very stable; also characterized by low moisture content and absence of clouds.

stratus. A low, gray cloud layer or sheet with a fairly uniform base; sometimes appears in ragged patches; seldom produces precipitation but may produce drizzle or snow grains. A stratiform cloud.

thermal low. A low-pressure area created by the heated, rising air from a land mass.

thunderstorm. In general, a local storm invariably produced by a cumulonimbus cloud, and always accompanied by lightning and thunder.

tornado (sometimes called cyclone, twister). A violently rotating column of air, pendant from a cumulonimbus cloud, and nearly always observable as "funnel-shaped." It is the most destructive of all small scale atmospheric phenomena.

towering cumulus. A rapidly growing cumulus in which height exceeds width.

trade winds. Prevailing, almost continuous winds blowing with an easterly component from the subtropical high pressure belts toward the intertropical convergence zone; northeast in the Northern Hemisphere, southeast in the Southern Hemisphere.

tropopause. The transition zone between the troposphere and stratosphere, usually characterized by an abrupt change of lapse rate.

troposphere. That portion of the atmosphere from the earth's surface to the tropopause; that is, the lowest 10 to 20 kilometers of the atmosphere. The troposphere is characterized by decreasing temperature with height, and by appreciable water vapor.

trough (also called trough line). In meteorology, an elongated area of relatively low atmospheric pressure; usually associated with and most clearly identified as an area of maximum cyclonic curvature of the wind flow (isobars, contours, or streamlines). *Compare with* ridge.

upwelling. The rising of water toward the surface from subsurface layers of a body of water. Upwelling is most prominent where persistent wind blows parallel to a coastline so that the resultant wind-driven current sets away from the coast. Upwelling is a strong climatological influence because it brings colder water to the surface, and in contact with the lower levels of the atmosphere.

virga. Wisps or streaks of rain or ice particles falling out of a cloud but evaporating before reaching the earth's surface. Virga is frequently seen trailing from altocumulus or altostratus clouds, but also is discernible below the bases of high-level cumulus clouds, from which precipitation is falling into a dry subcloud layer.

vortex. In meteorology, any rotary flow in the atmosphere.

vorticity. A localized rotation in a fluid flow, in this case the atmosphere. Strong vorticity "spins up" any nearby low pressure, and helps create or intensify fronts, storms, or cloud layers.

warm front. Any nonoccluded front which moves in such a way that warmer air replaces colder air.

whiteout. A loss of visual reference in conditions where all terrain and weather presents a white appearance.

wind shadow. An abatement of wind speed downwind of high terrain.

wind shear (windshear). The rate of change of wind velocity (direction and/or speed) per unit distance; conventionally expressed as vertical or horizontal wind shear.

Bibliography
and Recommended Reading

Books, monographs, and research papers

Atkinson, B.W. *Meso-scale Atmospheric Circulations.* London: Academic Press, 1981.

Bailey, Harry P. *Weather of Southern California,* California Natural History Guides, 17. Berkeley, Los Angeles, London: University of California Press, 1975.

Banta, Robert M.; Berri, G.; Blumen, William; Carruthers, David J.; Dalu, G.A.; Durran, Dale R.; Egger, Joseph; Garratt, J.R.; Hanna, Steven R.; Hunt, J.C.R.; Meroney, Robert N.; Miller, W.; Neff, William D.; Nicolini, M.; Paegle, Jan; Pielke, Roger A.; Smith, Ronald B.; Strimaitis, David G.; Vukicevic, T.; Whiteman, David C. "Atmospheric Processes over Complex Terrain." *Meteorological Monographs* 23:45. Boston: American Meteorological Society, 1990.

Benjamin, Stanley G.; Brundage, Kevin J.; Morone, Lauren L. "The Rapid Update Cycle, Part 1: Analysis/Model Description." *The Technical Procedures Bulletin, Series No. 416.* Washington, D.C.: U.S. Department of Commerce, National Oceanic and Atmospheric Administration, 1994.

Buck, Robert N. *Weather Flying. Revised Edition.* New York: Macmillan Publishing Co., Inc., 1978.

Byers, Horace R.; Braham, Roscoe R. *The Thunderstorm, Report of the Thunderstorm Project* (A joint project of four U.S. government agencies: Air Force, Navy, National Advisory Committee for Aeronautics, and Weather Bureau). Washington, D.C.: U. S. Department of Commerce, Weather Bureau, 1949.

Cagle, Malcolm W.; Halpine, C.G. *A Pilot's Meteorology. Third Edition.* New York: Van Nostrand Reinhold Company, 1970.

Caracena, Fernando; Holle, Ronald L.; Doswell III, Charles A. *Microbursts: A Handbook for Visual Identification.* U.S. Department of Commerce, National Oceanic and Atmospheric Administration, Environmental Research Laboratories, National Severe Storms Laboratory, 1989.

Carney, Thomas Q.; Bedard, A.J., Jr.; Brown, John M.; McGinley, John; Lindholm, Tenny; and Kraus, Michael J. *Hazardous Mountain Winds and Their Visual Indicators.* University of Colorado at Boulder Press, 1993. Project of the NOAA's Environmental Technology Laboratory (NOAA/ETL), with assistance from the National Center for Atmospheric Research, the National Severe Storms Laboratory, and the Federal Aviation Administration. (This handbook was reprinted by the FAA and is available as an Advisory Circular. Write to: Advisory Circular 00-57, FAA, Office of Communications, Navigation and Surveillance Systems, Washington D.C.)

Chaston, Peter R. *Weather Maps, How to Read and Interpret All the Basic Weather Charts.* Kearney, Missouri: Chaston Scientific, Inc., 1995.

Collins, Richard. *Thunderstorms and Airplanes.* New York: Delacorte Press/Eleanor Friede, 1982.
———. *Flying the Weather Map.* Charlottesville, Virginia: Thomasson-Grant, Inc., 1992.

Dane Clark, J., ed. *The GOES User's Guide.* Washington, D.C.: U.S. Department of Commerce, National Oceanic and Atmospheric Administration, National Environmental Satellite, Data and Information Service, 1983.

Day, John A.; Schaefer, Vincent J. *Peterson First Guides: Clouds and Weather.* Boston: Houghton Mifflin Company, 1991.

Doviak, Richard J.; Zrnic, Dusan S. *Doppler Radar and Weather Observations.* Orlando: Academic Press, Inc., 1984.

Fujita, Tetsuya Theodore. *Spearhead Echo and Downburst near the Approach End of a John F. Kennedy Airport Runway.* SMRP Research Paper 137, Satellite and Mesometeorology Research Project (Department of Geophysical Sciences). The University of Chicago, 1976.

Fujita, Tetsuya Theodore. *Andrews AFB Microburst.*
    SMRP Research Paper 205, Satellite and Mesometeorology
    Research Project (Department of Geophysical Sciences).
    The University of Chicago, presented at Andrews AFB,
    December 5, 1983.
———. *The Downburst, Microburst and Macroburst.* University
    of Chicago, 1985.
———. *DFW Microburst on August 2, 1985.* University of
    Chicago, 1986.

Gilliam, Harold. *Weather of the San Francisco Bay Region,*
    California Natural History Guides, 6. Berkeley, Los Angeles,
    London: University of California Press, 1962.

Grenci, Lee M., and Nese, Jon M. *A World of Weather:*
    Fundamentals of Meteorology. Second Edition.
    "A text/laboratory manual." Dubuque, Iowa:
    Kendall/Hunt Publishing Company, 1998.

Holley, John. *Aviation Weather Services Explained:*
    The Companion Workbook to AC 00-45D. Newcastle,
    Washington: Aviation Supplies and Academics, Inc., 1996.

Johnson, Kent; Mullock, J. *Aviation Weather Hazards of British*
    Columbia and the Yukon. Canada: Minister of
    Environment, 1996.

Kessler, Edwin, ed. *The Thunderstorm in Human Affairs.*
    Second Edition, Revised and Enlarged. Volume 1 of
    Thunderstorms: A social, scientific, and technological
    documentary. Norman and London: University of
    Oklahoma Press, 1988.

Kocin, Paul J. and Uccellini, Louis W. *Snowstorms Along the*
    Northeastern Coast of the United States, 1955 to 1985.
    Meteorological Monographs (22:44). Boston:
    American Meteorological Society, 1990.

Krishna Rao, P.; Holmes, Susan J.; Anderson, Ralph K.; Winston,
    Jay S.; Lehr, Paul E., eds. *Weather Satellites: Systems, Data*
    and Environmental Applications. Boston: American
    Meteorological Society, 1990.

Lankford, Terry T. *Cockpit Weather Decisions.* New York: McGraw-Hill, 1998.
———. *The Pilot's Guide to Weather Reports, Forecasts, and Flight Planning,* 2nd Ed., New York: McGraw-Hill, 1990.

Lester, Peter F. *Aviation Weather.* Englewood, Colorado: Jeppesen Sanderson, Inc., 1995.

Loebl, Thomas S. *View from Low Orbit. A photograpic tour of North America and its weather by satellite.* Hubbardston, Massachusetts: Imaging Publications, 1991.

McKinley Conway, H.; Liston, Linda L., eds. *The Weather Handbook. Revised Edition.* Atlanta: Conway Research, Inc., 1974.

Munn, R.E. *Descriptive Micrometeorology.* (Suppl. 1 to Landsberg, H.E., Van Mieghem, J., eds., *Advances in Geophysics*). New York: Academic Press, 1966.

Parker, Thomas R. with Raak Veblen. *Flying in Northern California.* Carmichael, California: Thomas R. Parker, 1987.

Ray, Peter S., ed. *Mesoscale Meteorology and Forecasting.* Boston: American Meteorological Society, 1986.

Sanders, Frederick. "Upper Level Geostrophic Diffluence and Deepening Surface Lows." *Weather and Forecasting,* 8:3, Sept. 1993. Boston: American Meteorological Society.

Taylor, Richard L. *Aviation Weather: Forces to be Reckoned With.* Greenwich, Connecticut: Belvoir Publications, 1991.

Townsend, John W., Jr. (Chairman). *Report of the Committee on Low Altitude Wind Shear and Its Hazard to Aviation.* Washington, D.C.: National Academy Press, 1983.

Wallace, John M.; Hobbs, Peter V. *Atmospheric Science, An Introductory Survey.* New York: Academic Press, Inc., 1977.

Williams, Jack. *The Weather Book.* (USA Today) New York: Vintage Books, 1992.

Conference papers

NEXRAD Product Improvement Program. Papers Prepared for the 77th Annual Meeting of the American Meteorological Society, 13th International Conference on Interactive Information and Processing Systems (IIPS) for Meteorology, Oceanography, and Hydrology. Long Beach, California, 2–7 February 1997.

Final Report on the Joint Doppler Operational Project (JDOP) 1976–1978. NOAA Technical Memorandum ERL NSSL-86. Norman, Oklahoma: National Severe Storms Laboratory, 1997.

Papers from the *Monthly Weather Review* (MWR), a journal publication of the American Meteorological Society, Boston, MA

Chen, Yi-Leng and Nash, Andrew J. "Diurnal Variation of Surface Airflow and Rainfall Frequencies on the Island of Hawaii." MWR 122 (January 1994): 34–56.

Karyampudi, V. Mohan; Kaplan, Michael L.; Koch, Steven E.; and Zamora, Robert J. "The Influence of the Rocky Mountains on the 13-14 April 1986 Severe Weather Outbreak. Part I: Mesoscale Lee Cyclogenesis and Its Relationship to Severe Weather and Dust Storms." MWR 123 (May 1995): 1394–1422.

Levinson, David H. and Banta, Robert M. "Observations of a Terrain-forced Mesoscale Vortex and Canyon Drainage Flows along the Front Range of Colorado." MWR 123 (July 1995): 2029–50.

Nachamkin, Jason E.; McAnelly, Ray L.; Cotton, William R. "An Observational Analysis of a Developing Mesoscale Convective Complex." MWR 122 (June 1994): 1168–88.

Wilson, James W. and Megenhardt, Daniel L. "Thunderstorm Initiation, Organization, and Lifetime Associated with Florida Boundary Layer Convergence Lines." MWR 125 (July 1997): 1507–26.

Ziegler, Conrad L.; Lee, Tsengdar J.; Pielke, Roger A., Sr. "Convective Initiation at the Dryline: A Modeling Study." MWR 125 (June 1997): 1001–26.

United States government publications

Federal Aviation Administration (F.S.S.), National Oceanic and Atmospheric Administration (N.W.S.). *Aviation Weather, Advisory Circular 00-6.* Revised 1975. Washington, D.C.: U.S. Dept. of Commerce, U.S. Dept. of Transportation.

Federal Aviation Administration, National Oceanic and Atmospheric Administration (N.W.S.). *Aviation Weather Services, Advisory Circular 00-45.* Revised 1995. Washington, D.C.: U.S. Dept. of Commerce, U.S. Dept. of Transportation.

U.S. Air Force, 4th Weather Wing (Brissett, Donald T., CMSgt; Everson, Clarence E., Climatology Branch, Aerospace Sciences Div.). *Climatic Atlas of North America Flying Weather.* 4th Weather Wing Technical Paper 69-2. Ent A.F.B., Colorado, May 1969.

U.S. Dept. of Commerce, and National Oceanic and Atmospheric Administration (NOAA) publications:

Climatic Atlas of the United States. Reprint, 1993. U.S. Dept. of Commerce and NOAA, 1968. Available from National Climatic Data Center (NCDC), Asheville, N.C.

Daily Weather Maps. (Vars. issues, 1995 through 1999.) Weekly publication of the NOAA/National Weather Service (NWS).

Storm Data. "Outstanding Storms of the Month: Hurricane Iniki Strikes Hawaii"; and "Damage Survey of Hurricane Iniki in Hawaii." Fujita, T. Theodore. September 1992 (Vol.34, No.9). *Storm Data* is published by the NOAA, and available from the NCDC.

Storm Data. "Outstanding Storms of the Month: Heavy Rains Cause Flooding in Pacific Northwest." February 1996.

Storm Data. "Outstanding Storms of the Month: Strong Thunderstorm Winds Cause Damage in Arizona." August 1996 (Vol.38, No.8).

Storm Data. "Outstanding Storms of the Month: Outbreak of June 2nd and 3rd." June 1990 (Vol.32, No.6). Maps of tornado paths were provided to *Storm Data* by Brian E. Smith, NSSFC.

Index

About the Author

Tom Horne brings a unique blend of experience as a pilot, flight instructor, and author to his new book, *Flying America's Weather*.

With over 3,500 hours of experience in some 200 different airplanes, with commercial and flight instructor certificates, and with instrument, multi-engine and glider ratings, Tom knows and understands the business of piloting light aircraft. His logbook entries include lengthy stints as a flight instructor, a photogrammetrist-pilot, and a trans-Atlantic ferry pilot with 14 crossings in single- and multi-engine airplanes.

As an author he has more than 650 magazine articles to his credit, including articles for the *International Herald Tribune*, authorship of three books for Time-Life publications, and two book-length safety reviews published for the AOPA Air Safety Foundation. He has written on the subject of aviation weather regularly for over 16 years, as a contributor and editor of *AOPA Pilot* magazine. From 1982 to 1984, Tom served as editor to *Ultralight Pilot* magazine, and he is a past winner of the Earl D. Osborn Award for Excellence in Aviation Journalism.

Add to these credentials a unique understanding of what makes weather work, from both the meteorologist and pilot perspectives, mix in a capable and accessible style of writing, and the result is a book that few other people could have written—*Flying America's Weather*.